The Aircraft Designers:
A Grumman Historical Perspective

The Aircraft Designers:
A Grumman Historical Perspective

Michael V. Ciminera
Northrop Grumman
Vice President (Retired)

LIBRARY
OF FLIGHT

Ned Allen, Editor-in-Chief
Lockheed Martin Corporation
Bethesda, Maryland

Published by
American Institute of Aeronautics and Astronautics, Inc.
1801 Alexander Bell Drive, Reston, VA, 20191-4344

Photographs and quoted materials (including letters and *Grumman Plane News* articles) reprinted with permission of Northrop Grumman Corporation.

American Institute of Aeronautics and Astronautics, Inc., Reston, Virginia

1 2 3 4 5

Library of Congress Cataloging-in-Publication Data
Ciminera, Michael V.
   The aircraft designers : a Grumman historical perspective / Michael V. Ciminera ; Ned Allen, Editor-in-Chief.
      pages cm. – (Library of flight series)
   Includes bibliographical references and index.
   ISBN 978-1-62410-177-9 (alkaline paper)
1. Grumman Aircraft Engineering Corporation–History.   2. Airplanes–United States–Design and construction–History.   3. Grumman Aircraft Engineering Corporation–Employees–Biography.   4. Aeronautical engineers–United States–Biography.   5. Designers–United States–Biography.   I. Allen, Ned. II. Title.
   TL686.G78C56 2014
   338.7'6237460973–dc23

2013044607

ISBN 978-1-62410-177-9

A Note from the Editor-in-Chief

It must have been the summer of 1992 with the Grumman plant at Bethpage, Long Island near peak activity that I timidly approached the office of Grumman's then Vice-Chairman for Technology, Renso Caporali for an appointment arranged by the Defense Advanced Research Projects Agency. I was seeking Grumman collaboration on an advanced aircraft design project the little company I then headed was leading. While I left without a definitive agreement, it was that meeting and Caporali's penetrating insights that first impressed upon me the great significance of sagacious visionaries in the advance of American aerospace research.

In this book, Michael V. Ciminera recounts key elements of the story of Grumman's creative aircraft engineering people from the beginnings in 1929 through the merger into the Northrop Grumman Corporation in 1994. Ciminera examines Grumman engineers' foundational contributions to the growth of U.S. Naval aviation power during and after WWII, the definition of the canonical configurations for business aviation with the Gulfstream heritage, and Cold War development of assertive avionics missions of Early Warning aircraft, Intelligence, Surveillance, and Reconnaissance (ISR) aircraft, and of Electronic Warfare (EW) types. Grumman's design and engineering creativity extended well beyond aircraft, of course, to spacecraft including the Apollo mission's historic Lunar Module and even to canoes and surface vehicles, though they are not the focus of this book. Ciminera's portrait of these engineers and their projects sketches their diverse and rich contributions to the technoculture of aerospace today. As such, this book properly belongs in the Library of Flight.

The Library of Flight is part of the comprehensive portfolio of information services from the American Institute of Aeronautics and Astronautics. It extends the Institute's offerings with the best material in a growing variety of topics in aerospace from policy, to histories, to law, management, and beyond. The Library of Flight documents the crucial role of aerospace in enabling, facilitating, and accelerating our technological society and its global commerce, communication, and defense.

Ned Allen
Bethesda, Maryland
July 2013

v

Where Did We Get Such Men?

Why is America lucky enough to have such men?
They leave this tiny ship and fly against the enemy.
Then they must seek the ship, lost somewhere on the sea.
And when they find it, they have to land upon its pitching deck.

James A. Michener

Nothing great was ever achieved without enthusiasm.

Ralph Waldo Emerson

This book is dedicated to
Mike Pelehach, chief designer of the F-14A,
who was my boss, my mentor, and my friend for 40 years;
to all the aircraft designers and
their design teams who created and contributed
to so many technical innovations and exciting aircraft;
and to those young minds who have the
aspiration, dedication, and imagination
to conceptualize, conduct research, design, and build new aircraft.

– Michael V. Ciminera

CONTENTS

PREFACE

Many of the readers of this book who are members of the aerospace industry past and present—aviation enthusiasts, aeronautical–mechanical engineering students, historians, and so forth—know about the "giants" of aircraft design. Names that come to mind are Orville and Wilbur Wright, Glenn Curtiss, Chance Vought, Donald Douglas, William E. Boeing, Jim McDonnell, Jack Northrop, Leroy Grumman, Kelly Johnson, Lee Atwood, Willy Messerschmitt, Reginald Mitchell, Igor Sikorsky, Marcel Dassault, Artem Mikoyan, and Andrei Nikolaevich Tupolev, to mention a few.

In *The Aircraft Designers: A Grumman Historical Perspective*, I have attempted to tell a story about the aircraft designers and their key teammates who created, and contributed to, so many innovative exciting aircraft and their variants. It is important to remember them and record their names because each one devoted so much time and intellect to what is one of the most demanding technological industries.

Rather than writing about the aircraft, I wish to concentrate on those who provided the vision and leadership to create the aircraft or aircraft weapon system. My initial research began as a broad look at all the world's aircraft manufacturers and finding people's names as they became available. My sources have been books in my personal aviation library, museum books, communication with members of the aviation industry and my peers, many personal interviews, the Internet, magazines, visits to museums, and communication with company historians.

Based on some sound advice from my wife Donna; Irv Waaland, retired chief of design for the Northrop Grumman Corporation; and Dr. Brian Hunt, retired Northrop Grumman chief engineer, I have concentrated on individual U.S. companies, with Grumman being the first company to be investigated. This has allowed me to dig deeper and develop a more extensive list of names, what each person accomplished, key design considerations and issues relating to each aircraft, and anecdotes.

Since I began my research, I have been encouraged by aerospace company historians, aviation pioneers, active aerospace employees, and retired aerospace veterans to continue my quest to identify as many people as possible who helped create each aircraft design with its integrated avionic and weapon system and major derivatives. I have attempted to establish the chief of design, the chief engineer/aircraft designer, the key engineers, the project engineers, and the program managers who developed the conceptual design and carried it through to preliminary design, proposal, and the beginning of full-scale development, as well as the development of important aircraft system derivatives during an aircraft weapon system's life.

In some cases this same team was responsible for creating the design and building the demonstrator and/or first prototype aircraft. My most important objective in writing this book was to identify and recognize as many of the key team members as possible who contributed to the creation of a new design and its evolution. In that regard, my job will never be done because I will not have been able to find every name; however, my quest will continue.

The design could evolve as a team effort, with the preliminary design personnel, the project engineer, and/or the program manager working closely and adjudicating issues with all key functional engineering and corporate/division departments. At times one or more people would be responsible for the preliminary design and the final inboard profile, and another person would be responsible for building the first flying article (demonstrator/prototype) with a relatively small well-integrated team. One general observation is that aircraft designed in the past bore the earmark of the chief engineer/designer, in contrast to today's complex aircraft weapon systems that require a significant team effort.

Pertinent disciplines could include personnel from aerodynamics, structures, propulsion, avionics, subsystems, systems analysis, software, simulation, testing, research, advanced development, integrated logistics support, reliability and maintainability (R&M), manufacturing, prototype shop or product development center, model design, flight test, proposal operations, contracts, cost estimating, procurement, cost, and so on, with inputs streaming in from business development and field service as well as corporate and division offices located in Washington, D.C., and government agency sites.

Business development played a key role during the evolution of a new design and subsequent derivatives of an aircraft. Business development personnel knew each customer through relationships forged over many years as the young officers or civilians came up through the ranks. Previous experience as service pilots and officers, test pilots, engineers, program managers, or field service representatives, to mention a few, served the business development personnel well. These employees worked hand in hand with the design teams to make the right contacts in the military, government agencies, and laboratories; helped secure important seed money contracts;

participated on proposals; and were also key members of each program management team, such as the F-14, S-2, A-6, EA-6B, and others.

Today the chief engineer and his or her team spend years evolving system requirements and specifications with government and military input based on extensive operations analyses to determine the most cost-effective solution and detailed systems analysis trade-off studies to determine system and subsystem requirements.

The aircraft of yesterday have become today's "integrated weapon system platforms." These aircraft weapon systems are the result of an integrated effort among airframe, propulsion, subsystems, avionics, radar, observables, systems analysis, systems engineering, software, antenna system design, and other groups that are responsible for architecting, designing, simulating, building, and testing the preferred system concept. Once a program reached flight status and production, many important derivatives or variants were conceived, simulated, tested, and proposed to the U.S. government. I have also attempted to identify the people responsible for these developments.

I have used appropriate biographical information and anecdotes interspersed with pictures of the designers and teammates where appropriate. I will discuss what motivated them to become aircraft designers and what they contributed to the field. I also mention key people in the government as well as military engineers where available, like George Spangenberg, Evaluation Division Director, Naval Air Systems Command, who I had the good fortune and privilege to know and work with in the late 1960s.

Were the designers active pilots, structural engineers, or flight test engineers? Were they model builders as youngsters? Where did they go to school, or were they self-educated? Were they with other companies or associated with other designers? What was their span of time leading new designs, and how many aircraft did they design or influence? So many questions arose during my research, and I attempt to answer as many as possible within these pages.

I also discuss how preliminary design or advanced systems were structured and what it was like to work in this environment, as well as what aircraft the design teams were responsible for. I also summarize and try to generalize the various design philosophies that each design team and manufacturer utilized in developing their aircraft designs. I provide some insights about the leadership, technical skills, longevity, designer traits, and lasting contributions of the designers and discuss the role of the designer in the future.

Mike Ciminera
Palos Verdes, California
August 2013

ACKNOWLEDGMENTS

Donna Ciminera, my wife, for her patience, wise counsel, knowledge of the aerospace industry, early recommendation to concentrate my research on one company at a time (starting with Grumman), and helping me to fulfill my passion to remember the aircraft designers and their teammates.

This book will never be complete. I did my best to dig deep and find as many people as I could who contributed to the creation of the aircraft.

Larry Feliu, manager of Northrop Grumman History Center in Bethpage, New York, for his constant support and encouragement over two years, many helpful visits to the Northrop Grumman History Center, digging out a ton of data, and lots of photographs.

Thomas Griffin, volunteer at Northrop Grumman History Center, for his untiring research into numerous *Grumman Plane News* articles, finding many aircraft and personnel photographs, and his invaluable knowledge of the F-14B engine development.

Robert Tallman, volunteer at Northrop Grumman History Center, for finding, preparing, and sending me hundreds of pictures of all Grumman "X" aircraft, operational photographs, historical photographs, and design drawings of Design 711 (the last proposed amphibian).

Lynn McDonald, volunteer at Northrop Grumman History Center, for finding biographies of many Grumman designers and founders.

Ken Speiser, volunteer at Northrop Grumman History Center, for his efforts to find Dick Hutton's historical letters relating to his early designs.

David Arthur, AIAA acquisitions and development editor, for being instrumental in selecting my draft for publication, wise counsel, and editing.

Pat DuMoulin, AIAA senior editor of books, for managing the entire manuscript to printed book process and keeping the chapters focused on their intent.

Toni Zuccarini Ackley, project manager and copyeditor, for her excellent detail editing and great ideas on chapter organization.

I was able to discover and read letters and documents and obtain unique photos that captured the lives of the designers and their key teammates. Long personal interviews and exchanges of information with many senior

Grumman personnel, some lasting for many months, resulted in many names and anecdotes. For those people I did not find, I encourage you to contact me with your stories or anecdotes so that at some time in the future this book may be updated.

Vinny Milano, for many discussions about preliminary design, good anecdotes, and his detailed review and endorsement of my book.

John Norris, for good conversations about the F11F-1F Super Tiger development.

Irv Waaland, one of Grumman's leading aerodynamicists who became Northrop's chief of design, for access to his AIAA Wright Brothers Lecture, good suggestions as to how to accomplish the research of this endeavor, and reading and endorsing this book.

Dr. Brian Hunt, for his friendship, wise counsel, many discussions, and in-depth review of the draft and endorsement.

Leonard "Sully" Sullivan, for his letter to Joe Lippert, written in 1985, about his recollection of his role as director of Preliminary Design (PD) and Operations Analysis and identification of key designers and their accomplishments during the 1950s and 1960s.

Renso Caporali, for good conversations, encouragement, reading and endorsing the draft, and comments on how the F-14 Mach Sweep Programmer and the Central Air Data Computer (CADC) came about, as well as his role as mediator between structures and propulsion.

Mark Siegel, for his enthusiastic responses and good words about all the aero guys contributing on many aircraft developments.

Dick Kita, for what aerodynamacists did, good anecdotes, and his recall on the development of many aircraft and key people involved.

Bob Salzmann, for long phone conversations about how the airborne radar jamming system and EA-6B came about, his valuable insights and critiques, and providing historic data and video that were sent on to the Northrop Grumman History Center.

Bob Scholly, for an excellent detailed story about Grumman's electronic warfare history, developments, and personnel photos from the EA-6A to the EA-6B programs.

Hank Janiesch, for very caring and detailed emails, letters, and organization charts about how many of Grumman's top programs developed (including RGWS, F-14A plus, F-14D, and EA-6A).

Jerry Norton, for long detailed histories, anecdotes, names, and accomplishments on the AF-2S/W Guardian, E-1, E-2 family, and Joint STARS as well as access to his excellent brochure, "From Concept to Combat."

Jim Glover, for opening the door to many Joint STARS veterans like Jerry Norton and much insight into Pave Mover, the beginning of Joint STARS, and anecdotes.

Pat Reilly, for good phone conversations and recall on Pave Mover and Joint STARS.

Alan Van Weele, "Mr. Energy," continues to move at his fast pace and provided the concise history of Joint STARS Boeing 707 modification and refurbishment at Melbourne and Lake Charles, as well as good conversation.

Bob Nafis, for his detailed remembrances of people, anecdotes, and what they did. (Bob was involved in the evolution and led the system development of many of Grumman's programs.)

Jerry Madigan, for very detailed insight into the early phases of Joint STARS development and key people who became the core of Joint STARS's success.

Don Terrana, for his blog on the TFX evolution, good conversations, and several reports on how preliminary design operated, how the Gulfstream I started, the early phases of the TFX/F-111 proposal, and anecdotes.

Norm Lewin, for long conversations about Grumman's history and who were some of the key "guys."

Ellen Moss, for her kind words about her husband Hal's health as well as research to find good articles about operations analysis and Hal's contributions to advanced vehicle design.

Jack Ingold, for good conversation and his recall about how Grumman became the integrator of the E-2 system.

Mike Lombardi, Boeing historian, for his encouragement to undertake this project to remember the designers and their teammates.

Pat McGinnis, Douglas historian, for her encouragement to undertake this project to remember the designers and their teammates.

Jerry Huben, Northrop Grumman's longest tenure employee, for providing me with a detailed history of Grumman, a long conversation with his wife Dorothy and him, and giving me a portion of his aviation library.

Louis Lee, owner of J.D. Hobbies in San Pedro, California, for access to his extensive aviation library, his contributions of historical aviation books, and his continued support of my research.

Aldo Spadoni, for his imaginative draft cover design, enthusiasm, and continued encouragement.

Joe Cagnazzi, for his in-depth look at who were the key personnel involved in the A-6 family of derivatives.

Joe Ruggiero, for his excellent recall of preliminary design, history of the A-6 and Gulfstream programs, and unique photos of the first A-6A and the A-6F personnel.

Joel DiMaggio, for his recall of the Mohawk and Airborne Radar Jamming System demonstration program.

Bill Bischoff, for his attempts to remember those hectic days in Engineering.

Jack Saxe, for trying to remember those old Preliminary Design days, and his recall about the size of the S-2F proposal.

Keith Wilkinson, for remembering almost all the names of the X-29 design team.

Howie Schilling, for remembering how the F-14 was designed and many key names.

Carlos Paez, for his wonderful article about the design evolution of the F-14 wing center section and who were some of the key personnel.

Harvey Eidenoff, for his detailed insights as to how the F-14 structure was designed and for contacting Harry Armen about Grant Hedrick's biography.

Harry Armen, for sending me articles and letters about Grant Hedrick that provided valuable insight into not only his technical achievements, but also his deep concern for and care of Grumman's people.

Bob Aberle, for his early advice on this undertaking and his sustained belief that such a story would be of interest to readers and model aircraft builders.

Bob DeVoe, for his good advice and help in opening doors to key Joint STARS personnel like Jim Glover, Pat Reilly, and Allan Van Weele.

Paul Weidenhafer, for his enthusiasm and helping me find Dick Lu.

Dick Lu, deep thanks to this 93-year-young friend who provided a six-page handwritten account of his days at Grumman and Republic Aviation.

Jim Dante, for his meticulous research, lots of emails, and good conversations about the key people who made the F-14A, F-14B, and F-14D happen.

Neil GilMartin, many thanks for talking to me about the history of the F-14 program and key people, and trying to help.

Joe Rodriguez, for his broad history of how Grumman became a system integrator and manager of weapon system development, his recall on how Grumman became a leader in systems engineering, and his recall of the early days on the A-6, Mohawk, and F-14.

Don Roberts, for his patient and detailed review of the rough draft, his encouragement to continue, and guidance in writing style.

Karl Jackson, retired Garret AiResearch vice president, for his good anecdotes about the F-14A team when he was program manager of the Central Air Data Computer (CADC).

Jim Flemings, for sending me the inspirational book *Through The Back Doors of the World in a Ship that Had Wings*.

John Ohler, for his friendship over these many years and his remembrances of testing the XF10F-1 Jaguar variable sweep aircraft.

Roy Schering, for his excellent articles on Joint STARS weapon system guidance tests and his recall of key Joint STARS personnel.

Frank Dellamura, for our detail discussions about the improvements in the preliminary design process and all the fine preliminary design engineers who created countless conceptual designs.

Nick Dannenhofer, for his contributions as a project engineer in preliminary design starting in the dynamic 1950s at Grumman, and his recall of the contributions of many key personnel.

Stan Kalemaris, for his excellent recall of preliminary design and advanced systems history and good discussions on many designer and teammate contributions.

Lou Hemmerdinger, for his memories about Larry Mead and the early days on the A-6 program.

Kathy Henry, for securing excellent photographs of Joint STARS personnel and obtaining release for their use from the U.S. Air Force.

John McCabe, for his encouragement when reading the draft and his thoughts about advanced systems design teams.

Dr. Dick Scheuing, for his recollections of the research department's contributions to Grumman's aircraft designs and technology.

Connie Blyseth, for his help in understanding the evolution of software department at Grumman, and for sharing lots of pertinent data and good anecdotes.

Al Kuhn, for his excellent recall of the C-2A program and how the reprocured C-2A program evolved.

Joe Tieng, for his wonderful recall of the S-2T TurboTracker program and key personnel, as well as contacting old friends for me.

Dan Pliskin, for being one of the stalwarts of the integrated logistic support (ILS) community that keeps the guys together, and helping me tell the F-14 ILS story.

Don Schlegel, for finding some unique pictures of the S-2T TurboTracker.

Carol Nelson, for her caring and sustained interest in Grumman retirees and help at the Cradle of Aviation Museum on Long Island.

Josh Stoff, curator at the Cradle of Aviation Museum, for access to at the museum's archives.

In Memoriam

Joe Gavin, who began to recall the 1950s and early 1960s in Preliminary Design, but unfortunately passed on before he could finish.

Corky Meyer; Dorothy Meyer tried to help her ex-husband Corky, Grumman's chief test pilot, respond to my request before he became ill and passed on.

Bob Kress, for having the privilege of reading his notes at the F-14 retirement dinner on Long Island in 2006 when he was ill, sending me his published articles and unfinished papers, and using these notes in telling his story on the design evolution of the F-14 before he left us.

Bob Smyth, for good conversations before he became ill and passed on.

Ernie Ranalli, for good conversation about the days at Grumman and his attempt to give a "stress man's view," but unfortunately an accident took him from his family and all his friends.

Larry Canonico; Karen Canonico, Larry's wife, for sharing her memories, pictures of Larry, and other invaluable data.

Bill Rathke; John Rathke, his son, for speaking to me and trying to find some of Bill's old files.

Mike Pelehach; Linda Pelehach, his daughter and good friend, for looking through her father's old papers and making them available to me.

Grant Hedrick; Mrs. Hedrick and the former wife of Joseph Hubert (Grumman's senior aerodynamicist and designer from Messerschmitt) for finding unique preliminary design photos from the 1950s.

Larry Mead, for letting me have total access to his autobiography, which is, in itself, a history of Grumman; many conversations; and anecdotes. He was the oldest surviving member of Grumman's senior team at the age of 94 (he was hired in June 1941).

Fred Tiemann's *Memoir 11*; thanks to the Northrup Grumman History Center, I was able to access Fred's amazing history of his involvement with the E-2 program and gain tremendous insights into the details of airborne early warning technology, challenges, and people.

Chapter 1

THE EARLY YEARS

IN THE BEGINNING

LOENING AERONAUTICAL ENGINEERING

The story of Grumman's aircraft designers begins with Grover Loening. During his career, he became an assistant to Orville Wright (shown on the right in Fig. 1.1) and went on to become the chief aeronautical engineer for the Army Signal Corps in World War I. In 1917, Loening formed Loening Aeronautical Engineering, and there he designed a destroyer-launched plane and the M-8 pursuit plane featuring rigid strut bracing—a pioneering first. He went on to design and build flying or air yachts and the Loening Amphibian featuring the first "practical" landing gear (see Fig. 1.2).

LEROY R. GRUMMAN

While Loening was building his aircraft factory, Roy Grumman was finishing up at Cornell University. In 1916, Roy Grumman enlisted in the U.S. Naval Reserve. However, according to his son, David, "His first intent on joining the Navy was to become a submariner, due to his familiarity with boats and the sea." But an opportunity arose for him to apply for preflight training at Massachusetts Institute of Technology (MIT). He took the test and passed, but his physical exam was a different story. "He actually failed the eye exam, but someone made an administrative error and entered him in ground school anyway." Roy Grumman said nothing about this oversight and went on to become a pilot: naval aviator #1216 (Fig. 1.3).

Besides being an excellent aircraft designer, Loening had a real knack for finding the best and brightest engineers for his company. In 1919, the Navy stationed a young Lieutenant Grumman at the Loening factory at 31st Street and the East River in New York City. He was to be the project engineer and supervise construction of the M-8 monoplane (Fig. 1.4). In 1920, Leroy Grumman joined Loening after leaving the Navy, and rapidly rose through the ranks as test pilot, aircraft designer, and finally general manager responsible for aircraft design. Mr. Loening also hired Leon "Jake" Swirbul and William T. Schwendler.

Fig. 1.1   Grover Loening and Orville Wright (courtesy of CHIRP, 1969).

The Loening hydro-aeroplane set an altitude record of 19,500 ft with a crew of four and achieved a speed of 130 mph (Fig. 1.5). Many aircraft of this type began production during the 1920s; meanwhile, the Navy was looking for a replacement. Loening merged with Keystone Aircraft in 1928, which later became the Loening Aeronautical Division of Curtiss-Wright.

GRUMMAN AIRCRAFT ENGINEERING CORPORATION

In 1929 a very bright, innovative, and industrious group of Loening employees left Loening Aeronautical Engineering to form the Grumman

Fig. 1.2   Loening OA-1A.

GRUMMAN, LEROY R.
Ensign
Huntington, L. I., N. Y.
Mass. Inst. of Tech., Miami.
Pensacola,   N. A. F.
Phila. N. A. No. 1216.
HTA.   Fig. 1.3   Ensign Leroy R. Grumman.

Fig. 1.4   Rollout of a Loening monoplane with a pusher-mounted Liberty engine. Grumman is far right in a dark overcoat with Loening to his left. Julie Holpit, a leading figure in manufacturing at Grumman, stands right of the wing sponson in tan coveralls.

b)

a)

After descending from its record breaking climb, the monoplane takes to the water.
ANOTHER RECORD SMASHED.—A monoplane designed by Grover C.
Loening established a new altitude record for hydro-aeroplanes by

Dave McCullough, pilot (left), G. C. Loening and passengers.
mounting to a height of 19,500 feet, carrying four men. Prior to accomplishing the feat the machine attained a speed of 130 miles per hour,

Fig. 1.5   a) Loening hydro-aeroplane taxiing after a record-setting flight; b) Roy Grumman (far right) stands next to Grover Loening.

Aircraft Engineering Corporation on Long Island, New York. Leroy Grumman, who had been the general manager at Loening, in concert with his coworkers Jake Swirbul, William Schwendler, Julius Holpit, Albert Loening, and Ed Poor, struck out on their own. The Grumman Aircraft Engineering Corporation (Grumman) was financed by Grover Loening, his brother A.P. Loening, Leroy Grumman, Swirbul, Poor, and E. Clinton Towl, and provided with the manufacturing rights to the Loening retractable landing gear hull and float designs. Towl was a close friend of Poor's; he was involved in a Wall Street brokerage and had an appreciation of engineering.

FLOATS

Grumman's first U.S. Navy contracts entailed the development and production of the Model A and B floats for the Vought O2U and O3U observation aircraft. The floats were a new design that featured monocoque structure with a new landing gear scheme that allowed the wheels to be recessed in the floats (see Fig. 1.6). The Navy considered the floats of unconventional design because they seemed too light and might collapse. To prove their point, Roy Grumman and Jake Swirbul climbed into the aircraft with the Navy pilot at the controls and successfully catapulted from a battleship.

Roy Grumman and Bill Schwendler became the chief designers of many of Grumman's early aircraft. Expanding the horizon of designing advanced floats led them to begin designing amphibians as early as 1930 (Fig. 1.7). Although Schwendler's early amphibian design was not built, a long line of excellent amphibians was to emerge in the late 1930s and continue well into the 1950s. The team of Grumman and Schwendler went on to design and to lead design teams that turned out many Grumman aircraft, as described in ensuing chapters.

Fig. 1.6   A float for the Vought O2U and O3U observation aircraft that allowed the wheels to be recessed during flight.

Fig. 1.7   Bill Schwendler with a side view drawing of one of his first designs signed off on by Roy Grumman in 1930.

XJF-1 TO J2F DUCK SERIES

The Grumman XJF-1 to J2F Duck series was the first of many Grumman amphibians created by Roy Grumman and Bill Schwendler. Jack Neady also became part of Grumman's young expanding engineering staff. He came to Grumman from Loening via Bristol Aircraft and was a very accomplished and adaptable engineer whose specialty was hydrodynamics. He became the chief designer on the XJF-1 (Fig. 1.8), a redesign of the Loening/Curtiss-Wright XO2L-1. Construction of a prototype was ordered in 1932. The Duck exhibited good speed for an amphibian and good handling characteristics. From the XJF-1 [military designation], G-7 [Grumman designation] design evolved a series of Duck variants, namely the JF-2, G-9; JF-3, G-10; and J2F, G-15.

XFF-1

In 1930, the Navy became interested in Grumman's design of a high performance two-seat fighter that became the FF-1, G-5 (Fig. 1.9). Roy Grumman and Bill Schwendler did the preliminary design that embodied some very advanced and robust design features. Schwendler gave a hint of what was to come in his future aircraft designs when he created the first practical retractable landing gear for an amphibious float, and followed that up by designing the first retractable gear for a fighter—the Grumman FF-1, nicknamed Fifi. Although the retractable landing gear made the FF-1 much heavier than other military fighters, the reduced drag permitted the plane to fly some 20 mph faster than any of its contemporaries, a remarkable

Fig. 1.8   Grumman Design 7 that became the XJF-1(1932).

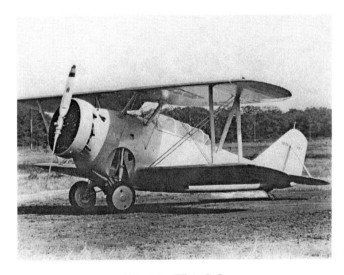

Fig. 1.9   FF-1, G-5.

accomplishment at the time. It was the first Navy fighter equipped with retractable landing gear, and it featured an innovative aluminum wing spar design; an all-metal, monocoque fuselage; and an innovative new gun mount for the gunner's seat.

This was followed in 1933 by the XF2F-1, G-8 (Fig. 1.10), a single-seat fighter, and the XF3F-1, G-11 (Fig. 1.11), also a single-seat fighter, in 1935.

Fig. 1.10   XF2F-1, G-8, single-seat fighter.

Fig. 1.11   XF3F-1, G-11.

JULIE HOLPIT

Julius "Julie" Holpit (Fig. 1.12) is well remembered as the wizard who headed the experimental department when Grumman was in its infancy. He worked hand-in-glove with Bill Schwendler, Roy Grumman, Jake Swirbul, and a few engineers to make the designs a reality. Holpit laid out the work for each person who represented his respective department in experimental design.

Holpit began working at the age of 14, and joined Grumman in Baldwin, New York, on the first day of business for the new company. Holpit brought with him over 12 years of experience that he had gained while working at Loening, Keystone, and L.W.F. (Lowe, Willard and Fowler) Aircraft. His tight team of carpenters, metal workers, and mechanics built the mockups and first articles, and rebuilt crashed or damaged aircraft in record time. He was probably Grumman's first field service representative, as well as the first in a long line of remarkable people who headed experimental design manufacturing shop, later called the prototype shop, and eventually the product development center. Holpit said, "In the early days we used tin snips for cutting out skins, and I brought my sewing machine from home to sew wing fabric. In the thirties the Company was poor—we were really poor."

Holpit recalled working on the XF3F-1:

> The pilot was very well known: Jimmy Collins. He cracked up. He had been hired to test this plane. It was built to withstand about 12 *g*, but he

Fig. 1.12   Julius "Julie" Holpit.

pulled it out too fast (it went to 15 *g*), and the airplane fell apart in the air. I said, "Why don't we build another airplane?," and I remember Mr. Grumman saying, "What did you say?" And I said, "We've still got two months before we have to deliver to the Navy. We'll build it in six weeks." So we started. All the men in Experimental were crackerjack mechanics. We all worked together like clockwork. So we got it out in six weeks. We had a pilot by the name of Lee Gellbach to dive this second airplane. And he dove it right. But he takes it up to about 18,000 ft and it goes into a spin. The motor stalled. Comes down.... And the pilot jumps. Well, Gellbach survived but the airplane cracked up. So then Jake Swirbul gets on the phone, "What happened, Julie?" "Bad news."

The next day at the Bureau of Aeronautics all the brass was there. Jake came down. Admiral Ernest King was in charge. They showed the pictures taken in the air. Admiral King came over to me. "Julie," he says, "when do you think you can build another airplane?" "Well, I think in 21 days." So I went back, and we built an airplane in 21 days... and we got the order for 54 airplanes. That's the story.

Julie Holpit also remembered an incident from just before World War II began. They were building the TBF (Torpedo Bomber, F, the Navy's designation for Grumman), and someone came along and said,

"Julie, we've got to move the engine 10 inches. The thing is tail heavy." So that day we worked everything out, moved the whole engine, the whole bulkhead and all, and put a piece in that section, right behind the main bulkhead—and we did that in 24 h and had it out. We had to cut all the controls, the wires, everything. Had to do this and put this section in. We built every TBF after that just like that. Airplanes were simple in those days, don't forget. Nothin' to the darn things: a motor, a fuselage—that's all.

G-22, GULFHAWK II

Roy Grumman and Bill Schwendler developed the design of the Gulfhawk (Fig. 1.13) by combining the fuselage of the F3F-2 with the biplane wings of the F2F-1. This was an attempt to develop some commercial sales by designing an aerobatic airplane for air shows, air races, and sport flying. The first Gulfhawk was built for Major Al Williams, who had a distinguished record as a naval aviator, airplane racer, and stunt pilot. The Gulfhawk was very maneuverable because it was stripped of military equipment carried on the F3F Navy fighter. It was powered by a Wright Cyclone R 1820 engine rated at 1000 hp and could reach 290 mph with a landing speed of 66 mph. During the concept design of the G-22, Grumman and Schwendler adopted a lightweight approach by covering the fuselage with thin aluminum alloy skins, but strengthened the fuselage to allow high g maneuvers during aerobatic airshows. The staggered, biplane wings were also of aluminum construction with fabric skins. George Titterton was the project engineer on the Gulfhawk. The Gulfhawk flew from 1936 to 1948, and during that time it

Fig. 1.13 Grumman Gulfhawk.

was flown in Europe, used as a flying laboratory to test new devices and lubricants, and used to inspire young aviation aspirants and cadets.

In 1980, a Gulfhawk was flown into the Bethpage airport facility and exhibited during the annual Grumman stockholders' meeting. During the meeting, Titterton, who eventually retired as senior vice president and a member of the board of directors, recalled the events and excitement of producing the high performance aircraft.

> Al Williams was a famous stunt flyer... who flew for Gulf Oil, and in 1936 we put this aircraft together for him. In those days we were building the F3F (with a wing span of 32 ft) that was a little bit bigger than the F2F. Al wanted the F2F wings with a wing span of 28 ft so that the plane would be easier to flip around the sky. He also wanted a snappier looking cowling but we couldn't do anything like that for the Navy. And, my God, it was a beautiful thing! We were very proud of it.

Titterton said, "It was a small company then. Everyone knew everyone else's name. But the spirit of the place hasn't changed. What got this company through 50 years is the abiding belief in good hard work... getting the job done, and not making excuses. It's been a pleasure watching it grow." This philosophy combined with open access to management, giving constructive criticism to help rather than belittle, led to the free flow of creative ideas for new aircraft concepts.

GOOSE

In 1936, a group of wealthy businessmen approached Grover Loening to design and build an updated air yacht. Loening recommended that they contact the Grumman Aircraft Engineering Corporation. As a result, Roy Grumman and Bill Schwendler did the preliminary design of the Goose G-21 (Fig. 1.14), a two-engine amphibian, to meet their specifications. Ralston Stalb, as the project engineer, laid out the design of the two-stepped hull. He was a naval architect by training and became chief engineer at Loening before coming to Grumman. Stalb was one of the foremost hull designers in the United States, and he was directly involved in the whole series of Grumman amphibians. Tom Rae was also part of the design team.

Interestingly, in 1981, Joe Gavin, then president of Grumman Aerospace, was approached by a group of Alaskan bush pilots who had been flying the Goose for many years. They held conversations with Fred Rowley in regard to the design of a replacement for the Goose. Rowley, along with Carl Alber, was a highly regarded test pilot with considerable amphibian experience throughout the industry. Chapter 7, Future Systems, discusses Grumman's

Fig. 1.14   A Goose G-21 in a commercial paint scheme.

imaginative attempt to design a Goose replacement, Design 711, that reached full-scale mockup.

XF4F-2

In 1936, Roy Grumman, Bill Schwendler, and Dick Hutton, who was to become chief of production design, designed the XF4F-2, G-18 monoplane fighter. Julie Holpit and his prototype manufacturing team built the wooden mockup in 1936 that showed a mid-wing location and an inboard arrangement (Figs. 1.15 and 1.16).

Hutton began his career in aviation as a mechanic at Loening Aeronautical Engineering Corporation in New York City in 1928, and two years later became the 21st employee of Grumman. He had already begun engineering

Fig. 1.15   A mockup of the XF4F-2, G-18 monoplane fighter.

Fig. 1.16   An early flight test of the XF4F-2, G-18.

studies in the School of Science at Pratt Institute; he completed these night courses in 1935. Bob Hall was the test pilot, and an excellent designer and experimental engineer in his own right. He had designed the Gee Bee for the aircraft manufacturer Granville Brothers, and would play a lead role in some of Grumman's later aircraft designs.

CONCLUSION

During the startup years from 1929 to the beginning of World War II, Grumman was a small, tightly knit company that was blessed with superb, imaginative technical leadership and financial acumen that kept the company going as it began to design and build rugged, good-performing aircraft. Initially, Grumman was not one of the U.S. Navy's preferred contractors like Chance Vought. The float successes followed by the Duck, FF-1, XF2F, XF3F, the Goose, and the indestructible XF4F (in the eyes of many Navy pilots who flew it in World War II) gained Grumman its share of Navy aircraft programs. The human relationships of this success were forged at Loening. There was a unique blending of conceptual aircraft designer/engineer/test pilot—Grumman; Schwendler, a chief engineer experienced in every aspect of aircraft design; Swirbul, a production genius, people motivator, and true salesman; Holpit, a builder of aircraft and field support wizard; and the calm, Wall Street financial prowess of Towl and Poor.

Chapter 2

THE WAR YEARS

GRUMMAN'S EARLY DESIGN PHILOSOPHY

One of the unique aspects of a well-integrated design team is how they conceptualize and work out design issues. Roy Grumman's office was small, and there were about 160 aircraft models suspended from the ceiling. He and Jake Swirbul, cofounder, ran Grumman in an informal manner that the Navy and Grumman workers liked. Grumman also designed his aircraft in the same manner. An oft-told story is indicative of Grumman's design genius. He was trying to figure out the most compact way of folding carrier aircraft wings in order to fit the most possible aircraft onto a carrier deck.

"With his feet cocked on his desk," he used a gum eraser and a bunch of paper clips to figure out how best to fold the wings. By putting paper clips in the eraser and "working them back and forth" (Fig. 2.1) he came up with the solution that allowed the Hellcat's wings to be folded like a bird's wings. This was the skewed axis concept that was worked out in detail by the Grumman engineers and was used for the first time on the production F4F-4 Wildcats. The overall span decreased from 38 ft to 14 1/3 ft.

As chief engineer, Bill Schwendler conducted design review meetings twice a week, a process he continued well into the 1970s. Larry Mead, in his autobiography, recalled that Bill Schwendler was a master at doing intuitive tradeoffs in his head to come up with the best compromise among the many competing demands for performance, weight, cost, pilot safety, and so on. He was a true systems engineer. He used to say that "the best new design was the one with the least experimental features."

Much has been said and written about the Grumman Iron Works in numerous Navy pilot speeches, excellent books, periodicals, and other works. This aircraft design philosophy embodied a very rugged structure with reliable systems able to sustain significant damage that would allow the pilot to complete his mission and return home safely. This philosophy and resultant design guidelines were inherent in all Grumman aircraft as they were being created in Preliminary Design and then engineered by the design team. This philosophy was put in place by Roy Grumman because of his deep conviction that the "pilot was more important than the airplane." Jake Swirbul called Roy Grumman "as practical

Fig. 2.1   Roy Grumman working out his unique wing folding scheme with an eraser and paper clips.

an engineer as there ever was." This assessment lends itself to Roy Grumman's credo: "Build it strong, keep it simple and make it work."

Every new designer at Grumman was inculcated with two guiding principles. Grumman's edict was "the last part of the aircraft to fail will be the cockpit," in order to increase survivability in a carrier crash landing and in aerial combat. Schwendler's guidance was to "judiciously apply a factor of 2 (the Schwendler factor) to a structure that met specifications to make it twice as strong as needed." These overarching design principles manifested themselves in a robust structural design philosophy. The result was that the static and fatigue strength of the structure had many redundant load-carrying structural paths that addressed combat damage, fire, and crash landings. This resulted in a long structural life for prolonged carrier operation in the harsh marine environment. An F6F-3 Hellcat that crash landed on an Essex class carrier off Peleliu Island in 1944 broke apart due to severe damage to the wing; however, the forward fuselage with the cockpit was intact and the pilot had only minor injuries (Fig. 2.2).

Three other examples highlight the results of these design philosophies. The first occurred in aerial combat in the Pacific between the Grumman F4F Wildcat and the Mitsubishi Zeke 52 "Zero." A Zero had put over 500 rounds into a Wildcat that "still kept flying even with its rudder and tail in shreds," as compared to a Zero that would have disintegrated. In the second case, Carl Alber, one of Grumman's renowned test pilots, flight tested the F4F-8 in a

Fig. 2.2   The cockpit of a crash-landed Hellcat remains intact on the carrier deck.

dive and pulled 12.5 g in his final dive attempt! In the third case, the G-21 Goose made several wheels-up landings on land during its long life, and the hull structure, though designed for water, was totally intact with only a few dents and scratches. The aircraft returned to flight status immediately.

In 1941, Dick Hutton was the head of Experimental Design; according to Larry Mead, he was a "true" aircraft designer. Mead had been hired in 1941 by Charlie Tilgner, who was head of stress at the time. It should be noted the design studies of more advanced, single engine fighters based on European experiences continued in experimental design at Grumman.

Grant Hedrick joined Grumman in 1943 as a stress analyst. He began a 50-year career at Grumman that not only carried on the Grumman and Schwendler design philosophies, but also elevated Grumman engineering to world-renowned levels of excellence. Hedrick was involved in the design and development of literally every Grumman aircraft.

He performed pioneering research into high strength aluminum alloys used in future naval aircraft, developed a method to determine water impact loads on sea planes in rough seas, and developed a detailed analytical structural fatigue methodology that has been adopted worldwide. These efforts culminated in the F11F-1 Tiger being the first aircraft in which fatigue life was a design requirement and the first aircraft tested to destruction under a comprehensive Navy-specified spectrum of repeated loads. Hedrick became chief of Structures after World War II, chief technical engineer in the late 1950s, and vice president of Engineering in 1963. In these positions he was responsible for the structural design, analysis, and testing of all Grumman aircraft.

PRE–WORLD WAR II DESIGNS

In 1939, as World War II approached, Roy Grumman, Bill Schwendler, and Dick Hutton were managing development of three new preliminary designs—the Widgeon, G-44; the XF5F-1, G-34; and the XTBF-1 Avenger, G-40. Larry Mead was hired in June 1941, and remembered an open house for all Grumman employees to celebrate the opening of Plant 2 facility at Bethpage, Long Island, on December 7, 1941. At the time, TBF Avengers were being assembled in Plant 2 and initial drawings were being released to the shop for the XF6F-1 Hellcat. Mead arrived with his fiancée, and future wife, Janet at the plant and enjoyed a sandwich lunch with all the Grumman personnel. On the way back to New Jersey, where his fiancée lived, they heard the radio broadcast about the attack on Pearl Harbor. The next day, at the direction of the U.S. Navy Bureau of Aeronautics (BuAer), Grumman put the whole shop on two 10-hour shifts per day and engineering on a 60-hour week.

WIDGEON, G-44

Roy Grumman and Ralston Staub designed the Widgeon, G-44—a smaller version of the Goose. It was a good design, and Roy Grumman did the test flying himself. During his early employment with Grumman, long-time employee Tom Rae, who spent many years working in amphibians, recalled, "Mr. Grumman would drop by with design ideas (e.g., a rudder control system) for the Widgeon jotted down on the back of an envelope. The Widgeon was his pet design, and he contributed a great deal to it." The timing of its introduction not only attracted private and foreign customers, but also fulfilled the needs of the Coast Guard and Navy for coastal patrol, rescue, and transporting of light cargo.

XF5F-1, G34 AND XP-50, AND G-46

The Grumman design team of Bill Schwendler and Dick Hutton focused its attention on the next-generation fighter design philosophy based on close collaboration with the Navy, National Advisory Committee for Aeronautics (NACA), and Curtiss-Wright. This effort resulted in the XF5F-1, G-34 (Figs. 2.3 and 2.4) and the follow-on XP-50, G-46 (Fig. 2.5) for the Army Air Corps. The resultant designs blended an aluminum stressed skin wing construction with a twin engine configuration and twin tails for added directional stability and single engine control. The XF5F-1 had an excellent rate of climb and maximum speed exceeding 380 mph; however, stability and aircraft carrier suitability performance (a most critical design issue) were marginal because there was inadequate vision over the nose.

Dick Hutton (Fig. 2.6) prepared the following letter on the design philosophy of the XF5F-1 in 1986, in response to a request from the *Journal*

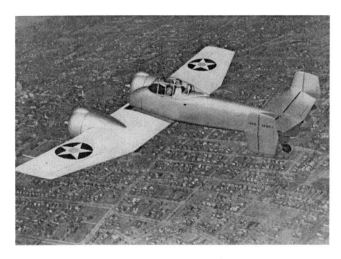

Fig. 2.3   Side view of the XF5F-1.

of the American Aviation Historical Society, some 40 years after he designed the aircraft. This reflects his balanced design approach while introducing new technology.

> In reply to your request for info on the F5F, I offer the following—things get a bit hazy as one tries to recall events 40 years ago but, for what they are worth, here they are.

> Two engine safety was always a desirable goal, but resulted in a larger aircraft, span wise, for parking on the carrier. By eliminating the width of the fuselage, the engines could be located close together as shown in this interesting nose shot of the XF5F.

> By locating the guns on the center-line, the bore-sight problem could be eliminated. Landing visibility from the cockpit could be improved. Good

Fig. 2.4   XF5F-1.

Fig. 2.5   XP-50.

space coverage of the wing by the slipstream would improve the takeoff. Engines close together made single engine operation, along with the twin vertical tails in the slipstream, easier.

Location of the guns on the center-line and close to the center of gravity permitted various gun combinations to be accommodated. 30 caliber, 50 caliber and cannons were considered and tried out.

Engines used were about the lowest power-to-weight ratio and by having two (engines), total power would give good performance.

Fig. 2.6   Dick Hutton.

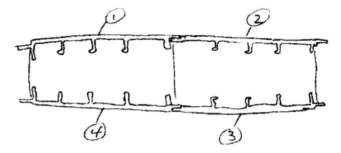

Fig. 2.7   Hutton's hand sketch of the wing box with four numbered extrusions.

At about the time the F5F was being thought of, large aluminum alloy extrusions were becoming possible, and to take advantage of this development, the wing box beam structure was conceived using the largest extrusion at the time to make the box of four identical extrusions with integral stiffening [see Hutton's hand sketch of wing box with four numbered extrusions in Fig. 2.7]. This was the same idea as is practiced today of leaving one sheet stiffener integral with the structure (today it is usually manufactured so as to avoid the restructure of having the same cross section throughout the span).

This box structure was the integral fuel tank (an item which restricted the application of self-sealing tanks in the aircraft, one of the items considered undesirable and leading to no production of the F5F). The structure was also good from a gun fire damage standpoint.

As originally laid out, the aircraft did not have a bubble canopy, but I think this was changed on the mockup.

The U.S. Army Air Corps (now Air Force) was interested in the aircraft and this led to the development of the XP-50; modifications included a nose gear instead of a tail wheel and turbo-supercharging for the engine.

XTBF-1 AVENGER

The XTBF-1 Avenger, G-40, utilized the 1900 hp Curtiss-Wright R 2600 engine. Here again, Bill Schwendler led the preliminary design effort and Arthur Koch, a "lightning fast configuration layout man" according to Joe Lippert of the Preliminary Design team, created a winning design for a torpedo bomber. Lippert and Koch were contemporaries and key members of Preliminary Design. This feat was accomplished, with no experience in designing such a type of aircraft, even though Grumman was working against 13 competitors.

However, Grumman did have outstanding carrier design experience. Grumman and Chance Vought squared off in a design competition for the

Navy's new torpedo bomber to replace the aging Douglas TBD-1 Devastator. Bob Hall, assistant chief engineer for experimental design, sketched out the shape of a large-volume, aerodynamically shaped fuselage that featured a mid-wing design like the F4F and a large bomb bay to accommodate a torpedo or 2000 lb of bombs.

The Avenger featured a hydraulic system that powered the landing gear, wing flaps, wing fold mechanism, bomb bay doors, engine cowl, and oil cooler flaps. In addition, the rear gun turret was electrically powered. Oscar Olsen was working with the Navy, and looked at various types of electric motors that could work smoothly at varying flight conditions and at high g. He proposed this approach to Bill Schwendler, who gave the go-ahead with the warning the he did not want to see "a 4 ft hole in the top of the fuselage when the plane was finished." Olsen and Bud Gillies, a Grumman test pilot, worked with Grumman's research department to come up with a rugged and reliable electric motor design that would be more capable than hydraulic and mechanical systems, and would meet the Avenger prototype schedule.

Along with being assistant chief engineer for experimental design, Bob Hall was chief experimental test pilot, so he flew the Avenger for the first time. Upon landing, he ordered an immediate redesign by adding a large dorsal fin forward of the vertical tail to improve directional stability (see Fig. 2.8). The Avenger also featured a large, rugged fuselage that accommodated a bomb bay and a high seating position for the pilot, allowing good carrier visibility.

In November 1941, Gordon Israel was on a test flight of the XTBF Avenger with pilot Bob Cook when the airplane caught fire. Both men bailed

Fig. 2.8   XTBF-1 Avenger.

out. Cook landed safely, but Israel sustained a broken ankle. He had a limp from that injury for the rest of his life.

WORLD WAR II DESIGNS

During World War II, the Navy's technical branch was pushing Grumman to look at more powerful engines made by Curtiss-Wright and Pratt & Whitney, namely the R-2600 at 1700 hp and the R-2800 at 2000 hp, respectively. (U.S. intelligence on a captured Zero influenced the Navy and Grumman to opt for the higher horsepower.) The team of Roy Grumman, Bill Schwendler, and Dick Hutton conceived Grumman Design G-50, which became the XF6F-1 Hellcat (Fig. 2.9).

XF6F-1 HELLCAT

The Hellcat first flew in 1942, and was the first new fighter designed after Pearl Harbor. Schwendler's succinct statements about the requirements for the Hellcat are noteworthy for the credit they gave to combat pilots: "The early Pacific battles... all served to write, through experience, the requirements for the type of fighter needed by the Navy" and "... the specifications were roughly drafted by such men as Thach, Flately, O'Hare and Gaylor of the Navy and Smith and Carl of the Marines. With the insistent demands of these men, the Hellcat was engineered to provide greater rate of climb and speed over the Wildcat, with heavier fire power and armor protection for the pilot and vital parts of the airplane."

Fig. 2.9   Bill Schwendler and a young Dick Hutton working on an early concept design of the G-50.

"In the beginning of World War II," said Schwendler, "I established some ground rules with Pete Erlandsen [head of structures]. We were going to build an airplane that nobody could break up, nobody could shoot down. That was our philosophy. Some of them did break up, of course, but I think we had the reputation of building a pretty strong machine." So the Grumman Iron Works grew out of their design philosophy.

The resulting design (Fig. 2.10) featured a low wing configuration housing rearward-retracting landing gear, with the cockpit located over the fuel tank in the fuselage and the canopy located high on the fuselage. (The engine and prop orientation improved vision over the nose.) In terms of size, the Hellcat was only a bit smaller than the Republic P-47 Thunderbolt; however, its wing area was larger than the P-47(334 vs. 300 ft^2), to keep carrier approach speeds as low as possible.

XF7F-1 TIGERCAT

The preliminary design of the XF7F-1, G-51 was carried out by Dick Hutton, Gordon Israel, and Bob Hall. After the demise of the XP-50 for the Army Air Corps, the design team continued design studies that led to G-51, the XP-65 (a concept for a future convoy fighter). These studies were terminated in favor of a long-range Navy fighter that could outperform all fighters and carry more offensive firepower in terms of cannons/machine guns and bombs. The resultant design was over 70 mph faster than the F6F Hellcat at sea level. Admiral Frederick Trapnell, one of the Navy's most highly regarded test pilots, called the XF7F-1 the "best damn fighter I've ever flown."

Fig. 2.10   XF6F-1.

Fig. 2.11   The beautiful lines of the experimental version of the F7F.

The design was a twin engine, single seat aerodynamic "beauty" with the engines in large nacelles ahead of the wings (Fig. 2.11). The main landing gear was housed in the back of the nacelles, and was attached to the rear wing spar.

Carrier suitability was a problem with early configurations due to high approach speeds and high landing loads; this resulted in a major wing redesign and redesign of the tail hook supporting structure. The F7F was successfully employed by the Marines for land operations during the Korean War.

XF8F-1 BEARCAT

The G-58 design requirements were laid out by Roy Grumman based primarily on a flight test report of a captured German Focke-Wulf, Fw-190, that Bob Hall flew in 1943. On their trip to England, Roy Grumman, Bud Gillies, and Bob Hall found the Fw-190 to have excellent performance and handling qualities with a weight of about 9000 lb and 1700 hp, compared to the Hellcat, which was 3200 lb heavier with 2000 hp. According to Corky Meyer's *Flight Journal*, the Fw-190 did not have good vision over the nose for good gunnery accuracy or carrier approach visibility, nor was the structure designed for carrier operations.

The preliminary design of the XF8F-1 Bearcat, using the Pratt & Whitney 2400 hp R-2800C engine, was done by Bill Schwendler, Dick Hutton, and Bob Hall. Hall was an aeronautical engineer, aircraft designer, and experimental test pilot when he joined Grumman in 1936. He already had

10 years of experience designing aircraft and flight testing them with the
Fairchild Engine and Aircraft Company, Granville Brothers, and Stinson
Aircraft. In addition, he designed, flight tested, and raced several Thompson
Trophy aircraft. He became assistant chief engineer in 1939 and contributed
heavily to the designs of the F4F Wildcat, F6F Hellcat, and F8F Bearcat. By
1950, he had become chief engineer and was involved with the F9F Panther
and F9F-6 Cougar developments. In 1954, Hall was promoted to vice
president of Engineering and oversaw all of Grumman's Marine engineering,
and programs in hydrofoil research and development of hydrofoil vessels for
both commercial and military applications.

The midwing design of the F8F and the resultant aerodynamic
performance enabled the F8F to operate from the smallest aircraft carriers
with excellent carrier suitability. The design featured a bubble canopy
(Fig. 2.12) and a wide landing gear track due to inward retracting gear that
greatly enhanced land and carrier operation. Drag was reduced due to the use
of flush rivets, and the structure used spot welding and a heavy gauge
aluminum alloy skin. To further reduce weight, the internal fuel capacity was
reduced by 35%, four guns were utilized versus six, and the seat was an
integral part of the cockpit structure. In addition Oscar "Pete" Erlandson,
who was chief of Structures at the time, came up with a novel design that
saved about 250 lb of wing structural weight. His wing design involved
having wingtips that would break off when the fighter was pulling high g and
entered the buffet boundary with compressibility effects. The tips would
break at about 7.5 g, leaving the remaining wing structure with sufficient
aileron control for safe carrier recovery (Fig. 2.13).

Fig. 2.12   F8F Bearcat.

Fig. 2.13   F8F Bearcat with left wingtip broken off.

Bob Hall performed the first flight of the XF8F-1. Upon landing, he immediately ordered a change to the stabilizer span to correct a longitudinal stability deficiency. The resultant performance was remarkable because the XF8F-1 weighed 20% less than the F6F, had a 30% greater rate of climb, and was 50 mph faster. Hall blended his exceptional aircraft designer's prowess with vast experimental test flying expertise from his arrival at Grumman through 1944. During this intensive prewar and wartime period, he performed the first flights of eleven Grumman aircraft: the XF4F-2, XF3F-3, the Goose, XF4F-3, XTBF-1, XP-50, XF6F-1, XF6F-3, XF7F-1, F7F-3, and XF9F-1. Indeed, his was a record of remarkable accomplishment.

AF-2S AND AF-2W GUARDIAN

The evolution of the AF Guardian, which reached operational status in 1950, began in 1942 when the Navy Bureau of Aeronautics (BuAer) requested that Grumman look at a more capable replacement for the successful Avenger design. The team of Bill Schwendler, Dick Hutton, and Bob Hall designed a large, twin engine torpedo bomber, the XTB2F-1. In 1944 it reached the full scale mockup stage shown in Fig. 2.14. The XTB2F-1 had a payload of up to 8000 lb (torpedoes, bombs), had a range in excess of 3500 miles, and could operate from larger aircraft carriers.

The preliminary design team also developed a "derivative" of the F7F called the XTSF-1, but it was less capable than the XTB2F-1. In addition to

Fig. 2.14   A full scale mockup of the XTB2F-1.

these configurations, the preliminary design team, which soon included
Arthur Koch, initiated design G-70, the XTB3F-1,-2 Guardian that featured a
dual propulsion system consisting of a 2300 hp engine with different
Westinghouse turbojets (subsequently scrapped). Navy requirements also
were changing from dedicated torpedo attack to a broader anti-submarine
warfare (ASW) mission consisting of submarine detection and attack. From
these requirements, two versions of the XTB3F series were designed and
flown in 1948–1949: the XTB3F-1 (Fig. 2.15) and the XTBF-1S/2S
(Fig. 2.16). The XTBF-1S "hunter" had a crew of three and a large belly-
mounted search radar; the XTBF-2S became the "killer," with a bomb bay,
searchlight, and radar. Earl Ramsden was the project engineer of the
Guardian series. These aircraft were redesignated the AF-2S, AF-2W, and

Fig. 2.15   XTB3F-1 with the bomb bay doors open.

Fig. 2.16   XTBF-1S and XTBF-2S in flight.

AF-3S [with a magnetic anomaly detection (MAD) system and boom] when they entered production in 1950.

Harold Kressly and his avionic group were responsible for the Guardian avionics. Their task was to pursue and get rid of installation interference [radio frequency interference (RFI)] issues between government-furnished equipment (GFE) during production. Most of the avionic engineers monitored the GFE vendors and the installation requirements/provisions, and they had no responsibility to make various pieces of GFE work properly and together. According to Bob Nafis, the avionic team's main job was to get production aircraft accepted and to chase down fixes. In that vein, they worked well with shop personnel in solving development and production problems.

Bob Hall was a principal aircraft designer who "created the design" that consisted of a Grumman airframe with government-supplied engines (GFE). The avionics, consisting of radar and other major equipment, were GFE, and Kressly's team was responsible for fixing the electrical/electronics (avionics) problems. Kressly was a reserved person and an excellent boss, and hired some good people who worked well with the experimental and production shops in solving development and production problems. Jack Erickson was the group leader for communications, radar, and all antenna design. Ren Witte (ex-Navy captain) provided communications, and George Klaus, also ex-Navy (eventually Reserve Admiral), knew more about magnetics and the ASW problem than anyone in the country. He was a genius in coming up with compensation for the onboard equipment interference. Ed Pholig ran the electrical group that designed the installations (wiring) of everything except radio, data link, Interrogation Friend, Foe (IFF), and radar. Basil Papa worked for him on the Guardian AF series, the WF-2, and then the E2 series.

These were the days before Grumman was responsible for procuring avionics as contractor-furnished equipment (CFE) and integrating the total system as the prime contractor. During the WF-2 and subsequent aircraft system programs discussed in coming chapters, Grumman became one of the nation's leading aircraft weapon system prime contractors. In 1945, Oscar Olsen, Grumman's avionics manager, asked Kressly to form a Systems Engineering group in anticipation of the time when Grumman would have to supply all the avionics, or a good portion thereof, as CFE.

The jet era at Grumman began in earnest after World War II. Vought, McDonnell, Bell, and North American Aviation (NAA) had already flown the XF6U-1 Pirate, XFD-1 Phantom, XP-59 and XP-83, and XFJ-1Fury, respectively. However, it should be mentioned that even though Roy Grumman, Bill Schwendler, and Dick Hutton were very much involved in the Wildcat, Hellcat, Avenger, and Bearcat programs, they conducted preliminary design studies in 1943–1944 on designs that were pure jet and mixed piston/jet. These studies led to the G-57, a design utilizing an R2899 piston engine and a small jet engine; the G-61, which utilized an F6F Hellcat with a tail-located turbojet configuration; the G-63 and G-71 single engine turbojet designs (Fig. 2.17); and the G-68 design utilizing a TG-100 turboprop engine.

CONCLUSION

As the war was ending, Roy Grumman, Bill Schwendler, and Jake Swirbul were facing several challenges: how to keep a portion of their highly skilled workforce employed, identifying and pursuing new airplane markets (e.g., small private aircraft, amphibians), leveraging U.S. and German

Fig. 2.17   G-71 single engine turbojet design.

aerodynamic research to design higher performance fighters, and continuing to attract the best and brightest engineers that would become the next generation of aircraft designers. From 1941 through 1943, Grumman hired Larry Mead, Bernie Harriman, Gordon Israel, Bill Rathke, Joe Lippert, and Grant Hedrick, all of whom went on to become chief designers and contributed to many Grumman aircraft. Joe Gavin came on board in 1946 from MIT after serving in the Navy, and went on to play a key role in the Cougar and Tiger fighter projects. In addition, Grumman instituted a full scholarship program for the best and brightest students interested in engineering, and Bob Kress won one of these scholarship in 1947, graduated from MIT, and contributed to and led many successful aircraft design efforts. In the postwar years, Grumman pursued radical designs utilizing the variable sweep wing and adapted advanced research from the NACA to fighter designs like the Tiger. Grumman also recognized the need for more avionic engineers and began to organize a systems integration group in 1945, in anticipation of avionics equipment increasing in capability, size, complexity, and weight, and thus requiring significant integration capability.

Chapter 3

POSTWAR YEARS: FIRST JETS

XF9F-1 PANTHER

In September 1945, Grumman began design studies on the XF9F-1 (G-75). In response to a Navy request for proposal (RFP) for a two-seat night fighter employing radar and 20 mm cannons, the G-75 was based on the F7F planform with mid-wing-located twin engine pods utilizing four 3000-lb-thrust Westinghouse engines and a nose-mounted radar. Douglas Aircraft won this competition with the XF3D-1 Skynight.

Bill Schwendler and Dick Hutton had also been pursuing a smaller, single engine fighter configuration designated G-79 that was presented to the Navy when further design on the G-75 revealed inadequate performance. Schwendler visited the Navy and was able to persuade them to amend the contract from building two XF9F-1 prototypes to building three XF9F-2 Panthers (Fig. 3.1), a static test article, and design data on a swept wing version. One of the key developments in the design of the Panther was the engine selection. John Karanik, who was head of propulsion at the time, was investigating many new U.S. engines as well as English engines made by Rolls Royce (RR). Karanik went to England and recommended the RR Nene engine due to its higher thrust and good reliability. Grumman recommended this engine to the Navy, and they accepted its incorporation into the Panther design. Pratt & Whitney also built the engine under license in the United States.

XF9F-6 COUGAR

Joe Gavin (Fig. 3.2), who was a design engineer on the XF9F-2, became the project engineer on the G-93, the XF9F-6 swept wing Cougar. Several factors influenced the Navy's and Grumman's forward thinking: German research into swept wing technology, Russian access to the RR Nene engine technology, and the advent of the excellent MIG-15 in Korea. As a result, Gavin and the preliminary design team laid out a modified F9F-5 Panther with a 35-deg swept wing, swept horizontal tail surfaces, and improved chord length of the leading edge slats and flaps. The resultant configuration, shown

Fig. 3.1   XF9F-2 (rear) in flight with the XF9F-3.

in Fig. 3.3, had a critical Mach number of almost 0.9 at 35,000 ft and retained good carrier handling characteristics compared to the F9F-5 Panther. Another notable change to the Cougar was an all-flying horizontal tail that eliminated a control reversal tendency at high transonic Mach numbers.

G-73 MALLARD AND XJR2F-1 ALBATROSS

Grumman continued its line of successful amphibians with the G-73 Mallard and the XJR2F-1 Albatross. Early in 1945, Grumman made the

Fig. 3.2   (R to L) Joe Gavin, Dick Hutton, and Joe Lippert in preliminary design, with Howard Weinmann in the background working on a conceptual design.

Fig. 3.3   XF9F-6 Cougar.

decision to develop a new postwar amphibian for executive and industrial transport that offered the "greatest utility and flexibility for diverse operations," according to Fred Rowley, one of Grumman's most experienced test pilots and flight test directors. In 1945 the preliminary design for the Mallard was developed by Gordon Israel, Hank Kurt, and Ralston Stalb. The general performance requirements called for a cruise speed of at least 180 mph at 60% power, excellent single engine rate of climb, a cruising range of 1000 miles, and a payload based on two pilots and six passengers. Conceptual design studies indicated that at least 1400 hp would be required, and three engines were evaluated. The Pratt & Whitney R-1340 rated at 600 hp was selected. Wing sizing was based on design tradeoffs of maximizing single engine rate of climb, and achieving maximum cruising speed and the lowest stall speed. The eventual Mallard design, shown in Fig. 3.4, featured a 10- to 12-passenger cabin with a beautifully shaped, deep hull that was longer than previous amphibians. It was, and remains today, one of the finer looking aircraft of its class.

The design requirements for a utility transport with air–sea rescue capability resulted in the XJRF2-1 Albatross (Fig. 3.5), the largest amphibian built by Grumman (30,000 lb category with almost 3000 miles range). Bill Wange and Ralston Stalb designed the Albatross. This was Ralston Stalb's last design. He left a long legacy of excellent amphibians including the Loening Air Yacht, Widgeon, Goose, Mallard, and Albatross. In his later years at Grumman, Stalb was afflicted with severe arthritis that impacted his mobility, but not his acute design abilities. Vincent Milano, who at the time was project weights engineer on the SA-16 Albatross, recalled working with Stalb: "He had arthritis and walked slowly. He would come to see me about

Fig. 3.4   G-73 Mallard.

something and while still 25 to 30 feet away would begin his conversation with me. Sometimes someone would have to alert me if I was deeply involved in something to pay attention to his words." The Albatross was adopted by the U.S. Navy, Air Force, and Coast Guard as well as several foreign countries' militaries.

Tom Rae was also associated with the Albatross as a senior member of the engineering and program staff, and was project engineer on versions of the

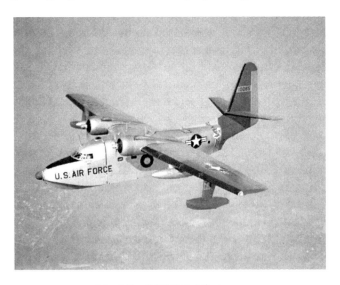

Fig. 3.5   XJRF2-1 Albatross.

Fig. 3.6 A rare image of the Widgeon, Goose, and Mallard flying in trail formation.

Albatross. Rae spent a vast portion of his career designing and being a project engineer on many versions of Grumman's long line of amphibians from the Widgeon to the Albatross (Fig. 3.6). At his retirement in 1969, after almost 40 years with Grumman, Rae was asked to reminisce about the planes that were the bread and butter of the company before and after World War II—the amphibians. Rae recalled being a summer student at Loening Aeronautical Engineering Aircraft in 1927. Roy Grumman was general manager of Loening at the time, and took some time out of his busy schedule to correct a mistake in a paper Rae was writing. On another note Grumman stated, "The Mallard (a 12 place amphibian) was a great plane but the commercial market we expected after the war failed to develop... because the services released 500 surplus amphibians at low cost. Would you believe these figures? From 1937 to 1942 we built 345 'Geese.'... We built 1146 amphibians altogether." About the Albatross, Rae recounted, "We originally built it for the Navy and the Air Force for rescue and the Coast Guard for search and rescue, hospital and transport. The big modification was when we converted 36 Albatrosses for foreign countries."

G-63 AND G-72 KITTENS, AND G-65 TADPOLE

During 1943, Roy Grumman, using company funds, began developing small remotely controlled land and amphibian aircraft conceptual designs that would be the United States' answer to the Japanese "kamikaze" aircraft. These aircraft would be designed to dive upon Japanese warships and land

Fig. 3.7   G-63 Kitten.

installations in many areas of the Pacific theater, including ocean and coastal areas. This effort was carried out in a special closed design, construction, and test area where the aircraft would be built and undergo static test.

As a result, the Grumman Aircraft Engineering Corporation designed and flew a series of light, two-place conventional and amphibious aircraft during the 1944–47 period. The Tadpole and the Hepcat Kitten were flown in 1944, and the Kitten I and Kitten II were flown in 1946 and 1947, respectively. The G-63 Kitten, the G-65 Tadpole amphibian, and the G-72 Kitten, shown in Figs. 3.7 through 3.9, were designed by Roy Grumman, Dayton T. Brown, David B. Thurston, and Hank Kurt. Thurston was a gifted designer who left Grumman relatively early in his career. Dr. Dick Scheuing remembers visiting him at his home and seeing a large drawing board in the living room, similar to those found at Grumman. Scheuing was very impressed with Thurston's dedication to aircraft design, and that he had married a very understanding woman. Sperry developed the remote control units for the

Fig. 3.8   G-72 Kitten.

Fig. 3.9 G-65 Tadpole amphibian.

G-63. The G-63 initially featured a tail sitter landing gear configuration, but it was redesigned to a tricycle gear arrangement for the G-72. The G-72 tail design was also changed from the G-63 to twin vertical tail surfaces that avoided slipstream effects on the vertical tails. This design feature, which was successfully flight tested, allowed "co-ordinated two- control operation" and simplified remote control operation. The G-65 amphibian was designed for coastal water operation.

Roy Grumman was known as a very calm person with a quiet demeanor. However, Dave Thurston recalls an incident when Roy Grumman threw two Navy Commanders out of his closed area, where the Tadpole and Kitten were being designed. When the Navy personnel entered, he quickly advised them that the Navy did not own this plant and that they seemed to have difficulty reading the restricted area notices!

Hank Kurt made the first flight of all three aircraft, along with Roy Grumman, in the G-75 Tadpole. Although good designs, these aircraft were not ordered into production in the postwar period because of price, strong competition (e.g., the Beechcraft Bonanza in 1946), and not achieving the desired market penetration. These aircraft were probably designed and built using Grumman Iron Works' military aircraft design guidelines to some degree versus the lower cost manufacturing techniques utilized by commercially based private aircraft manufacturers at the time.

XF10F-1 JAGUAR

The evolution of the XF10F-1 Jaguar began in 1947 when Grumman submitted Design 83, a fixed, swept wing, "T" tail fighter design for the Navy. This slowly evolved into a variable incidence swept wing design. The

Fig. 3.10   A full-scale mockup of the XF10F-1 Jaguar in 1947.

final design configuration featured a translating variable sweep design that moved from 13 1/2 deg for landing to 42 1/2 deg for combat (Figs. 3.10 and 3.11). The project engineer, Gordon Israel, was in charge of the overall preliminary design effort, and Gene Wade was head of aerodynamic development. Joe Hubert played a lead role in aerodynamic design. Al Munier was chief of structures at the time and developed the structural concept.

Gordon Israel (Fig. 3.12) was a gifted, self-taught engineer who designed, built, and flew his own racing aircraft in the 1930 Cleveland Air Races when still under 21 years of age. He began his career in 1928 as a draughtsman and worked part time with Jules LaGrave on the design of an airplane. In 1929 he worked with Benny Howard on the design and construction of a small racing

Fig. 3.11   The XF10F-1 Jaguar flying in 1952.

Fig. 3.12   Gordon Israel (right) with Grumman test pilot Fred Rowley.

airplane. Here he learned all the crafts to build an aircraft, and also saw firsthand how modifications were made to improve performance or make an aircraft good or bad. In 1930 he learned to fly, and as a result the self-taught designer and builder now could test and race his own aircraft designs. He successfully raced in the 1934–37 period with an aircraft that he and Howard designed. Israel also worked for Stinson and at Howard Aircraft, where he became vice president and chief engineer in 1940, before being hired by Grumman.

Gordon Israel worked for Grumman from 1941 to 1953 and was probably hired due to his friendship with Bob Hall during their air racing days. During his employment, he was a project engineer on at least four Grumman airplanes—the F7F Tigercat, the Mallard, the F9F Panther, and the XF10F-1. Joe Lippert recalled working with him in the late 1940s. "He was a nice man and generally easy to get along with. He did have a gift for designing pretty airplanes. When streamlining was the right way to go, his pretty airplanes sure did go." The "good lines" on the F7F, Mallard, and early F9F Panther series are attributable to Gordon, and these airplanes were outstanding in their appearance and gracefulness.

The Grumman Aircraft Engineering Corporation was definitely pushing the state of the art in aircraft design with the Jaguar concept, and the final preliminary design seemed to violate Bill Schwendler's philosophy that "the best new design was the one with least experimental features." It was an ambitious undertaking for anyone in those days because there was little technical data to support the design of near-sonic airplanes. This fact, coupled with the limited performance of the Westinghouse engine, resulted in an airplane that could not succeed operationally.

Don Terrana, who was a young engineer assigned to the project, marveled at the aircraft concept and stated "mechanically it was a beautiful design." The Jaguar was not a pivoted variable sweep design [this concept was later developed by John Stack at the National Advisory Committee for Aeronautics (NACA) and applied on the TFX discussed in Chapter 6], but was a translating variable sweep design to keep the proper relationship between aircraft center of gravity and the wing center of lift. Terrana described the wing attachment to the fuselage as a rather complex structural arrangement. A wing-pivoting post was located on the fuselage, attached to a sliding fitting on the wing. As the wing rotated on the post, it could also slide forward. The key structural element of the swing wing was a "huge" aluminum pivot forging that was jokingly called the "clip," which in aircraft parlance is usually a very small sheet metal part used to attach small assemblies.

In addition to variable sweep wings that showed remarkable aerodynamic performance improvements over comparable fixed wing designs like the F-3H Demon, the XF10F-1 employed a novel, untried, aerodynamically (rather than hydraulically) boosted flight control system that was Israel's design. The horizontal tail design created by Joe Hubert was not adequate for the critical takeoff and landing phase. At low speeds, the air pressure on the aerodynamically balanced horizontal tail control surface was so small that the response rate was much too slow for adequate control. According to Larry Mead (Fig. 3.13), who was Gordon's assistant project engineer at the time, this system had intuitive appeal, but was a failure. Israel would not believe the PhD, college-trained dynamicists, who had correctly predicted that this ingenious system would not work based on analyses done on early electronic computers that Grumman had just acquired.

The entire XF10F-1 control system was manual (cables) except the wing sweep mechanism and, here again, the design philosophies of the Navy and the chief designer at the time did not match the unique requirements of the Jaguar. It was too bad that Israel could not have stayed with Grumman, but it was not to be after the XF10F debacle, said Joe Lippert in 1985 as he was discussing Israel's career. Perhaps if he'd had a better understanding of certain fundamental principles of physics, Grumman would not have failed with the XF10F.

John Ohler, one of Grumman's senior aerodynamacists at the time who went on the become president of Grumman Solar Systems, recalled his days

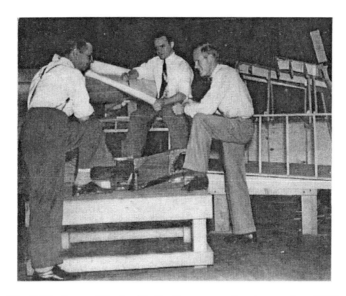

Fig. 3.13 Larry Mead with the Jaguar mockup team, circa 1949.

spent testing the XF10F-1. The story that the test team was told about the control system was that the Navy was resisting going to power systems like the Air Force was because they didn't trust anything that was new and unproven. The entire control system was manual, except the wing sweep mechanism. The lateral system was one of the most complicated things he had ever seen. It had to, in effect, "shift gears" when the wing swept to keep the throws (deflections) smaller. The lateral system and the rudder seemed to work fine mechanically. It turned out the aircraft had aerodynamic coupling problems laterally and directionally that no one really anticipated, or knew how to handle, at that point. These issues masked the longitudinal problems entirely. The manual longitudinal control system relied on a spring tab to move the servo plane that, in turn, moved the stabilizer and its geared tab. This approach was clever conceptually, but incurred a great deal of lag. The records of the taxi runs performed by Corky Meyers were incredible (over 222). Ohler said, "Meyers likened this [lag in system response] to 'chasing snakes all over the cockpit.' The local mechanics used to walk by the aircraft in the hangar and ask when do we fire the missile at the tail!"

Israel was a great prankster. During an XF10F-1 layup for maintenance, the Grumman engineers in Bethpage, Long Island, came up with a big bungee-type tie down that was supposed to keep the tail down until the servo could take over. The test team waited breathlessly for the shipment. Finally the expected box showed up. They could finally get in the air or at least on the runway to taxi again. The guys were standing by to work all night, if

Fig. 3.14 Powered model of the XF10F.

necessary. The box was eagerly opened and—there were two bricks in it. Israel had his big joke, but the air in the office and hangar was as "blue" as Ohler has ever seen it. The correct part did arrive a few days later.

One valuable preliminary design technique is to build scaled flying models, either powered or glided, that emulate the basic flying characteristics of the design in question. Joe Lippert, one of Grumman's lead aerodynamicists and designers, built a powered model of the XF10F (see Fig. 3.14), and it displayed poor longitudinal flight qualities and characteristics that were also verified during wind tunnel tests.

This process is extremely valuable today to give engineering design teams practicable hands-on knowledge in parallel with the preliminary design process. For example, during World War II, Ulrich Stampa, a Focke-Wulf designer, built a model of the TA-183 that eventually became the MIG-15. During the late 1970s, the X-29 design team built a flying model of a forward swept wing configuration. Today, a NASA/Boeing team are test flying a high fidelity model of a blended wing transport, the X-48B.

Many positive lessons were learned on this program that would be applied on the F-111B and F-14A variable sweep fighter programs. One of the best lessons learned was to keep the solution as simple as possible.

CONCLUSION

Three generations of aircraft designers, Schwendler, Hutton, and Gavin, created the solid Panther and Cougar series that gave the U.S. Navy rugged, higher performance operational jet aircraft that performed well during the post–World War II and Korean War time period. Success was also achieved with the third-generation Mallard and Albatross amphibians, which achieved multiservice, foreign, and commercial service and continue to fly today. Schwendler and Grumman, with the Navy's blessing, permitted an all-new, cutting edge, yet unsuccessful Jaguar to be designed and tested. Gordon Israel drove the creation of the Jaguar with pre-World War II and next generation aerodynamic teammates, including Joe Hubert and Gene Wade, that explored the feasibility of the variable sweep wing combined with untried lateral and longitudinal control systems.

The transition of engineering and chief designer leadership to Bob Hall and Dick Hutton, respectively, was underway as the 1950s began. Creativity was unleashed under their leadership, with rapid expansion of the preliminary design and operations analysis departments to meet the myriad requirements from the Army, Navy, and Air Force for aircraft weapon systems, as well as to expand into the commercial executive aircraft market. This resulted in the ascendancy of the aircraft designers and operations analysis personnel, including Leonard Sullivan, Walter Scott, Bill Rathke, Larry Mead, Mike Pelehach, Bernie Harriman, Dan Lynch, Russ Murray, Hal Moss, and Doug Hill.

Chapter 4

THE DYNAMIC 1950s AND 1960s, AND THE GULFSTREAM LEGACY

XF9F-9, XF11F-1 TIGER

In January 1953, in an engineering staff meeting, the perennial gripe about too much airplane had been aired. "There ought to be smaller, simpler, faster fighters." But that day the discussion was more pointed than usual. Dick Hutton, chief engineer (Fig. 4.1); Joe Gavin, project engineer; and Walter Scott, chief of Preliminary Design spent the next several days in each other's company. At the next staff meeting this team revealed the subject of their activities—a new conceptual fighter designated Design G-98 (Fig. 4.2). They described all of the unique features of the concept, and subsequently briefed Grumman management. The go-ahead was received for Preliminary Design (PD) to develop a design proposal to the Navy for the new fighter. Joe Gavin had the job of coming up with a small compact fighter with extremely thin wings. His problem was to relocate or eliminate anything that caused a thick wing, such as ducts, landing gear, folding mechanisms, or controls.

Dick Hutton supervised the preliminary design of the G-98, which was later renamed the XF9F-9 Tiger. Joe Gavin was the project engineer, and put together a design team including Bob Miller, chief of Aerodynamics, and Bob Mullaney, chief of Propulsion in PD. Larry Mead came on board in 1953 as assistant project engineer. Tom Kelly, who would achieve subsequent fame for leading the design of the Apollo Lunar Module as chief engineer, designed the inlets for the supersonic Tiger. The Research department made significant contributions to the design evolution of the XF9F-9, notably:

- Control system design and analysis: Arnold Whitaker
- Flight simulator (analog computer driven): Dr. Richard Kopp and Tom Keller
- Dynamic longitudinal and lateral stability analyses: Dr. Henry Kelley, Robert Kress, and Norm Lewin
- All flutter and vibration work on wing and stabilizer, using basic structural data from Engineering: Gene Baird and Ed Kelly

Fig. 4.1   An early meeting between Dick Hutton (right) and Bob Hall to discuss the initiation of the Design G-98 project.

• The thinness of the wing and tail necessitated great caution, especially in view of the lack of reliable transonic aerodynamic theory. Therefore, experimental corroboration was sought, employing rocket-powered sled tests at Edwards Air Force Base at speeds up to Mach 1.25. Joe Hubert led the effort with Gene Baird and Ed Kelly.

The Research department had been formed in 1947 with about 20 engineers and applied mathematicians, and was directed initially by Dr. Ralph Tripp, who turned the reins over to Dr. Charles Mack, Jr., a year later.

Fig. 4.2   A full-scale mockup of Design G-98.

From 1947 to 1957 or 1958, the Research department was responsible for exploring, developing, and applying the cutting-edge engineering technologies of flutter and vibration, dynamic stability and control, analog computer–based simulation, and supersonic flow theory. Management's logic, according to Dr. Dick Scheuing, was to initially place the responsibility for these technology and engineering disciplines in Research, because there were applied mathematicians in the department who better understood these relatively new areas. Following completion of the Tiger/Super Tiger design activities, all of the engineering responsibilities in these areas were transferred to Engineering. As the XF9F-9 design evolved in Preliminary Design, Research contributed to its successful creation by performing up-front analyses and tests that added to the design's maturity as the preliminary design was being solidified prior to detail design.

Norm Lewin, Bob Kress, Arnold Whitaker, Gene Baird, Ed Kelly, and Joe Hubert were all part of Research initially, and while there were involved in several aircraft designs, most notably the XF9F-9 Tiger. Each of them made significant contributions to many future aircraft during their careers in engineering.

Dick Cyphers was involved in the structural design of the Tiger. The wings of the Tiger needed to be thin [thickness-to-chord (t/c) ratio of 5%] to achieve the right cross-sectional area for supersonic flight; George Petronio was instrumental in developing a new form of wing construction. Upper and lower wing skin covers were milled from aluminum alloy slabs with integral stiffeners to reduce weight, as opposed to traditional construction of skins riveted to ribs and spars.

Many configuration studies were performed that stemmed from the previous Cougar design (F9F-7) and led to a supersonic, swept wing configuration employing the Richard Whitcomb [National Advisory Committee for Aeronautics (NACA)] area rule principle (coke bottle fuselage) that greatly reduced transonic drag with the Curtiss-Wright J-65 engine. Bob Miller did all the hand calculations on the area rule shaping of the wing and fuselage. Dick Hutton stated during an August 1954 demonstration to the Navy that, "The coke bottle design of the fuselage is one of its most novel features. Little if anything was compromised on this design—it was done the best aerodynamic way." Gavin and Mead worked closely with the dynamists and their computer simulations, leading to an aircraft with superb flying qualities. Indeed, the Tiger was used by the Blue Angels from 1957 to 1968 because of its excellent handling characteristics.

The resulting XF9F-9 (XF11F-1) flew in July 1954 only 16 months after the finalized three-view drawing and specification were released (Figs. 4.3

Fig. 4.3   An early test flight of the XF9F-9 (XF11F-1).

and 4.4). The Tiger was such an excellent configuration that a growth configuration evolved called G-98J, the F11F-1F Super Tiger (Fig. 4.5). Mike Pelehach was a key member of the design team and maintained the excellent lines of the Tiger configuration while incorporating larger air inlets, wing fillets, and a fuselage extension to accommodate the afterburning GE J-79 engine. Bob Miller was chief of aerodynamics and Bob Mullaney was chief of propulsion. Both contributed to the design and flight test success of the Super Tiger. The F11F-1F achieved Mach 2+ performance and set the world's altitude record in excess of 76,500 ft. (It actually reached altitude in excess of 80,000 ft.)

Fig. 4.4   Corky Meyer, Grumman test pilot, receives congratulations from Admiral Soucek, chief of the Bureau of Aeronautics (BuAer), and Joe Gavin, project engineer.

Fig. 4.5   G-98J, the F11F-1F Super Tiger.

As a group leader for internal aerodynamics research, Robert Bower and his team (which included Professor Antonio Ferri, a Grumman consultant and well-known specialist in supersonic theory and experiment) pursued a suggestion to develop the necessary theory and computer program to design inlet precompression bumps. Properly designed, such bumps offered the advantage of precompressing incoming air through a series of oblique shock waves, weakening the normal shock at the inlet, while simultaneously diverting the fuselage boundary layer around the inlet. This team applied their capability to the successful design for the XF11F-1F, the first aircraft known to have incorporated such a feature. It enabled the aircraft to achieve Mach 2+ with fixed inlet geometry. Research also performed zoom climb flight path optimization studies and minimum-drag fuselage shape tests at supersonic speeds.

A2F-1 AND A-6A INTRUDER

Based on Korean War experience, during late 1956 the U.S. Navy developed requirements for the VAX, an all-weather attack bomber with a very long range and high payload capability. Prior to about 1955, most of the Navy aircraft suppliers were asked to come up with designs that responded to current requirements laid out by the aircraft desk at the Bureau of Aeronautics (BuAer). These requirements usually included the engine or propeller programs and current electronics, communications, and missile systems being specified by the Bureau. The request for proposal (RFP) then included these items to be included as government furnished equipment (GFE). The RFP also included the type specification (TS 149), which specified a carrier-based, all-weather, two-man attack aircraft capable of flying a 1000-mile interdiction mission with a specified payload and with a maximum speed of 500 kt. The type specification also called for short takeoff and landing (STOL) capability.

Douglas Aircraft broke the mold with the A-4, which included a large percentage of contractor furnished equipment (CFE) and lightweight component designs incorporating an ejection seat and electrical systems that were not Navy developed. One of the major problems was that the Navy developed systems in separate departments within the Bureau that were self- contained, resulting in a lot of duplication of sensors, inputs, cockpit instruments, panel controls, and the like. The VAX program was the first to propose that the contractors do the integration, contract for the equipment (except the engines), and operate under a fixed price incentive fee/cost plus incentive fee (FPIF/CPIF) contract, the details of which were to be proposed by the contractor.

Larry Mead headed up the preliminary design as project engineer and was proposal team leader for the VAX design competition. Richard "Bugs" Waldt developed the basic Design 128 layout as configuration design engineer. This was the first time the Navy requested a total weapon system concept proposal including airframe, electronics, and logistic support system supplied by the prime contractor, with proposals due during August 1957. PD was headed by Walter Scott and assisted by Leonard "Sully" Sullivan. Sullivan did a phenomenal job of keeping all the Grumman departments focused. Mead brought together an excellent team including Horace Moore, assistant to Larry; Bill Murphy, aerodynamics; Bob Nafis, avionics; and Gene Bonan, weapon systems. Irv Waaland, one of Grumman's most experienced and talented aerodynamicists, recalled that the resultant A-6 design was considered the Navy's safest operation carrier aircraft and was the subject of a Navy study on which factor(s) contributed most to that assessment. Although the A-6A evidenced outstanding stability and control with low approach speed and exceptional visibility over the nose for carrier landing, the winning factor was the landing gear design. The Grumman Iron Works scored again as the rugged and durable landing gear accommodated the usual growth in landing weight incurred by all military aircraft during their service life.

Mead also worked very closely with his Navy counterpart at BuAer, Commander Bill Ditch, A-6A Class Desk Officer. Ditch had flown TBF Avengers off aircraft carriers in World War II and became an aeronautical engineer after World War II. He and Mead hammered out the details of the pre-award specification prior to the start of full-scale development. When Ditch retired from the Navy, he came to work at Grumman and helped Grumman win the VFX (F-14A) proposal discussed in Chapter 6.

The VAX also required a means to track moving targets, and a sensor for terrain clearance at low altitudes. The Bureau also wanted applications of the Army Navy Instrumentation Program (ANIP) and ergonomics to be proposed, along with a short field takeoff. Sullivan pushed the tilting tailpipe for Design 128, Grumman's VAX proposal design. Bob Nafis was the lead engineer in the systems group, and had to come up with a computer that could provide the memory and power to handle the equations for the integration of all the sensors and displays. Gene Bonan, Bob Carbee, and Newt Spiess did all the weapons delivery computations. Bill Beese, Bob Watson, Larry VanDercreek, Herman Wenz, and Lou Arsenau handled the navigation, instrumentation, air data, and interfacing computation and equipment. Dan Collins was one of the original people from a relatively small team working on the A2F proposal in late 1957 to early 1958. He worked under Harold Kressly, Bob Nafis, and Bill Beese in what was originally the avionics group of the Engineering department. Ren Witte and Joe Rodriguez were in charge of the communications and radars.

A2F-1 Number 1 was built in the prototype shop in Grumman's Plant 5 Bethpage, Long Island, facility (Fig. 4.6). Larry Mead is shown in the lower right corner of the picture. On the day this photo was taken, Mead remembered that he was in charge of the shop mechanics because the shop foreman was sick. Because Grumman was non-union this was accomplished without a hitch. Jake Swirbul, in the white shirt and tie standing on the right, is overlooking the assembly. Joe Ruggiero at the time was a 19-year-old technician going to college at night and working in Grumman's Plant 2 Long Island facility making parts for the A2F-1 leading edge. Joe is

Fig. 4.6   A2F-1 Number 1 in the prototype shop.

standing with his back turned on the work stand near the leading edge of the wing.

Lou Hemmerdinger remembers Mead for being not only an excellent aircraft designer, but also a good engineering manager to get the A-6 into the air from contract go-ahead.

> A lot of the unique characteristics of the plane were from Larry Mead. What I really enjoyed about him was his engineering management. He knew what was needed, gave direction, listened to the approaches and made decisions. Those were the days we were on mandatory 56 hour weeks (without real overtime pay—$2 extra per hour), dinner in the Plant 2 (Bethpage, Long Island) cafeteria while getting the plane to fly within 2 years.

Grumman ultimately ditched the Kaiser see-through vertical display and the large horizontal mapping display that were originally planned because of illumination and other technical problems; instead they used high intensity storage tubes that successfully achieved the ribbon-in-the-sky flight path control. A ribbon-in-the-sky flight path refers to a path the pilot flies to minimize risk associated with major topographical features such as mountains ahead of the aircraft. This can be seen visually on a vertical situation display and could also include other waypoints ahead of the aircraft, threats, and the like. Grumman also developed a whole line of vertical tape instruments for systems where fast monitoring comparisons were desired, as well as large vertical display indicator (VDI) repeaters for pilot and bombardier navigators (BN). The digital computer and inertial platform provided position and attitude accuracies that allowed unprecedented delivery solutions. It also made the design team very aware of the training and maintenance problems introduced into the fleet by the new fully integrated system approach to get weight out and performance up. This led to the inclusion of automatic checkout and testing equipment in subsequent aircraft derivatives (e.g., A-6E).

Bob Nafis recalled a very significant series of events involving Newt Speiss, who became one of Grumman's outstanding avionic visionaries. Bill Beese and Gene Bonan had both flown TBFs (Avengers) in the Pacific, and for a time were both on the same carrier, but had never met. Newt Spiess had been chief engineer for National Dairy before he came to Grumman. He got so frustrated listening to Beese and Bonan discuss the finer points of weapon delivery that he took flying lessons and got his license to better understand the pilot's point of view. Grumman was having difficulty programming the pilot's vertical display with the superimposed "pathway in the sky" representation, particularly when the roll entry and azimuth radial spokes were changing rapidly. Speiss spent several weekends conducting experiments during the winter when the large Jones Beach parking lots on Long Island were empty, but the parking line grids were visible. He mounted a camera on a car and the Cessna that he flew did runs on the car from many aspects. As a result, he decluttered the display and simplified the programming to everyone's satisfaction.

In 1958, the computer memory available to engineers was very limited. A computer drum at that time could handle about 30 target tracks and had the capacity of less than 1% of that available in a modern-day cell phone. The computer drum speed set the iteration rate. Everything was a tradeoff with accuracy including radome thickness as a function of deflection angle, the shock and vibration design of the inertial platform, fast disconnect mount adjustments, and optical jigging of the aircraft structure. No one person had the genius to make all the judgments. Fortunately, Grumman had the mix of experience and skills in engineering and manufacturing tooling to come up with answers.

Operations analysis performed VAX sizing and cost-effectiveness studies that provided a series of selected design points. Jerry Ryan and Bob Harvey did a lot of the cost-effectiveness studies on VAX alternatives based on VAX parametric aircraft inputs from Hal Moss's vehicle sizing group and Doug Hill's cost analysis group. Mead then spent several weeks with his small team solving a multidimensional puzzle to select the desired VAX configuration that resulted in Design G-128, A2F-1 (Figs. 4.7 and 4.8). Various configurations were laid out with different wing geometries including an "M" wing, tails, fuselage shapes, engines, radars, crew accommodations, weapons carriage, and so on. Each configuration was

Fig. 4.7   First flight of the unpainted A2F-1 with Bob Smyth at the controls.

Fig. 4.8   A rare picture of the A2F-1 prototype with tilting tail pipes to enhance takeoff performance.

sized to meet mission radius, payload, maximum speed, endurance, maneuverability, and carrier suitability requirements. In addition, each configuration met structural strength criteria, handling qualities, reliability and supportability factors, and all-weather weapon system performance and payload accuracy. Grumman won this competition that involved 12 competitive designs from seven companies, and the Navy designated the Grumman Design G-128 as the A2F-1.

After the contract award in spring 1958, Dan Collins became very involved in the development of the A2F system and derivatives (e.g., A-6E). Collins gravitated to the development of the ASQ-61 digital computer and ASN-31 inertial platform systems, and his experience broadened to cover the entire weapon system. During the early 1960s, Collins was involved with the A-6 avionics/weapon system flight development program conducted at Grumman's Calverton, Long Island, flight test facility. He became quite proficient at operating the system cockpit controls, and during Navy trials he could be seen in the cockpit instructing Navy flight personnel on the system operation. He had a flair for addressing the Navy's technical questions to their satisfaction—a trait that served him well throughout his career. Collins spent almost his entire career with the A-6 program, which culminated in his becoming the A-6 program vice president. His experience and longevity on the A-6 rightfully gave him the nickname Mr. Air-to-Ground Attack Systems at Grumman.

Design 128, which became the A-6A (after it won as the A2F-1), had many variations over a long operational life that extended from 1963 to 1997—a total of 34 years. Major variants were the A-6B, A-6 TRIM, KA-6D tanker, A-6E, and A-6F/G. The A-6A featured the high technology (for

THE DYNAMIC 1950S AND 1960S, AND THE GULFSTREAM LEGACY

its day) Digital Integrated Attack/Navigation Equipment (DIANE) system that provided excellent day/night/poor weather bombing accuracy by utilizing several radars: APQ-92 search radar, APG-46 tracking radar, APN-141 radar altimeter, and APN-122 Doppler navigation radar. Radar inputs were fed to the Litton ASN-31 inertial navigational system. (An interesting personal note is that Bob Nafis's daughter's name was Diane.) All the information was provided to the bombardier navigator in the right seat via an air-data and ballistics computer.

The A-6C TRIM (Trails-Roads Interdiction Multi-sensor) was designed to hit North Vietnamese supply routes at night. It had a low-light-level TV and specialized receiver equipment that was designed to pick up enemy truck exhaust emissions. Don Cook put the concept and proposal together with Bill Fehrs as program manager.

Dan Collins was the leader of the A-6E program that built or converted a total of 445 aircraft into this configuration out of a total 693 A-6 aircraft of all variants produced. The search and fire control radars of previous models were upgraded to the much more reliable APQ-148 multimode radar with new computers, the new ASN-92 inertial navigation system, and Carrier Aircraft Inertial Navigation System (CAINS). The "E" variant was also upgraded with a Target, Recognition and Attack Multi-Sensor (TRAM) system tied into new Norden APQ-156 radar.

The final version of the A-6 line was the A-6F, which utilized the new synthetic aperture radar (SAR) APQ-173 radar and some of the key system improvements developed and incorporated into the F-14D, notably the Control Data Corporation AYK-14 central computer, the Kaiser display processor, and cockpit multifunctional displays. The big airframe/engine change was accomplished with the nonafterburning GE F404 engine used in the F-18 Hornet that would provide significant improvements in thrust available on takeoff and in combat, as well as specific fuel consumption (SFC).

According to Joe Cagnazzi, who was responsible for systems, software, and avionics development on the A-6F/G, the "brains" behind the systems and avionics was Walter Smrek. As discussed previously, some of the A-6F avionics were used in common with the F-14D, and the F-14D program had the primary development lead for the common items (central computer, display processor, and cockpit displays). On the A-6F/G side, the lead software designer was Rich Capria. The F-14D and A-6 F/G missions were different, so the software requirements were vastly different. Capria did a great job of developing and implementing those requirements. Smrek, along with Capria and his team, made the A-6F program a technical success. On the vehicle side of the A-6F/G, Joe Ruggiero, who was one the A-6 program's most experienced program managers, recalled that Dick Feyk was the lead. Feyk (Fig. 4.9) was a seasoned veteran with a vast

Fig. 4.9   Roll-out of the A-6F with (L to R) Joe Ruggiero, Dan Collins, Dick Feyk, and Jim Richter.

structural design and analysis background combined with advanced systems program management and development experience. His personal interest in the engineering force was an inspiration to all who worked with him.

Hank Janiesch remembered a near miss involving the A-6. The first complete weapon system A2F aircraft (number 4) flew from Bethpage to Calverton early on the morning of November 30, 1960. Many of the engineering team had worked through the previous day and night and into the wee hours of the morning installing and checking out all the equipment of the aircraft for this major milestone. Some members of the tired, dedicated team then drove from Bethpage to the Calverton facility to share in the Navy/Grumman first system flight ceremonies and festivities. The A2F aircraft was on display with the radome up, all avionic equipment radar equipment installations on display, and viewing stands positioned along both sides of the cockpit. Dan Collins was sitting in the pilot's seat pointing out various controls and displays to both Navy and Grumman VIPs. Janiesch and Bob Branstetter, another Grumman engineer, were walking around the fuselage and stopped right under the arresting gear while Janiesch described how it was designed. No sooner had they moved out from under the gear, then it dropped with a loud, resounding "thud" on the hangar floor! Collins had inadvertently activated the arresting gear and the tail hook safety pin had not been installed by the plane captain. Needless to say they were shaken up and took the rest of the day off.

Due to the nature of a total weapon system concept desired by the Navy, Dick Hutton, then vice president of engineering, instituted a new engineering process in which a cross-section of all departments was "welded" into the core preliminary design team. This process allowed for the optimum blending and tradeoffs of technical, logistic, reliability and maintainability, cost, and life cycle cost factors at the same time, very much along the lines of how integrated performance teams (IPTs) perform today.

S2F TRACKER

Grumman submitted Design G-89 in response to a Navy RFP in 1950 for a single airframe and antisubmarine warfare (ASW) system to replace the AF-2S/2 W "hunter killer" aircraft. Bill Rathke was the proposal manager for this widely contested competition, and Joe Lippert was involved in the aerodynamic design of the configuration. Joe Boettjer was the avionics lead on the project. The resultant XS2F-1 was a compact, rugged, carrier-based, four-man crew, aircraft design. It featured a foldable high wing; two Wright 1525 hp engines; and a sizeable bomb bay that housed torpedoes, bombs, mines, and depth charges. The ASW system was housed in the fuselage with a retractable radome and magnetic anomaly detection (MAD) boom, as shown in Fig. 4.10. George Klaus (Fig. 4.11) was a legend at Grumman and in the Navy for knowing how to clean up and compensate for the random magnetic fields that affect MAD gear. He was instrumental in the S-2F MAD gear design and added hundreds of yards to detection depths. Jack Mooney and Skip Courtney (a blind engineer) worked closely with George in developing and testing MAD gear and applicable ASW technology. Klaus was a commander in the Naval Reserve and one of Grumman's most experienced avionics engineers. His team worked for 4 years to eliminate

Fig. 4.10   S2F Tracker.

Fig. 4.11   George Klaus in the ASW laboratory briefing (L to R) Jim Harbilius; Dr. V. Stantius, director of NASA; and Bill Athas.

unwanted aircraft magnetic field distortion and maneuver noise that resulted in good performing and maintainable MAD gear for the U.S. Navy. Jack Saxe, one of Preliminary Design's lead aerodynamicists, who worked on the S2F proposal, remembered the whole written proposal was about "a 1/2 in. thick." Oh, for those simpler days!

According to Leonard "Sully" Sullivan's letters, Grumman spent years in the 1950s and 1960s trying to sell product improvement versions of the S2F family. Grumman proposed a "clever design for twinned" GE T-58 turboprop engine nacelles. Bob Bram was the project engineer, Dane Lamberson did the aerodynamic and performance workup, and Bill Tebo, Preliminary Design propulsion head, worked with GE to install twin T-58 engines in each nacelle. Other turboprop engine configurations were investigated as well. In this book, I have elected to discuss only those designs that reached hardware or full-scale wind tunnel testing, or mockup phase. However, in the case of the S2F, a turboprop version did reach flight status some 30 years later and was sold to the Republic of China Air Force (ROCAF).

In 1983, Grumman proposed the S-2T TurboTracker, utilizing Garrett/Honeywell TPE-331-15AW turboprop engines with four-blade propellers, to the ROCAF, and 27 aircraft were converted with deliveries beginning in the late 1980s (Fig. 4.12). Gerry Maurer was the proposal manager, Dick Crowell played a major role in the proposal and logistics, Herman Wenz was in charge of the avionic suite development, and Joe Witko was responsible for the power plant installation.

Fig. 4.12 S-2T TurboTracker.

C-1A TRADER

Bill Rathke's preliminary design team developed new versions and missions for the S-2F because it had excellent range in excess of 1000 miles and could carry up to 7000 lb of payload and equipment. The author and Vinny Milano, head of PD weights and analysis at the time, believe that the PD team included Joe Lippert (aerodynamic configuration), Lloyd Skinner (structural layout), and Roy Wood) group leader, structural design). The TF-1 design, redesignated the C-1A, emerged based on an enlarged and deepened fuselage with port side cargo and cabin doors and more streamlined engine nacelle (Fig. 4.13). The Trader, which first flew in late 1952, had a long service life, lasting until 1988. It provided the Navy with excellent carrier on-board delivery (COD) performance with up to 9 passengers and 3500 lb of cargo.

MOHAWK

During 1956, the Grumman Preliminary Design team, headed by Mike Pelehach and including Don Terrana, Configuration Design, and Bob Kress, lead aerodynamicist, responded to the Army Type Specification 145 to replace the Cessna L-19 Bird Dog with Design G-134.

The tri-service requirements of the Army, Navy, and Marine Corps were very demanding:

• Army: Short takeoff and landing (STOL) from small, unimproved fields; observation; artillery spotting; and emergency resupply

Fig. 4.13   C1-A Trader.

- Navy: Operate from Jeep escort carriers; naval target spotting
- Marines: Perform close air support (CAS) with a variety of armament and store pylons; land at sea and taxi to island beaches using skis
- High speed, high maneuverability, and high crew survivability relative to the L-19

The resultant design was very rugged (high structural load factor) with a low wing loading, and featured a streamlined, "bug-eyed" canopy with an armored cockpit (Fig. 4.14). The wings had a fair amount of dihedral with large area flaps, full-span leading edge slats, and a tail configuration that featured three vertical fins. The engines were slightly canted outward for good single engine control performance and the props were fully reversible, the result being high agility and controllability, low stall speed, and excellent short-field performance.

The YAO-1 prototype weighed 9900 lb; the final version of the Mohawk weighed 20,000 lb—a testament to the growth capability designed in from the beginning.

Nine variants were built over 37 years of service, from first flight in 1959 to retirement in 1996. During the early testing of the prototype, Mike Pelehach's philosophy was to fly with Ralph Donnell, the chief test pilot, and personally evaluate the basic design for any "early fixes." Although the original design life expectancy was projected to be about 10 years, it turned out to be almost four times that amount. This reflected the basic design philosophy that Bill Schwendler established and incorporated in the early Grumman aircraft.

Fig. 4.14   First flight of the YAO -1.

The OV-1C was developed with the AAS-24 infrared (IR) surveillance system, but the IR system was not meeting specifications initially. It needed two successful system flights prior to deployment to Vietnam. Bill Zarkowsky, president of Grumman, called Joe Rodriguez into his office and said, "I want you to get your ass down to Florida and get the OV-1C to work!" Rodriguez spent two weeks at Grumman's St. Augustine production facility, where the Mohawk production line was located, and solved the IR system problems. Jim Peters was the Mohawk test pilot who flew all the test flights with Rodriguez. After the second consecutive test flight, Peters barrel rolled the Mohawk about 200 ft over the runway to celebrate the event, much to the shock of Rodriguez.

Larry Canonico was the Advanced Systems project engineer for the OV-1D variant that included in-flight refueling, a message drop chute, 300-gal drop tanks to enable ferry flights to Europe, and forward firing camera installations. Ed Harris and Jonas Bilenas of Advanced Systems developed engine IR suppressors for the Mohawk. These installations were done in the Product Development Center (PDC) under Herb Grossman, and the flight tests were successful. In addition, Ed Harris was instrumental in developing a prototype of the OV-1E that employed a modified APS-94 Scanned

Looking Airborne Radar in which the antenna could be mechanically "yawed" to allow larger standoff electronic surveillance of the battlefield.

PRELIMINARY DESIGN: OPERATIONS ANALYSIS

The beginning of the Cold War, following the Korean War, was an exciting time to be involved in the design of military weapon systems at Grumman. Practical engineering was pushed aside for new generations of more sophisticated machines carrying tons of even more sophisticated electronics. During this period, Grumman assembled many world class design teams that worked across a broad front of projects, namely supersonic fighters, attack aircraft, patrol aircraft, seaplanes and hydrofoils, vertical takeoff and landing (VTOL) aircraft, commercial aircraft, tactical missiles, space vehicles, air-cushion vehicles, commercial trucks, and commuter trains.

Preliminary Design (PD) was greatly expanded under the leadership of Dick Hutton, who became chief engineer in 1954. Walter Scott and Leonard Sullivan ran PD from 1954 to 1964. During this time PD, including operations analysis, was expanded from about 30 personnel in 1954 to 300 in 1964. Figure 4.15 shows PD in the mid-1950s, with Dick Hutton in the foreground (third from left, standing) working with a design team consisting of (L to R) Joe Lippert, Walter Scott, and Joe Hubert around a drawing board with an early model of Design 98. Immediately behind them is Leonard Sullivan. Directly behind Sullivan is Dick Houghton, Advanced Space. Al Munier, Advanced Space, is to the right of Sullivan, with Howard Weinmann standing. Mike Pelehach is standing at a drawing board to the left in the background of the photo, and behind him is John Michel. Behind Al Munier on the far right is Art Koch at his drawing board, with Dick Thurston to the left sitting at his board.

Fig. 4.15   Grumman Preliminary Design in the mid-1950s.

In the far background to the right is the nucleus of the Operations Analysis group including Dan Lynch, Russ Murray (standing), and Hal Moss farthest back. In those days, Hal Moss did all of the generalized design studies of various types of aircraft and vehicles of all types, both military and commercial. Moss and Pete Schwartz developed an Aircraft Parametric Design Program that enabled generalized aircraft design studies to be performed rapidly with sufficient detail to initiate the design based on selected points. These sizing studies were usually a part of any operations analysis study that examined future requirements and effectiveness of new aircraft concepts. With these data, Moss and his team (of which the author became a member in 1959) interfaced with the chief aircraft designers, configuration layout designers, and aircraft specialists including aerodynamics, propulsion, weights, and structural design to lay out a 2-D, three-view drawing of the selected design from the sizing and operations analysis studies. These design points materialized into viable configurations and were verified and "massaged or iterated" to verify the design area being investigated.

The weights and propulsion groups in Engineering also developed parametric methodologies to estimate aircraft structural weight components (e.g., wings, tail, fuselage, etc.) as well as subsystem weights (flight controls, electrical, environmental control system, etc.) and to perform propulsion sizing. These efforts were led by Arnold Gersch, John Harvey, and John Protopapas. The programs known as WISE (Weight Integrated Sizing Estimate) and PSI (Propulsion Sizing and Integration) were extensively used in advanced systems from the 1970s on, and are still in use today.

All of these sizing programs complemented each other and resulted in balanced design with good weight estimates. These design points materialized into viable configurations and were verified and "massaged or iterated" to verify the design area being investigated. Many designs were created, though many never materialized into actual aircraft. The heads of aerodynamics, propulsion, weights, structural design, and other functional disciplines were all hand-picked to work in PD based on their vast engineering experience and unique expertise involved in creating a new aircraft. A long and distinguished line of engineers contributed to PD, and this book attempts to mention as many names as could be found related to the aircraft identified in this research.

Because Grumman was one of the foremost aircraft companies that specialized in carrier aircraft, its young PD engineers were sent to sea aboard operational carriers. In my case, I deployed on the USS *Forrestal* with Vinny Milano, chief of PD weight and balance, and Jack Saxe, lead PD aerodynamics. We spent a whole week at sea while the carrier was conducting carrier qualifications (CARQUALS) for the F-4 Phantom. My job was to familiarize myself with every critical operation on the carrier that affected the design of a new aircraft, including observing the flight deck in day and night operations, understanding how the catapults and arresting wire systems worked, familiarizing myself with all the "colored shirts" (the fuel, catapult, arresting, armament, etc. specialists) on the deck and the detailed training that was necessary to safely launch and recover aircraft, talking to the flight boss and understanding aircraft spotting on the deck, observing and talking to the maintenance officers and maintenance techs as they serviced and made repairs below decks while the carrier was underway, and prowling all over the ship with escorts to understand what it takes to operate an aircraft carrier. After a week at sea, working 12 hours per day, and sleeping in junior officer quarters under the forward catapults, you came away with a deep appreciation of what it takes to operate an aircraft carrier and the tough environment that the naval aircraft must operate in.

In 1955, Joe Hubert became a citizen of the United States, and PD celebrated the event, as commemorated in a photograph of Hubert with the American flag surrounded by his contemporaries from Grumman (Fig. 4.16). Hubert was a renowned aerodynamic designer from Messerschmitt who was sought after by the United States and Russia at the end of World War II. Don Terrana, one of Grumman's senior designers, said, "a nicer man you never met," and he was a real baseball fan who loved the Brooklyn Dodgers. In 1948 Hubert was sent to work at Grumman in the research department after spending two years at Wright Patterson Air

Fig. 4.16   Joe Hubert becomes a U.S. citizen.

Force Base in Dayton, Ohio. Dr. Dick Scheuing had just graduated from MIT, sat next to him for a few years, and developed a close working relationship with Hubert. Scheuing helped him with his report writing as he mastered his English composition skills, and remembers him for his kindness.

The individuals in Fig. 4.16 are (front row, L to R): Mike Pelehach (designer), Hal Moss (advanced vehicle design, operations analysis), Lloyd Skinner (structural design), Shirley Rouse (secretary), Willy Fildstedt (prototype shop and a friend of Hubert's from his Messerschmitt days), Joe Hubert, Fritz Dunmire (designer), Dick Houghton (advanced space), and Bob Englert (designer). In the back row are (L to R): Al Munier (advanced space), Roy Wood (structural design group leader), Dick Cyphers (structural design), Howard Weinman (preliminary design), Sam Rogers (avionics), Leonard Sullivan (deputy director, preliminary design), Russ Murray (deputy director, operations analysis), Vinny Milano (weights), Al Nichtenhauser (advanced space), Don Imgram (advanced space), John Michel (weights), Tom Barnes (advanced space) Joe Lippert (aerodynamics, design), and Pete Viemeister (preliminary design).

Joe Hubert was a very kind and caring person, and a good listener who would always invite a colleague into his office to discuss an aerodynamics or design issue. During the late 1960s, the author was leading the early VSX parametric design study effort that examined many aerodynamic and propulsion configurations. In our parametric design process at the time, the skin friction coefficient of drag associated with the total wetted surface area of the configuration (fuselage, wings, and tails) was being debated because attempts were being made to improve performance by aerodynamic shaping, smoothing the fuselage contours, and manufacturing tolerances. We had lengthy discussions with the configuration designers, structural design engineers, and aerodynamacists. I attempted to resolve the issue by asking Joe Hubert, hence my lengthy meeting with him to discuss the parameters used in our computer sizing program. At length, he opened a cabinet and brought out World War II era German aerodynamic wind tunnel data and design manuals, in order to give his views on what the skin friction coefficient range would be. He felt we could be more aggressive with the value of the parameters, and the matter was settled.

Nick Dannenhofer recalled that he built a detailed model of the ME 163 with a display case to present to Joe Hubert when he retired from Grumman in the late 1960s. Hubert removed the model from the case and marveled at the detail, especially because he could remove the tail to reveal the rocket engine. When he did this the first time, he said that the model rocket engine was not the right design—some recall after almost 40 years.

OPERATIONS ANALYSIS (OA)

A lead article in the *Grumman Plane News* from 1963 stated that the "Search for new concepts by OA engineers reaches far into future!"

> "After LEM and the F-111, what?" The question, according to Leonard Sullivan, Jr., Chief of Aircraft, Missiles, and Space Preliminary Design [Fig. 4.17], is neither as unrealistic nor as audacious as it may sound. "Grumman could hardly have grown and prospered as it has if there had not been a body of engineers always working ahead on the next generation of Company products," Sullivan said. "Whether our engineers are studying upcoming bid requests from the military or NASA, or originating suggestions of their own, their thinking helps give a sensible, organized framework for the Company's decisions, and this is what makes a strong program of work. This is what brings in sound contracts.

Sullivan's comments made in 1963 still apply to today's military requirements. Sullivan continued:

> In Operations Analysis, you find the widest sweep of planning for the future. The OA group is doing the same kind of thinking that the new group—sometimes called "the Whiz Kids"—in the Department of Defense is doing: by systematic analysis, trying to predict with some degree of probability what the next decade will be like, and how to get the best use out of the taxpayer's dollar. Our Operations Analysis engineers are asking questions on a very broad scale: What weapons

Fig. 4.17   Leonard Sullivan, chief of PD and OA, speaks with Dan Lynch, OA director, and senior group leaders—Hal Moss, advanced vehicle design; Doug Hill, cost analysis; and Hank Beers, NASA studies.

systems are going to be most useful for defense? For offense? In a cold war? A limited war? Atomic attack? What is the future of manned aircraft? Of VTOL? Of hydrofoil craft? Man will go to the moon, but after the moon, where? What are the military implications of space exploration? What are their total system costs including R&D, procurement and operating cost over the system life time and how do they compare with existing or other alternatives? The possibilities are endless, diverse and fascinating.

OA engineers performed many classified studies for the Navy that contributed heavily to future thinking in the areas of airborne early warning (AEW), attack, electronic warfare (EW), air defense, and ASW.

Key OA lead personnel, who were involved in all of Grumman's aircraft weapon systems and in many cases were "multihatted." I have attempted to identify many of the key personnel, namely Dan Lynch, director; Russ Murray, deputy director; Doug Hill, cost analysis group leader; Bruno Maiolo, Bob Evans, and Jim Tedesco, cost analysis; Gerry Ryan and Bob Harvey, attack studies; Hugh Lowery and Swede Hansen, air defense simulations; George Duffy, air defense studies; Fred Roffe, tactical defense fleet model (TFDM); Ed Schoenfeld, Navy studies; Tom Doherty, carrier aircraft maintenance and turnaround simulation; Hal Moss, advanced vehicle design group leader; Pete Schwartz and Mike Ciminera, advanced vehicle design; Sam Rogers, senior OA study manager; Tony DeRuggierio, Hank Suydam, and Al Glomb, ASW; Bernie Buc, senior OA study manager; Joe Cubells, system studies/Joint Primary Aircraft Training System (JPATS); Ed Conroy, campaign analyses, advanced tactical aircraft (ATA), OA director; and Harry George, system studies, OA director.

AG CAT

The mid- to late 1950s were a dynamic time in commercial aircraft design at Grumman. Roy Grumman was looking for commercial aircraft concepts and made his wishes known in PD as well as at the annual stockholder's meeting. One of Roy Grumman's unique strengths as an individual that also permeated all levels of the company structure was the accessibility he gave to upper levels of management in presenting ideas. Joe Lippert had been studying the crop duster market and saw that crop dusting was performed with modified private light aircraft with limited hopper capacity and performance. Lippert and Arthur Koch created Design G-164, which became the "Ag Cat" (Fig. 4.18).

Joe Lippert recalled how a crop duster and a new amphibian design evolved. In the mid-1950s, both Koch and Lippert were based in the preliminary design group. In spring 1955, Koch was enthused about

Fig. 4.18   Design G-164, which became the Ag Cat.

the idea of redesigning the G-21 Goose with a larger wing and stretched fuselage, and powered by four engines. In addition, a completely new twin engine amphibian design, to replace the G-21 and carry six to eight passengers, was laid out. This model never got beyond the preliminary design stage after Lippert made a survey of the need for such an aircraft. History repeated itself in 1980–81 with a new amphibian project, Design 711.

Lippert was interested in an agricultural aircraft design. Because their types of work were complementary, Lippert and Koch decided to combine talents and did preliminary designs for an amphibian and a crop duster together. In order to continue further work, they needed approval and funding. They had no success with immediate superiors, so they approached Roy Grumman directly. He was interested in both designs, and authorized a field trip to the U.S. Gulf Coast and Alaska to determine if a market existed. The survey showed a need for a duster, and they went on to design and build the Ag Cat (Fig. 4.19). According to Koch, a survey of the amphibian market was also conducted in Alaska, where the need for such an aircraft was great. The survey showed that the price of the new amphibian would be too high, however ($120,000 per copy then), and the project was dropped.

The Ag Cat was an all-new design that was created to maximize controllability, performance (stall speed as low as 56 kt to a maximum speed of about 130 kt), safety, spraying capacity, and economics. This was achieved by using a staggered biplane wing arrangement, a nose shape to maximize forward visibility, rugged landing gear with a wide

Fig. 4.19   Joe Lippert holds a hand-built model of an Ag Cat.

track (distance between main tires), and aluminum construction where needed in the fuselage. The basic design had good growth potential due to the lifting capability of the biplane configuration and a good basic center of gravity travel available with varying loads that enabled an increase in engine horsepower from 200 hp (reciprocating) to 600 hp (turboprop). Production was moved to a lower cost aircraft producer (Schweitzer Aircraft).

Joe Lippert was born in 1919 and received his first flight in a Curtiss Flying Boat in the 1920s. His father bought him a silk-covered, wire frame model from Macy's (imagine—made in Japan back in those days), and they tried to make it fly but it did not do well. After the Lindbergh flight in 1927, he began to build models for local people that flew very well, and even won some prizes in model building contests—one of them sponsored by New York University (NYU). He received enough prize money from NYU to purchase a real gasoline model engine; built a large flying model; and became intrigued by the NYU Guggenheim School of Aeronautics, in which he enrolled in 1936.

Lippert's career with Grumman spanned 28 years, of which 10 years were spent in Preliminary Design. He participated in the design development and testing of aircraft programs from the F4F Wildcat up to and including the F-14A Tomcat. He was a private pilot, a glider pilot, and a builder of radio-controlled aircraft, including the radio equipment.

According to Joe Lippert's remembrances of Arthur Koch (pronounced *coke*), Koch never really received the credit he should have for his work on the Avenger. Of the many designers Lippert worked with, he regarded Koch (Fig. 4.20) as one of the most talented, with a remarkable ability to quickly transform a collection of ideas into a design drawing. Koch was born in 1911 and, like Lippert, also attended NYU, graduating in 1933 with a mechanical engineering degree with an aeronautical option. Engineering jobs were scarce in those days, but Koch went to work for Grumman in

Fig. 4.20   Arthur Koch in front of an Ag Cat.

1935. He did power plant installations on the XF4F-1 fighter and the J2F-1 amphibian. During 1938, Koch was offered a job as chief engineer by the Dubois Martin Aircraft Company in Dubois, Pennsylvania, which was working on a torpedo bomber. Bill Schwendler wisely intervened to keep Koch at Grumman, raising pay and offering him the position of project engineer on a torpedo bomber. Koch was also the preliminary design engineer of this fairly large single engine airplane. His success marked him for further work on similar airplanes such as the AF Guardian series. He was also involved in several proposed designs, and a single engine design that was submitted along with Grumman's successful S2F-1 proposal. He also participated in the design of the G-21 Goose amphibian and made the first three-view proposal of the G-21 using hull lines of the J2F-1 amphibian with two Pratt and Whitney 450 hp engines. Koch stayed with the Ag Cat when production was subcontracted to the Schweizer Aircraft Corporation in Elmira, New York, and he made various improvements and redesigns of this very successful airplane.

C-2A GREYHOUND

Like the C-1A Trader, a derivative of the S2F, S-2 ASW series, the C-2A Greyhound (Figs. 4.21 and 4.22) was a derivative of the E-2A. Both the

Fig. 4.21   Early C2-A sketches and mockups.

Fig. 4.22   A C2-A carrier qualification test.

E-2A and the C-2A had the same Grumman Design 123 designation. The first two C-2As were actually converted from the original E-2A prototypes and retained the same Bureau of Aeronautics Numbers (BuNos). The first flight occurred in 1964. Nineteen of these cargo on deck (COD) aircraft were built between 1964 and 1968, and the Greyhound served in every theater of Navy operations, including Vietnam.

The C-2's primary mission was to transport high priority cargo of up to 10,000 lb with a range of over 1000 n. miles, or 39 passengers with 4 attendants. In land-based operations, the C-2 can carry up to 15,000 lb of cargo. The C-2 design utilized the E-2A wing with its side-folding wing design for carrier stowage, and initially the E-2A's T-56-A-8 turboprop engines. It featured a new, widened fuselage with an integrated rear loading ramp, increased fuel capacity, a strengthened nose gear, and an auxiliary power unit (APU) for engine starting and remote operations. The tail assembly was also redesigned and featured four vertical stabilizers to meet carrier hangar height restrictions. The rudders were positioned in the prop slipstream for adequate single engine control during take-off and landing.

Bill Rathke was the project engineer on the C-2A design, and Mike Pelehach did the initial configuration layout. Frank Perley was in charge of the aerodynamic design. Lloyd Skinner influenced the structural design of the fuselage, according to Paul Weidenhafer, and eliminated all unnecessary escape hatches and other access panels from the W2F-1 (E-2A design). Jim Brennan was involved with the E-2A wing design, and probably was involved with the C-2A wing with Grant Hedrick "looking over the shoulders" of the entire PD structural and design efforts.

In the early 1980s, the Navy requested a proposal from Grumman to obtain a new batch of COD aircraft to replace the original aircraft. The only potential competitor to the C-2A program was a proposed wider-body cargo variant of the jet-powered Lockheed S-3. Grumman was awarded the contract to build 39 aircraft designated "Reprocured C-2A." The Navy designation was meant to imply that they were just buying more of the same, and hence minimizing/avoiding any congressional scrutiny and/or competition for a new design. The Navy decision was primarily cost driven, and the name was to imply that the Reprocured C-2A was a no-risk program, and did not entail any flight test or major development effort.

The Reprocured C-2A was in fact a new aircraft with substantial redesign of almost all systems and components. The only major feature in common between the two models was the external aerodynamic shape. This eliminated the need for any flight testing to evaluate handling characteristics and the like.

Among the many differences from the original C-2A are

- New engines and propellers
- New wing structure and fuselage beef-up for substantial increase in fatigue life
- New materials and finishes to reduce corrosion
- New solid-state modern avionic suite (about two dozen items)
- New APU with engine cross-bleed self-start capability
- New cargo cage with increased volume capacity and cargo winch
- Incorporation of new landing gear components from the E-2C

Al Kuhn joined the E-2 program in the early 1970s and eventually became the vehicle engineering manager. Kuhn worked closely with business development to market the follow-on C-2. When Grumman received the RFP, Paul Wiedenhafer and Kuhn were assigned to manage the technical proposal. Larry Canonico from advanced systems was the design manager, and led the effort on a conformal tank design to increase range, as well as a unique cargo cage design to increase cargo capacity for the proposal. Many key personnel from the E-2 program assisted in the winning proposal. After contract, Kuhn became program manager of the Reprocured C-2A program.

The C-2A and the Reprocured C-2A have had a long life with the U.S. Navy, totaling 45 years, and will probably continue in service well beyond 2015. They represent another example of a design that was created based on practicality, structural ruggedness, performance, and range to meet U.S. Navy far-reaching world commitments, as well as years of carrier suitability and integrated logistic support (ILS) experience.

THE GULFSTREAM LEGACY

G-I GULFSTREAM

During the mid-1950s, PD engineers and configuration designer Don Terrana began looking at versions of the TF-1, the transport version of the S2F, utilizing T-55 turboprops "that morphed into the G-I," according to Vinny Milano, head of PD weight estimating. When Don Terrana finished work on the Mohawk proposal, Mike Pelehach asked Terrana to look into replacing the piston engines on the S2F transport version, the TF-1(C-1A), with new Lycoming T55 turbo prop engines. The idea was simple: put a new wing on the old hull, pressurize the design, and keep the S2F/TF-1(C-1A) landing gear. In the initial design, the landing gear was just too short. However, Mike Pelehach insisted that the team try again. Terrana made several more layouts of the landing gear that showed the existing gear was not compatible with initial preliminary configurations. Pelehach finally gave in and the design, by that stage, became "pretty much brand new." Basically, the fuselage had to be made circular for pressurization and a new wing had to be designed for the turboprop engines.

The selection of the Gulfstream I design number—159—came into being when Don Terrana asked Jim Langley, the PD administrator, for a charge number because he was the only person working on the project at that time. According to Sullivan, "Langley tried his damnedest to be an Administrative Assistant." Normally the design numbers are selected in some numerical order, but in this case, Langley just invented a charge number for Terrana and selected 159, hence Design 159 was born administratively.

Charlie Coppi and Fritz Dunmire worked closely with Terrana during these early aircraft design studies, and they even built a balsa wood model of the cabin. After a short while, "word came down from the front office" (Grumman and Schwendler) that the aircraft was not to be a shipboard transport but rather an executive aircraft to replace many of the corporate DC-3 and Convair executive transports. PD, working closely with the prototype shop, built a rudimentary, full-size mockup that featured a high wing. When Leroy Grumman returned from a trip to Florida, he viewed the mockup and remarked, "It looks like a miniature Fokker Friendship. Take that damn wing off the top and put it on the bottom where it belongs!" The engineer/shop team accomplished the change in about 4 hours by sawing off the wing and bolting it on the bottom of the fuselage to create an instant low wing design. The preliminary design of the G-I then began in earnest.

Vinny Milano was also involved in the transition from the "stubby TF-1 to the sleek Gulfstream I executive transport." Like the Mallard, a predecessor executive aircraft, the Gulfstream I exhibited very clean lines.

Its final configuration flowed from early decisions on the body shape, highly efficient Rolls Royce Dart turboprop engines, Sullivan recommending oval windows, Leroy Grumman's decision to have a low wing vs. a high wing configuration, and the vertical tail. The final change on the vertical tail occurred when Dick Hutton came into PD and sat down with Bob Englert, who was doing G-I configuration layouts. Hutton looked at the inboard profile and said something like "that squarish rudder/rudder trimmer has to go!" So Dick Hutton sketched out a swept tail, which Englert added, and that was basically the G-I configuration that Bill Schwendler approved.

Grumman was a visionary and a thinker, and he contemplated a way to penetrate the civilian executive transport market to develop a broader aircraft line that would buffer decreases in military sales. At the same time Henry Schiebel, who was a confidante of Roy Grumman, a company commercial pilot, and a great salesman, was talking to a broad cross-section of private, executive, and commercial aircraft operators.

Don Terrana recalled that two of Grumman's bright young engineers, Pete Viemeister and Don Imgram, left Grumman to start their own consulting business at nearby Zahn's airport on Long Island. Bill Schwendler did not want to go ahead with financing an all-Grumman program without some assurance, so he contracted with them to do an industry survey. They sent out survey questionnaires to about 200 prospective clients, with the result being that less than 25 had any interest in buying the airplane. But the best part of the story, according to Don Terrana, is that Bill Schwendler proclaimed, "I don't put any faith in the study, let's just go ahead!"

The program was guided by Bernie Harriman as project engineer and Henry Schiebel; Charlie Coppi became the chief configuration designer of the Gulfstream I. According to one of his co-workers, Harriman was "a great guy and very funny in his special way." "Bernie and I worked together on the Gulfstream programs for 10 years," recalled Bill Sutton, program director for the Gulfstream I and II. "His efforts in the design and development of these aircraft made a tremendous contribution to the reputation of the Grumman Company as a designer and builder of commercial aircraft." Ed Clark, who at the time was Gulfstream engineering manager, said, "The Gulfstream is a monument to B.J.H. (Bernard J. Harriman)." Al Rogers was project aerodynamicist for the Gulfstream I, and during the summer of 1957, I was working in the Grumman subsonic wind tunnel as a student engineering apprentice helping to test a variety of wing root fillet designs for the Gulfstream I.

The Gulfstream I first flew in August 1958 (Fig. 4.23); it had a maximum speed of over 300 kt, and a range of 2200 n. miles. As of August 2006, 48 years after first flight, 44 were still in service after a production run of 200.

Fig. 4.23   First flight of the G-I.

The G-I was yet another example of a Grumman aircraft with a rugged structural design and long life in the tradition of the Grumman Ironworks. Grumman actually conducted hydrostatic tests of a full-scale G-I fuselage, fully submerged in a giant tank of water to verify the fatigue life design.

Significant variants of the G-I were the TC-4C, the bombardier/navigator trainer for the U.S. Navy (Fig. 4.24), and the G-159C, which was a stretched version to accommodate 35 passengers.

Bill Fehrs was the TC-4C program manager and Larry Canonico was the vehicle project engineer, with Larry Kipnis as avionics project engineer

Fig. 4.24   TC-4C bombardier/navigator trainer for the U.S. Navy.

Fig. 4.25   Larry Canonico, Larry Kipnis, and Jim Koschara during Navy mockup review of the TC-4C.

(Fig. 4.25). Nine Gulfstream I aircraft were modified and delivered to the Navy for bombardier navigator (BN) training. In order to win the development contract, Grumman built a full-scale mockup and performed extensive avionic and human factors studies with the Navy to maximize student BN proficiency.

G-II GULFSTREAM

The G-II, Design 1159 (Fig. 4.26), was created in the early 1960s in response to competitors' jet-powered business transports like the Lockheed Jetstar and Dassault Falcon. Bernie Harriman was project engineer on the G-II, Charlie Coppi was the configuration designer, and Irv Waaland was project aerodynamicist.

Weekly meetings with key Grumman vice presidents were held to discuss various engineering and manufacturing design issues. Bill Schwendler and Bernie Harriman conducted the meetings with Dick Hutton, Bob Hall, and Grant Hedrick in attendance. Schwendler generally sat at the head of the table and was very concerned about all aspects of the design as well as cost. He also directed that the wing have no leading edge devices and no yaw damper, and that the design would be capable of operating on a Federal Aviation Administration (FAA) balanced runway

Fig. 4.26   G-II Number 1 making its maiden takeoff.

from a 5000-ft field. Dick Hutton sketched out the vertical tail (size, shape, and sweep). Irv Waaland felt it was too large and would make the aircraft "too stiff directionally," so the tail was photographically reduced (dynamically scaled). Hedrick and Schwendler not only were very active during the conceptual design and preliminary design stages of the G II evolution, but also were intimately involved in the detail design and construction of the first prototype (Fig. 4.27).

Fig. 4.27   Grant Hedrick, Bill Schwendler, and George Doukas with the first G-II prototype.

The G-II wing design was done by Irv Waaland and Rudy Meyer. Waaland and his team utilized British and NASA research data on supercritical airfoil design that led to an "airfoil shaping approach to relieve wing-body compressibility interference on a passenger aircraft where area ruling was not practical." The wing also featured inverse camber inboard to prevent stalled wing flow from entering the engines and causing stalls and failure. Waaland was also responsible for having the horizontal tail incidence geared to flap deflection to trim out the pitching moment change and using elevators for flight control. In addition, the research data permitted the design of a vortex generator configuration that significantly delayed buffet onset. Dr. Gunther Buchmann was responsible for wing transonic shaping, and Ed Curtis did the performance estimates and calculations. Other significant contributions by Waaland's aero team, including Walt Valckenaere, were the placement and orientation of the engine nacelles, which had a significant impact on cruise drag and deep stall, as well as the T-tail configuration impact on deep stall. The resulting performance of the G-II was remarkable: max 0.85 Mach, a service ceiling of 43,000 ft, and a range of over 3300 miles. The Gulfstream line of aircraft has longevity of almost 50 years, with nine civil variants after the G-II, culminating in the G650 currently in flight test that has a range of 7000 miles. This does not include military variants and the shuttle training aircraft (STA).

According to Irv Waaland, during the G-II design effort, an F11F-1 crash landed in the trees alongside an emergency airstrip on Long Island. The pilot lost power and couldn't complete the turn onto the final approach. The pilot's only injury was a sprained ankle incurred from tripping while exiting the aircraft. The wings stayed on the aircraft, only crushing the leading edge back to the front spar of the wing as it was shearing trees prior to stopping. At the next G-II design meeting, Bill Schwendler and the design team debated what tree diameter they should use to design the wing spar of the G-II.

Joe Ruggiero recalled why the dorsal spine on top of the G-II fuselage was a bit longer when the G-II flew. A redesign of the aft fuselage of the G-II was necessary when the first three aircraft were in assembly. During wind tunnel tests with the final T-tail configuration, similar to the Boeing 727, Douglas DC-9, and BAC-111, it was found that the resulting bending moments from the T tail on the aft fuselage structure were underestimated. Bill Schwendler, George Titterton, and Grant Hedrick went ballistic and called for an immediate redesign. Bernie Harriman assigned Jim Brennan, chief structural engineer, and Don Bone and Ernie Ranalli of stress to design the fix. The double framing in a back-to-back arrangement resulted in a longer dorsal spine.

G-II: SHUTTLE TRAINING AIRCRAFT (STA)

Grumman competed against Lockheed and won the competition to build a plane for astronaut training in shuttle atmospheric reentry/energy management. The STA (Fig. 4.28) was a very significant achievement in aircraft design, flight controls, and propulsion.

G-IIs were extensively modified to include:

• Independent control of 6 deg of freedom (DOF) to mimic Shuttle motions in the cockpit via fast-acting direct lift controls (DLC).
• Fowler flaps were replaced with larger chord, quick-acting, plain flaps to simulate pitch control.
• Side force controls (SFC) were included on the underside of the fuselage to simulate yaw control (later removed due to low duty cycles and the potential of a wheels-up landing).
• In-flight reverse thrust (to match the low shuttle lift/drag).
• Model-following flight controls.

Mark Siegel (lead) and Dick Kita did the aerodynamics, Walt Kohloff was responsible for propulsion, and Bill Barnhart and Jack Klafin did the flight controls. Bill Gentzlinger was the program manager. Norm Lewin was vice president of engineering and conducted detailed engineering reviews consistent with the Schwendler/Hedrick style of reviewing engineering decisions that delved deeply into selected engineering areas and to keep things "copacetic" (running smoothly with all functional department inputs fully aired during discussions).

Fig. 4.28   G-II shuttle training aircraft (STA).

THE GULFSTREAM G-III

During 1976–77, Grumman began to plan for a successor to the G-II. The Gulfstream was being built by Gulfstream American, a subsidiary of Grumman located in Savannah, Georgia, and studies were initiated to increase the range and payload of the G-II at the Georgia plant. Initially, wing tip-mounted fuel tanks were designed and incorporated on a number of G-IIs to extend range by several hundred miles.

Subsequently, a major design effort began in 1976 combining the Gulfstream American design staff and a team consisting of Grumman Aerospace aerodynamics, structures, and other discipline personnel. Bill Gentzlinger was program manager, Steve Dondero developed the aircraft configuration, Dick Kita was project aerodynamicist, Paul Bavitz did the aerodynamic wing design with Richard Whitcomb from NASA as consultant on winglet design, and Ed Curtis did the aerodynamic performance estimates. It should be noted that this was the first use of winglets. Initially the wing design featured an advanced supercritical wing of composite construction. As the design matured, Gulfstream American took the lead and Pete Hellston, formerly from Grumman Aerospace, became the project aerodynamicist with Charlie Coppi as chief designer. The basic requirement was to achieve an increase of 1000 n. miles in range with more cabin volume. What resulted was the G-III (Fig. 4.29), which had a truly remarkable configuration that featured a new reinforced composite wing, a higher speed windshield, a 2-ft extension of the fuselage, a 26% improvement in aerodynamic efficiency, and a 1400-mile increase in range to 4000 n. miles.

Larry Mead was once again called on to lead a major company effort that would produce a mature preliminary design, and a cost and development schedule for the G-III. The composite wing would have saved 1000 lb in structural weight; however, the design was stopped due to the high price associated with testing and the uncertainty of obtaining FAA certification within the planned development schedule. Mead directed the use of the existing aluminum G-II wing with a new leading edge and winglets that resulted in a range of 3750 n. miles, enough for a nonstop New York to

Fig. 4.29   Gulfstream G-III.

London trip against 95% of the worst head winds. In May 1977, Mead's team had performed enough wind tunnel configuration tests and design studies of a composite wing to obtain board approval to proceed.

This period was one of the most productive and transitional in Grumman's history. Not only were 21 new aircraft and variants flown, but the company became an aircraft weapon system designer and integrator. Under Roy Grumman's technical leadership, the company not only conceived and created aircraft weapon systems like the A2F-1 (A-6A), but also attracted some of the top avionic engineers from the industry and recruited the best and brightest graduates from U.S. universities.

Subsequent chapters (Chapters 5, 6, 7, and 9) go into more depth on the evolution and lineage of airborne early warning, fighter, battlefield surveillance, and electronic warfare systems, respectively, and highlight the leadership and imaginative contributions made by many avionic engineers, as well the continuing creativity of Grumman aircraft designers.

Chapter 5

LINEAGE OF AIRBORNE EARLY WARNING SYSTEMS

The origins of airborne early warning (AEW) systems can be traced to the final months of World War II, when the Japanese mounted a campaign of kamikaze ("Divine Wind") attacks against U.S. naval forces. U.S. ships, equipped with relatively crude search radars mounted on mastheads, proved sadly deficient in detecting low-level attackers bent on crashing their airplanes into ships at the waterline. The Navy reacted rapidly to devise an AEW system, using as its basis available airborne radar with a new video data link developed by the Naval Research Laboratory (NRL).

For the airborne platform, the Navy designated the Grumman-designed, General Motors–built, TBM-3 W. The radar was to be installed in a bulbous radome beneath the fuselage (Fig. 5.1) that gave the AEW airplane a unique look and inspired its nickname of Guppy. Only 27 were modified before the war ended. None saw combat, but tests showed the plane's radar could detect low-flying aircraft out to a range of about 65 miles and ships out to about 200 miles. The TBM-3 W's bulging belly radome also was adapted for radar primarily designed to detect submarines on the surface. That system later was installed on Grumman's next radar platform, the AF-2 W Guardian, the hunter half of the postwar Navy's two-plane submarine hunter–killer team.

Early radar was susceptible to sea clutter (static caused by reflections from rough water) that was severe enough to mask an attacking aircraft. Grumman's studies showed that clutter effects could be lessened by a change to ultra-high frequency (UHF) radar operating in the 300-to-1000 megacycle range. However, the UHF radar in the Guppy layout suffered from distorted antenna patterns and coverage gaps because of reflected radiation from the aircraft's wings. The only feasible alternative was to mount the radar antenna above the fuselage. The NRL-developed radar was installed in the fixed overhead radome of the Grumman WF-2 (later redesignated E-1B) Tracer.

With the advent of the WF-2, followed by wins on the A2F-1, OV-1, and W2F-1, Grumman evolved from an airframe builder into a major aircraft weapon system development contractor responsible for total system performance. The WF-2 system integration task was the first undertaken

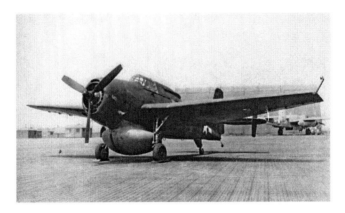

Fig. 5.1   TBM-3W with bulging belly radome.

by Grumman. This task included not only solving radio frequency interference (RFI) issues, but also resolving interface issues between avionic systems and components, and ultimately verifying performance requirements for the installed system. This transition necessitated a large staff of avionic and systems analysis engineers. Extensive simulation and test facilities were designed by Grumman and constructed to carry out total systems integration tests prior to flight test in order to make system flight testing successful. In the case of the W2F, General Electric (GE) was the original systems house and the Navy provided much of the avionics; however, over a relatively short span of time Grumman assumed the leadership role with the government customers (Navy, Air Force, and Army) in providing most of the key avionic components (e.g., radars, computers, etc.) as company furnished equipment (CFE). As each new aircraft weapon system was proposed to the customer, the key people identified as the "creators" of the aircraft expanded to include not only the aircraft designer, aerodynamic engineers, and other key airframe functional engineers, but also key avionic system engineers including such disciplines as radar, software, systems analysis, systems integration, and the like.

WF-2 TRACKER: E-1A AND E-1B

The evolution of the WF-2 Tracker (G-117) began in 1955 in preliminary design when Joe Lippert, an aerodynamic design engineer, and Sam Rogers, an avionics engineer, developed and evaluated many carrier-based configurations utilizing a new Hazeltine AEW search radar. The radar was installed in both the new airframes and the modifications of the AF-2S Guardian and S2F Tracker airframes, because increased fuselage volume was necessary within carrier performance and carrier stowage requirements. Significant wind tunnel tests were performed that led to the utilization of the cargo version of the S2F—the TF-1—with twin tails for increased fuselage volume; an overhead, aerodynamically shaped radome with a long tail to reduce drag; and twin tails for controllability (Fig. 5.2). The WF-2 ("Willie Fudd") had accommodations for two operators behind the cockpit. The radome housed the APS-82 *S*-band radar.

The installation of the huge radome (Fig. 5.3) dictated a complete redesign of the tail surfaces on aircraft such as the TF-1, to provide twin vertical tails situated at the tips of the horizontal stabilizer. The design of the tail assembly, resulting in a dual fin arrangement, was decided on to reduce possible radome wake effect on the tail surfaces. The large radome also precluded the use of the S2F, TF-1 wing fold scheme and led to the adoption of a "Sto-Wing" type of wing fold similar to that used on the AF Guardian and Avenger aircraft.

Bill Rathke headed the proposal team that won a contract for the WF-2 and became project engineer. Lloyd Skinner designed the radome support structure. Rathke was one of Grumman's finest engineers and program managers, and had a long career with Grumman after his graduation from Iowa State University in 1942. He began work on the F6F, followed by assignments on the TBF, F7F, Mallard, F9F, and F11F aircraft programs. In production design, he was project engineer for design and development of the

Fig. 5.2   Takeoff of the No. 1 WF-2 followed by the aerodynamic flight test WF-2.

Fig. 5.3   A close-up of the WF-2 illustrates the large size of the radome in relation to the fuselage.

S2F-1, S2F-2, TF-1, and WF-2 aircraft. This effort included technical direction of efforts of major electronic subcontractors as well as Grumman in-house efforts. He managed the engineering development of the S2F antisubmarine aircraft, one of the earliest successful airborne electronic weapon systems, whose design was a major step forward in submarine detection.

After first meeting Bill Rathke in production design in 1959, the author had the distinct pleasure of working with Bill 10 years later when he was program manager (technical) of the F-14A program. Rathke had just finished excellent work as the assistant chief engineer on space projects, including the Orbiting Astronomical Observatory (OAO), and as lunar module program manager. He was a quiet, unflappable man who was highly respected by all government agencies and military services for his technical excellence and integrity. Rathke's desk was always filled with tons of paper, much of which was written on in his excellent, flowing handwriting that was very legible.

In 1959, Rathke was project engineer on a proposal for the long-range missile fighter program called the Design 128E Missileer, which utilized a highly modified A2F (A-6A) with TF-30 engines. Grumman lost this competition to Douglas's F6D-1 project, which was subsequently canceled.

He directed the successful WF-2 Airborne Early Warning Aircraft Weapon System program that required the harmonious integration of a large search radar (a major subcontractor procurement) with the aerodynamic design of the aircraft while achieving the ruggedness, reliability, and maintainability required for naval aircraft carrier suitability. Rathke directed successful proposals for Models S2F-3 and W2F-1 aircraft (E-2A), the latter a highly sophisticated successor to the WF-2 featuring increased duration on station, a larger crew, and increased multitarget capability, and incorporating airborne interceptor control. Sam Rogers worked closely with him during the early planning stages of the WF-2, along with Bill Burns, avionic systems group leader, and John Lenz, experimental shop foreman (Fig. 5.4).

Fig. 5.4   Key members of the WF-2 team: (L to R) Rathke, Rogers, Burns, and Lenz.

When Grumman submitted the design for the WF-2 modification to an S2F, it included a contractor-furnished search and height-finding radar. This was the brainchild of Joe Gavin and Bill Rathke, with inputs from Sam Rogers, who had come over when the Rigel missile program was cancelled. (The Rigel missile was a Navy, M2.0, ramjet-powered, rocket-boosted, medium-range surface-to-surface missile that was successfully tested but canceled due to federal budget cuts.) Bob Nafis had the good fortune of finding sensors and an autopilot that could get 250 lb out of the weight, and the system had the angle accuracy needed for the radar and height finding.

Key engineers that helped the E-1B materialize were Bill Burns, Mark Mellinger, John Cunniff, Tom Wolfson, and Bob Watson. Burns was the lead avionics guy on the E-1B and a master of specification requirements. He was an avionics manager from the government furnished equipment (GFE) days, but a solid manager. Mellinger was Burns's assistant. Cunniff was the cognizant E-1B communications engineer, and Wolfson was the cognizant E-1B navigation engineer. Watson was also a key avionics engineer on the E-1B who helped create the E-1B and execute the program. Gerry Norton remembered a story about taking Jake Swirbul for a test hop in the E-1B one afternoon to demonstrate the avionic system for him. After the flight, Swirbul, thinking that Norton worked for Hazeltine, commented to Augie Walsky, his corporate assistant, "That is the kind of engineer we need to hire at Grumman."

The WF-2 was another tribute to the versatility of the basic S2F antisubmarine aircraft design. It was the third version, including the TF-1 cargo passenger aircraft.

W2F-1: E-2A TO E-2C

Between 1955 and 1960, the Navy took a leadership role in tackling and solving two key issues from before the W2F competition took place, namely, a solution to the WF-2 APS-82 *S*-band radar's total lack of sea clutter rejection capabilities, and computer-aided target tracking to avoid target overload for the operators because the Soviet threat consisted of both aircraft and missiles. The WF-2 normally operated at 10,000 ft (it was unpressurized) and was intended to provide an interim capability until the new AEW system became a reality. The Navy requirements and actions resulted in a new aircraft weapon system that included a new radar to address unwanted clutter from operating at 30,000 ft; a radar antenna housed in a rotating, flat, circular dish; and the airborne tactical data system (ATDS).

The Navy held the competition for the W2F program in 1956 among Grumman, Lockheed, and Vought. Grumman won with design G-123. Lockheed had experience in land-based AEW with no aircraft carrier–based design experience, and Vought had carrier design experience.

The W2F that became the E-2A Hawkeye was a large, all-weather, carrier-based AEW system platform with twin Allison T-56-A-8 turboprop engines and a crew of five (two pilots and three controllers), compared to four crewmen in the WF-2 Willie Fudd. Bill Rathke was the proposal manager and Mike Pelehach was the chief designer of the W2F-1. Leonard "Sully" Sullivan also helped in solidifying the preferred high wing configuration. Pelehach's original design had twin vertical tails, as shown in the proposed three-view drawing (Fig. 5.5). The propellers rotated in the same direction on both wings, resulting in significant slipstream curvature, impacting low speed direction stability and control. It was determined that additional fin area was required on the impacted side of the aircraft, and wind tunnel tests confirmed satisfactory performance with the change. The Navy insisted that the design be symmetrical, resulting in the addition of a fourth fin—two on each side (Fig. 5.6).

Frank Perley was lead aero on the W2F. Lloyd Skinner did all the work on the radar dish support, as he had on the WF-2. He was a real veteran, and came from Stinson Aircraft where he designed the Stinson SR7. Jim Brennan put a lot of effort into the wing design. Grant Hedrick promoted the use of

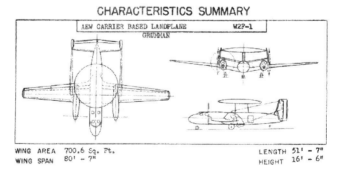

Fig. 5.5   Mike Pelehach's original design for the W2F-1.

Fig. 5.6   First flight takeoff of the W2F-1.

fiberglass epoxy composites for primary load-carrying structure in the rotodome and vertical tails of the E-2 aircraft; this was the first use of composite materials in primary structure.

The W2F-1 had a range in excess of 1600 n. miles, had a maximum speed of 320 kt, and carried a pylon-mounted, 24-ft-diameter rotating radar antenna dish on top of the fuselage. One of the most unique design aspects of the E-2A was that it carried a very large electronic payload of about 12,000 lb in an airframe that when empty weighed about 36,000 lb; its design takeoff gross weight (TOGW) was about 50,000 lb. The payload plus crew to TOGW ratio was 26%, which represents a trend of increasing electronics systems content for Grumman aircraft weapon systems.

Bob Nafis played a key role in the avionic system design concept for the proposal, and Fred Tiemann came on board in early 1957 just after the "win" to become the avionics project engineer. GE was supposed to be the systems manager because at the time the Navy perceived that Grumman did not have all the electronic skills and had to be "bolstered" by an electronic firm. In addition, the Navy's Bureau of Aeronautics (BuAer) traditionally contracted with the airframe primes for the airframe, and provided the engines, propellers, radars, radios, and other equipment as government furnished equipment (GFE).

Bill Zarkowsky became the "ramrod" leader as program manager. Leon Colyer, of the Navy's BuAer, was the Navy's overseer; he was the first of many excellent U.S. Navy representatives, both civilian and uniform, that provided leadership for the long time span of the E-2 program. Grumman had worked with GE on its UHF solution to clutter suppression and automatic height finding while scanning, and was inclined to develop the associated displays with GE, because of the complex information exchange between the radar operator's display and the radar processor. BuAer had for several years invested with Litton in developing display station/controls with symbology generation evolved through Navy Research Lab (NRL) and Naval Air Development Center (NADC).

Key government and civilian leaders that made the W2F-1 program a reality were: Leo Puckett, BuAer; Don Hemingway and Fred Staudaher (formerly with GE), NRL; and Chuck Curtis, NADC Johnsville. It was another company furnished equipment (CFE) program, and Grumman's Systems Group came up with the yellow line, or technical path, on a master interconnection specification that enabled Grumman to contract separately with GE and Litton. Once again, Grumman used the inertial system developed for the WF-2/A2F to reduce the fleet logistics and bench area.

Fred Tiemann, ex-Navy, was the muscle behind the project electronics systems team (Fig. 5.7). Fred played a very significant technical and leadership role with the Navy Program Office, BuAer Avionics Division, government labs, and key avionic contractors (GE, Litton, Dalmo Victor, etc.), as well as the new Grumman W2F-1 (E-2A) Hawkeye program management staff to make the E-2A and follow-on versions a success.

In 1968, Tiemann also worked with Jim Corbett in advanced systems to fund the coherent radar signal analyzer (CORSIGA) program to handle the overland radar clutter problem. According to Tiemann's memoir, this concept was the brain child of the TRG Company located in Rosemont,

Fig. 5.7   (L to R) Fred Tiemann; Gerry Maurer, assistant program manager; Ed Dalva, aircraft project engineer; and Bill Zarkowsky, program manager.

Pennsylvania. This talented group of people prepared a design concept for a feasibility demonstration, and the concept was eventually incorporated into the E-2C variant as Advanced Radar Processing System (ARPS). Joe Rodriguez and Bob O'Donahue submitted one of the early preliminary design proposals to BuAer on the ARPS concept based on meetings with GE and Leo Puckett of BuAer. O'Donahue was an "ideas and good antenna man," according to Rodriguez.

Gerry Norton remembered an interesting experience that occurred during lab testing of the first set of CORSIGA hardware. The hardware was installed in Grumman's Electronics Laboratory and connected to the E-2 antenna on the roof. Line of sight from the roof of Plant 14 was limited, but they were able to detect airplanes and, of course, lots of automobile traffic.

There were time limitations for when the test team could transmit from the rooftop antenna, so a live test was scheduled for 0600 h. When the system was fired up, the crew initially saw typical auto traffic, but a short time later most of the targets disappeared. This event puzzled the team, and they checked to make sure the equipment was still operating properly, which it was. They then found out that freezing rain had brought traffic near Grumman to a stand-still. This "suspect the equipment first" mentality is typical for an immature system like CORSIGA was at the time. This experience reminded Norton of something that Chuck Curtis of NADC had said to him years before: "You will know you have a mature system when you are no longer surprised that it works when you turn it on."

Alex Alexandrovich, who was the technical guru on radar systems, worked with Tiemann on technical problems as they evolved. Julie Cohen was the systems engineer, and the radome and antenna performance involved Bob O'Donahue and Barney Tichy. The problems facing the design engineers at Grumman were immense, and were compounded by the fact that the U.S. Navy insisted that the E-2A operate from the older World War II Essex class carriers. These requirements imposed various dimension and weight limitations on the design that initially impacted aircraft handling characteristics, and, more dramatically, caused serious problems with equipment reliability due to closely packed avionic systems and inadequate cooling. The initial E-2A systems that included the new GE *B*-band APS-96 radar were unreliable and did not fare well in official Navy evaluations. According to Gerry Norton, who had a lead role in the E-2 system developments, reliability was certainly an issue in the case of the matched filter circuitry for pulse compression, which required constant attention and adjustment. Equally significant factors were the velocity limitations of the E-2A system and the extensive sidelobe returns from nearby land masses. These factors helped spur the continuing evolution of the E-2, which would

Fig. 5.8   The E-2C in flight.

lead to the new TRAC-A antenna, CORSIGA/ARPS, and eventually, the E-2D developed by the Northrop Grumman Corporation.

Grumman and the Navy responded with the E-2B design, which was a vast improvement over the E-2A due to the use of a Litton L-304 digital computer that replaced the unreliable drum computer, and various other avionic upgrades. The E-2B replaced the E-1B in the carrier inventory. The next upgrade, the E-2C (Fig. 5.8), was greatly enhanced by a series of group developments that concentrated on the radar and computers.

- The basic E-2C employed the new GE UHF APS-120 radar that incorporated airborne moving target indicator (AMTI), additional computer capacity, and a passive detection system (PDS). Both the APS-96 in the E-2A and the APS-120 suffered from significant target velocity response limitations, in that only certain radial velocities could be detected reliably. These limitations spurred the development of CORSIGA and ARPS, discussed earlier in this section.
- Group 0 included the total radiation aperture control antenna (TRAC-A), the GE (later Lockheed Martin) APS-138 radar, enhanced computer capacity, a more secure communications system, and a new PDS. Up to 300 targets could be tracked.
- Group 1 featured the APS-139 radar that fed a new standard central air data computer (SCADC), additional cooling capacity, and more powerful Allison-T-56-A-427 engines. This allowed a 400% increase in tracked targets.
- The Group 2 configuration consisted of the APS-145 radar with ARPS housed in a new Randtron rotodome antenna group with a new interrogate friend or foe (IFF) system. In addition, the combat information center (CIC) was upgraded for the three controllers. This system allowed

simultaneous tracking of surface and airborne targets, and increased jamming resistance.

When the E-2C was integrated with the F-14A Tomcat/Phoenix system, outstanding air superiority effectiveness against present and future Soviet threats to the carrier air taskforce was achieved.

In the late 1950s, Grumman was not a hotbed of electronic engineering talent. There were many brilliant aircraft designers, but not so many "avionicers." Most of that category's skill was in the big electronic companies such as GE, Hazeltine, Westinghouse, Hughes, and Sperry. Most electronic equipment was provided GFE to the aircraft builders, and hardware suppliers supported Grumman in the integration/testing of that equipment. The E-1B and the E-2A changed that. These were the first big system integration jobs with Grumman as the system manager.

From the early 1960s to the early 1990s, a team of key Grumman personnel was instrumental in creating the improved system concepts that led to the development and testing of these new variants with the Navy and major subcontractors. Jerry Norton, who began his E-1 and E-2 career as a radar project engineer, became the E-2 systems project engineer and then deputy engineering manager for advanced development. Ken Koehler was initially the L-304 computer group leader working with Fred Tiemann on the E-2A. He became one of the few E-2A system operator experts, and is credited with having made the first successful automatic E-2A data link-controlled intercepts in which the E-2A sent a digital message to the F-14 with an intercept path to a threat aircraft. Koehler eventually became the E-2 program manager. Bernie Farber was instrumental in guiding all the independent research and development (IR&D) programs that led to improvements in the E-2C systems. Dennis Carter, the E-2C software project engineer, was also involved in all E-2 developments, and was highly respected by his U.S. Navy counterparts.

Paul Coco was the best flight test engineer on the E-2 program in the early 1980s. Coco had worked as an electromagnetic compatibility (EMC) engineer before leaving engineering to join flight test. Chuck Muller was a reliability engineer on the E-2A. He later was named a program manager for the E-2B/C upgrades. Dick Anderson started at Grumman in the electrical engineering group, and then joined E-2A engineering where he focused on special studies that GE was doing under the direction of Fred Tiemann. Anderson headed a team of analysts and soon became intimately involved with a U.S. Navy study group headed by Dr. Peter Waterman (the U.S. Navy's key civilian on E-2C development) that recommended improvements to the E-2 program. He went on to become the engineering manager of the E-2C, and was a well-respected and level-headed engineer according to his

Fig. 5.9   E-2C development meeting.

peers, major suppliers such as GE, and the Navy. Figure 5.9 shows an E-2C development meeting with Dr. Waterman seated third chair on the left. Dr. Charles A. "Bert" Fowler, Deputy Director Defense Research Engineering for Tactical Systems, Office of the Secretary of Defense, is seated second from the right at the table. Seated next to Dr. Waterman is Julie Cohen, program manager, and in the back row are Bob Barnard, Bob Higgins, Barney Tichy, and Bob O'Donahue. Behind O'Donahue are Dean Stone, Chuck Muller, Ken Koehler, Bob Bohner (E-2C engineering manager), Dick Anderson, Bernie Farber, and Dean Cassell.

Jim Murphy was the vehicle project engineer on the E-2. He played a key role in the E-2A aircraft carrier suitability effort, and later in the changes necessary in support of transition from E-2A to E-2B (a major impact on the airframe). Mike Kozak would take over for Jim later on in the E-2C. Marty O'Connor was an expert in system analysis. He worked very closely with Dick Anderson on special studies and supporting analyses for many of the system improvements. He was considered by many as the expert in E-2 operations and requirements. Dennis Carter was recognized as the expert software designer for the E-2 by Grumman and the Navy.

Sy Absatz was the major contributor to the design of the automatic tracking software program. Bernie Braun, Tony Guma, and Bill Austin were the brains behind the PDS system integration and development in the E-2. Tony Guma was, in addition, the L-304/display expert and ultimately took over E-2 systems leadership before being recruited for Joint STARS in 1986. Bill Kallansrude was a brilliant former Hazeltine APS-82 engineer who came to Grumman in the early 1960s. He became the top E-2 radar analyst on the

E-2A, B, and C. He was also an expert on GE's radar processor (computer detector) hardware and firmware, and subsequently became the resident ARPS engineering expert.

Tony Pacia became the communications/data links guru for E-2 engineering. He transitioned into the black (highly classified) world as the cognizant engineer on all the classified communication and links equipment. Dick Lebitz was regarded as the number-one Grumman E-2 radar engineer who primarily worked with the GE radar team in the evolving radar design of the APS-96, APS-111, APS-120 and APS-138. He was intimately involved with all radar ground and flight testing. He ultimately transitioned into the black world as the main designer for classified upgrades to the radar and IFF system. Larry Michelon became Grumman's key flight test manager and provided a critical interface with the operating Navy squadrons and with the Navy test community at Patuxent River, Maryland. "Deac" Jones transitioned from the E-1B program as flight test manager to becoming the first E-2A flight test manager. He played a key role as improvements were tested on the E-2A.

Jerry Norton (Fig. 5.10) remembered a great story involving Deac Jones and George Titterton, one of Grumman's more forceful leaders. Jones made a bet with Titterton that he could have all E-2As in existence at the time in the air at the same time, which was very difficult. He won the bet when all nine aircraft flew that day (eight of the aircraft flew from Long Island and the ninth aircraft just managed to get airborne in time from Naval Air Station Patuxent River, Maryland).

Jim McManus was an antenna engineer during the initial E-2A rotodome design with Dalmo-Victor. He then moved into the program office during the APS-111 development flight testing program. McManus was a funny guy and a great poet well known for his "odes." His most notable was the "Ode to an Involute Egg," which was a "Gunga Din" parody on the E-2A rotodome (Fig. 5.11).

Fig. 5.10 Jerry Norton discussing some flight test results with Larry Michelon.

"*ODE TO AN INVOLUTE EGG*"

You may talk of sidelobes low
When you're putting on a show
And writing penny specs for "AER" consumption
But when it comes to get 'em
You can strain and you can sweat 'em
And you'll wonder where you ever got the gumption

Now in Grummans sunny clime
Where I used to spend my time
A-serving up antennas for a fee
Of all the lousy planes
On which I racked my brains
There was none could top design one twenty three
It was Dome, Dome, Dome
You heavy, yagied, tilted rotodome
"Put another db in it
Or I'll cancel you this minute
You cockeyed, rotten egg-shaped rotodome

How Dalmo used to sweat
O'er the troubles they would get
When the model sidelobes seemed to hit the skids
They shuddered at the crash
When G.E. shouted "Cash"
And a dozen other vendors sent in bids
It was Dome, Dome, Dome
As the problems started hitting close to home
And it really was a mess
When we got the word from stress
All that structure lousing up our lovely dome

We had beams and we had splices
And a slew of dammed devices
And the tunnel tests all proved you were too big
With a tail to small to fly you
By the gods, we still stuck by you
And swore we'd see you someday in a jig

It was Dome, Dome, Dome
You misbegotten masthead, rotodome
Though we argued and we pleaded
Our advices weren't heeded
And you'll be a bloody memory. rotodome

```
We had Tschebycheff arrays
Which had all seen better days
And "Cigars" and "Dipoles" mounted by the score
We had helices and slabs
We got gain in dribs and drabs
And the weight was making project people sore
It was Dome, Dome, Dome
Though in one day Caeser couldn't build up Rome
Though we've pushed you and we've shoved you
And some even say we've loved you
You're an ugly plastic covered rotodome

So we took it to BuAer
And we thought they weren't fair
When they added extra spec on top of spec
"Displaced phase" and "Lobe suppression"
And wild talk of size compression
Made the whole damn project one big wreck
It was Dome, Dome, Dome
You will never see a Naval aerodrome
So we told old Leo Puckett
He could take his dome and _____ it
And we all began our weary march for home

So we'll see it later on
In the place where it has gone
With the F-10-F and all its motley crew
Where the heat will make us sweat
And we'll know that's what we get
For biting off much more than we could chew
It was Dome, Dome, Dome
You screwed us and tattoed us, rotodome
Though they've stressed you and they've weighed you
It was Avionics made you
You're a better Dome than Lockheeds rotodome
```

Jerry Norton had some great stories about the early flight testing of the E-2A. The first flight of the E-2A was a big deal, with a lot of folks from the papers and *Aviation Week* on hand at the Grumman facilities and airfield in Bethpage, New York. Norton was on the aircraft, and Tom Attridge was the pilot. Immediately after takeoff, the combined hydraulic pump let go and spewed gallons of hydraulic fluid into the aircraft. Attridge was not fazed by the situation. He flew the aircraft once around the field and then landed. All the writers on the ground looked up and were puzzled when they realized that the underside of the aircraft was pink not white, but they never knew why. In-flight emergencies were not unusual in the early days of the E-2A. The hydraulic pump failure on the first flight was just the first of several associated with a vibration issue, but there were other problems with the hydraulic system as well as with other systems.

Attridge was a terrific pilot but would do some bizarre things reminiscent of Hollywood stunts to get the job done. On one flight, a problem occurred in getting the rotodome to turn. Attridge quickly set the aircraft down at the Grumman Calverton, New York, flight test facility. He then opened up the pilot's overhead hatch and climbed out onto the fuselage *with both engines running* and pushed the dome to get it started. He then climbed back in, took off, and finished the mission successfully.

On another flight, when the avionic engineers were looking at the submarine detection capability of the E-2A, Attridge dropped down from 30,000 ft to near sea level to identify the sub visually. He was flying so low that salt spray from the ocean was covering the windshield. When the wipers failed to clear the windshield, he opened his overhead hatch and reached out and wiped the windshield clear less than 50 ft from the ocean surface.

Another story involved Walter Burndt, an E-2A test pilot. Norton recalled a flight test that involved evaluating a higher raised rotodome position to minimize aircraft effects on radar performance. In this flight test, the aircraft spent several hours at 30,000 ft and, as usual, when it was time to go home, Burndt would dive the E-2A at a high rate of descent to reach low altitude as quickly as possible. Well on this particular flight, when the E-2A reached 5000 ft, a "big bump" was felt that the crew could not identify. Upon landing, the ground crew looked up at the rotodome with faces aghast! The rotodome had imploded, leaving it with a hole big enough to fit a steel case desk through. The problem was caused because breathing holes, which allowed pressure in the rotodome to equalize, had been covered up in raising the dome.

In the mid-1960s, Ken Koehler, Jerry Norton, and a Navy officer were on board the E-2A preparing for takeoff during a Navy preliminary evaluation (NPE) test flight. The Grumman test pilot, Bill Bedell, was in the left seat and Fred Tiemann, the E-2A avionics project engineer and former Navy pilot, was in the right seat. Tiemann was at the controls during the takeoff, when he mentioned to Bedell that he was experiencing difficulty in keeping the aircraft properly aimed down the runway. After a brief exchange between the two about how difficult it was to maintain steering control, Bedell took control of the aircraft and the two managed to get airborne, albeit briefly. The pilot alerted us in the back end of the emergency and directed us to be prepared to bail out if necessary.

Hearing the alert, Norton quickly attached his parachute to his harness and put on his helmet, and then glanced back to see if Koehler and the Navy officer in the back of the plane were prepared. To his amazement, Norton saw that they were intensely focused on a display and completely unaware of the impending emergency. They both had apparently deselected the pilot on the intercom and had not heard the "prepare to bailout" directive. Norton managed to get their attention and when they turned and saw Norton ready to jump, they had an incredulous look on their faces, as if to say, "Is there something you know that I don't?" All Norton could say was, "Didn't you guys hear the pilot say be prepared to bail out?" The expressions of shock and surprise on their faces were unforgettable. Thank goodness the two pilots managed to get the aircraft safely back to earth without further difficulty. The incident was attributed to a failure in the stability augmentation system.

Perhaps the most memorable event was an overwater radar test flight in the middle of winter in the mid-1960s. The E-2A was about 300 miles south of Long Island at about 28,000 ft when the radar shut down unexpectedly, causing a huge electrical transient and power surge. This transient caused the fuel gauges to show a significant loss in the amount of indicated fuel in both fuel tanks. Tom Attridge, the test pilot, informed the crew in the back that he was concerned whether there was enough fuel to return to base, and requested Norton and the crew to give him a vector to the nearest landing area as soon as they could. When the crew got the radar back on line, there was no land being painted on the indicator because the E-2A was well beyond the line of sight.

Attridge headed for home and the crew finally could detect land, which was about 180 miles ahead. Fuel calculations needed to reach a place to land kept coming up a bit more than what was indicated. That prompted a discussion among the crew about bailout vs ditching options. No immediate action was necessary because the crew had at least half an hour before they would have to decide. Norton spent the next several minutes reviewing procedures for ditching and bailout. If they had to ditch at sea he would be the last back-ender out of the aircraft, and he made sure to connect his seat bottom containing a life raft to his harness, and that he had a knife and shark repellent. If the order to bail out was given, Norton would be the first out because he was closest to the main entrance hatch. He checked to make sure everything was in order—oxygen mask secured to helmet, knife and shark repellent handy, seat bottom life raft was secured to harness, and so on. He repeated his checklist over and over again until he was absolutely confident of any eventuality. Had he been told to ditch things probably would have worked out; however, he had left his parachute stowed in the aircraft. Fortunately, the E-2A landed safely with a few minutes of fuel remaining.

Tom Attridge, the E-2A project pilot, played a role in many of the anecdotes about the E-2A. Attridge apparently had confidence in the E-2A's autopilot—possibly more than was justified. He took pleasure in leaving the flight deck with some frightened avionics engineer in the right seat when he was the only pilot on board to see how the radar and tracking systems were working. It is reported that on the very first test hop of the aircraft, with only the pilot on board, Attridge went to the back end and turned all the systems on. Seeing him in the back of the aircraft was unnerving to most operators, and Norton was no exception. This situation was exacerbated even more because of a continuing problem with the crew compartment door. When closed, the door would lock, and could only be opened from the entrance side. Norton was not sure whether Attridge was aware of the problem with the crew compartment door, but when he showed up in the back end on a flight and pulled the door closed behind him, the crew was on the verge of cardiac arrest.

CONCLUSION

Grumman had become a major aircraft weapon system developer, integrator, and manager with all the inherent skills and dedicated facilities to create sophisticated solutions to complex mission area requirements of the services. The aircraft designer and his teammates from the traditional engineering disciplines (e.g., aerodynamics, propulsion, structures, sub-systems, weights, flight controls) were complemented by a bevy of operations and system analysts, avionic engineers, software engineers, and others as they examined thousands of tradeoffs to meet service requirements. Grumman avionic engineers contributed heavily to new AEW systems from the E-1 series through the family of E-2 derivatives culminating in the E-2C. Another key factor in the creation this long line of AEW aircraft was the sustained technical and program leadership of the U.S. Navy.

Mike Pelehach, Joe Rees, and some of the key avionic engineers who helped create and win the W2F-1(E-2A) Hawkeye would go on to help Grumman regain its role as a designer of world class fighter weapon systems with the development of the F-111B and F-14.

Chapter 6

THE F-111B AND THE LINEAGE OF THE F-14

TFX, F-111B

In late November 1962, the Department of Defense (DOD) announced the award of the TFX program to the General Dynamics (GD)/Grumman team. The resulting GD/Grumman F-111B (Fig. 6.1) flew for the first time in May 1965.

This award was the culmination of an intensive four-year program that involved breakthrough research by NASA and airframe, electronics, engine, and missile manufacturers; many pre-request for proposal (RFP) design tradeoff and cost effectiveness analyses conducted by DOD, the Air Force, the Navy, and manufacturers; and four proposal runoffs. Nine aircraft companies and three engine manufacturers were initially involved in the competition, with Boeing and GD/Grumman ultimately involved in the fourth proposal runoff.

The TFX story began in 1959 when U.S. Air Force (USAF) General Frank F. Everest, Commander of Tactical Air Command (TAC), wanted a new fighter bomber for the 1960–1970 time span that could fly nonstop from the United States to Europe and from the United States to southeast Asia with one refueling; perform a 1000-mph dash for several hundred miles at high altitude with tactical nuclear weapons; dash at 1700 mph on the deck; and operate from sod air fields with half the takeoff and landing distance of an F-105. John Stack, the assistant director of NASA's Langley Research Center, proved that a "pivot" variable sweep design (versus a translating variable sweep design on the Bell X-5 and the XF10F-1 Jaguar) was feasible. This concept resulted in a much lighter and less complex variable sweep installation due to the placement of the wing panel pivot points in a "fixed" location outboard of the fuselage. This significant development, in combination with the benefits of the TF30 turbofan with a modulated afterburner engine (a first for a fighter application), held the promise of achieving a great portion of General Everest's ambitious requirements. As a result, Secretary McNamara/Department of Defense Research and Engineering (DDR&E) agreed with the concept and directed that the TFX, which

Fig. 6.1   General Dynamics/Grumman F-111B.

was to become the F-111, fill the requirements of both the Air Force and Navy and result in the promise of reduced costs.

A great deal of work ensued as the Air Force and Navy wrestled with their requirements to achieve some form of baseline configuration that would meet their individual needs. The Navy maximum takeoff gross weight was raised to 55,000 lb and the Air Force lowered its takeoff gross weight to 63,000 lb by reducing the supersonic dash requirement to 200 n. miles and providing the Navy with almost five hours of time-on-station. The Navy wanted the Fleet Air Defense mission with six Phoenix missiles, superior fighter air combat capability based on Vietnam experience against existing Soviet and projected threats, and excellent carrier suitability. DOD cost-effectiveness studies were indicating that the Navy could defend the fleet with only standoff capability. As the design of the F-111B matured, achieving all these requirements became very difficult.

The final runoff proposal pitted GD/Grumman against Boeing. Grumman's role on the TFX program was very significant because of the three final contractors in the competition, only Grumman had vast carrier design and operational experience. This unique experience manifested itself as the preproposal and preliminary design studies began to mature and Grumman assigned some of its finest engineers to work on the pre-RFP and proposal effort program. Grumman's responsibilities on the program included all unique F-111B design, F-111B flight test, production and delivery of the F-111B, and the design, tooling, and production of all aft fuselages, landing gear, and the horizontal stabilizer for all F-111 aircraft.

Leonard "Sully" Sullivan, who led the Preliminary Design department for several years, was instrumental in helping secure the GD/Grumman win that became a strenuous joint design effort. He spent the better part of a year flying back and forth to the GD plant in Fort Worth, Texas, while also trying to convince the Navy that the F-111B would satisfy its requirements. Sullivan also led the winning effort with Bendix on the long-range Eagle missile program that was to be carried by the canceled F6D Missileer program, the predecessor to the F-111B for Fleet Air Defense. The Eagle missile program was also canceled. Sullivan subsequently led the charge by Grumman on its excellent Phoenix missile proposal that Hughes won on a close call. Sullivan was highly respected by the military as well as his peers at Grumman. He had unique technical, leadership, writing, and communication skills that enabled him to stir his design teams to think and do better. He spoke eloquently to anyone, flag officer to scientist, with command of any topic, and he could critique any aspect of a design or proposal in detail while often "grading" the effort in the process.

Sullivan left Grumman in 1964, and he and Russ Murray, at one time the deputy director of Operations Analysis, went on have outstanding careers in DOD. The Preliminary Design department, along with many friends from other departments and Grumman top management, gave Sullivan a rousing sendoff that featured the entire audience singing a Grumman rendition of the theme song from the musical "Hello, Dolly!" written by Fritz Dunmire (Fig. 6.2). At the end of the ceremony, Clint Towl, a Grumman founder and president, said, "and we hope you come back," which drew loud applause from the audience.

On the first TFX proposal, Grumman personnel went to Ft. Worth to work with GD on the Navy version. Gene Bonan was the team leader and Vinny Milano was his deputy. Dane Lamberson from Aerodynamics, Dick Feyk from Stuctures, and Ted Zach were also key members of the team. As the proposal effort grew and further proposal rounds occurred, Grumman brought in more senior engineers: Paul Anbro, design team lead; Mike Pelehach, lead designer; George Petronio, structures; Bob Roemer, mechanical systems/hydraulics; Bob Kress, aerodynamics; Irv Waaland, aero design and wind tunnel testing; Joe Rodriguez, radio frequency (RF) engineering; Paul Weidenhaefer, weight control preliminary design; and Don Terrana, configuration layout. Grant Hedrick and Dick Hutton also made key visits during the four proposal submittals.

The challenges in developing the preliminary design of the TFX were multifaceted:

- A pivoted, variable sweep wing that would allow very long-range cruise, endurance, and supersonic dash (200 n. miles at Mach 1.2)
- Wing aerodynamic design that incorporated high lift slats and flaps to achieve the desired carrier landing and takeoff performance while minimizing pitching moment
- Frontal cross-sectional area to minimize drag for supersonic performance with a fuselage that housed the large AWG-9 radar antenna, the crew escape module, a bomb bay, landing gear, and two turbofan engines

GOODBYE SULLY
(Sung to tune of "Hello Dolly")

Hel-lo Sul-ly, Well Hel-lo Sul-ly
It's so nice to have you here where you belong

You're looking swell Sul-ly
We can tell Sul-ly
You're still glow-ing, you're still grow-ing,
          you're still going strong

We know you'll soon be leaving
And we'll all be grieving
Potomac River you'll be seeing soon, So,

Take a beer fellas
Lets all give a cheer fellas
Sully's gonna sing the D.C. tune

Good-bye Sul-ly, Well Good-bye Sul-ly,
We'd like to keep you here where you be-long

It will be hell, Sul-ly, we can tell Sul-ly
You're still going, and we're knowing that it's wrong

We hear the dead-line call-ing
There's no time for stall-ing
Proposal time is almost drawing near, So

Gol-ly Gee Sul-ly, hell with DOD Sul-ly
You should never go away
You should never go away
You should never go away from here

Fig. 6.2   The original copy of the famous rendition.

- Internal stores in a fuselage bomb bay and wing-mounted stores on swivel pylons
- Efficient inlet/engine/exhaust nozzle design to incorporate afterburning turbofan engines and minimize drag
- Landing gear design for land and carrier operation that had to be housed in the fuselage to minimize frontal area in order to achieve supersonic performance requirements
- Incorporation of a crew escape module
- High-strength materials for the wing carry-through structure for the variable sweep wings

The F-111A weapon system had a minimal, smooth cross-sectional area that provided exceptional transonic capability. However, the successful flight test program of the F-111A uncovered other problem areas, as shown in Fig. 6.3 and discussed here:

- Base drag: The development of the aft fuselage was very critical in terms of drag. What was important was not simply the thrust of the engine, but the thrust-minus-drag created by the installation of the engine's exhaust nozzles in the aft fuselage.
- Turbofan engine/inlets: With the advent of the turbofan engine, pressure spikes in the fan engine could propagate forward and adversely affect inlet performance
- External store drag: Stores location, pylon/bomb rack design, and spacing between weapons took on increased importance in the effort to achieve transonic and supersonic performance
- Materials: The metal fatigue problem arising from the use of high-strength steel (D6AC type) for critical structures—the wing center section box and the horizontal tail carrythrough bulkhead—required a better understanding of the fatigue characteristics of material.

Other difficult issues also emerged that would require careful consideration as the pre-VFX studies in the 1960s began to yield the eventual VFX requirements:

- Guns: These vanished for a time because the United States was entering the missile era, only to return when it was found that the gun was a critically needed part of a fighter weapon system.

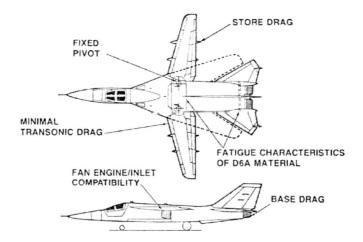

Fig. 6.3   F-111A problem areas.

- Missiles: These became the primary armament as their performance and reliability improved, but their full effectiveness was diminished in certain combat situations that required visual identification prior to firing.
- Corrosion and fatigue: Detailed studies and tests were devoted to corrosion problems as well as increasing the fatigue requirements (spectrum) for not only the wing, but all aircraft structural components. The fatigue spectrum of the F-14, in terms of allowed g exceedance per thousand hours, was increased by a factor of 10 over that of the F-4 Phantom.
- Cost: As the Vietnam War expanded, affordability began to surface as a major factor in aircraft design, planning, and procurement.
- High-low mix: This was the first reaction to rising wartime costs and the need to increase procurement of more aircraft. However, as each "low" aircraft concept was being developed, requirements creep took hold because it was necessary to increase combat effectiveness; hence, the cost benefits of a low side of the mix was never fully realized

The Grumman TFX design team had many interesting experiences in this demanding program, as recounted by some of its key members. Don Terrana recalled that once the crew station, nose radar, engine and inlets, and bomb bay were configured, all that was left was the landing gear. All of the aforementioned items pretty much dictated how much space was available for the landing gear, but fitting the landing gear into the little area (volume) that was available was the most difficult problem in the whole design. At the time, Grumman had some of the best landing gear designers in the industry because of all the carrier-designed aircraft, but no matter how many configurations were looked at by both Grumman and GD, no solutions were found. Finally, a GD engineer familiar with Ford cars came up with a design based on the Ford Motor Company front wheel suspension system, hence the name FOMOCO landing gear.

Terrana also recollected when the fourth proposal was submitted in fall 1963. Grumman and GD were at odds about the weight of the F-111B. GD held that the takeoff gross weight would be 60,000 lb, whereas Grumman estimated the weight at 65,000 lb—the actual takeoff gross weight of No. 6 F-111B with six Phoenix missiles was on the order of 79,000 lb. Grumman recalled the entire team of about 20 employees from GD and sent them home. After intense negotiation, Grumman agreed to have the team return and to keep the Grumman name on the proposal, with changes to the wording of the proposal reflecting Grumman's reservations on weight.

Phil Brice, an important member of Alexander Kartveli's engineering design team at Republic Aviation, came to Grumman in the 1960s and led various advanced system design projects—one of them being a Grumman performance improvement study of the F-111B. Don Terrana, configuration design, and Ed Waesche, advanced systems project engineer, worked diligently on this study, which was referred to as the Colossal Weight Improvement Program (CWIP). It showed some potential for performance improvement; however, the U.S. Navy was convinced that the F-111B did not offer sufficient air combat maneuverability (ACM) for the Fighter Escort Mission where Navy fighters would accompany attack bombers over enemy territory.

Irv Waaland was very involved in aero design and wind tunnel activity at Grumman, GD, and NASA facilities. Fioravanti (Frank) Visconti and Dick Kita were also engaged in aero work; Frank's specialty was low speed aerodynamics. Waaland recalled that Bob Kress had the unique job of looking at all the aero data and coming up with design variations or alternatives to meet aerodynamic requirements. Along with Charlie Jackson at GD, he created the leading edge slat design that allowed unprecedented extension of the lift-curve slope in the presence of powerful, double-slotted flaps. A considerable amount of wind tunnel testing occurred to try and achieve a maximum lift coefficient of 3.2 with acceptable pitching moment characteristics that had to be countered by large down loads on the horizontal tail. Another area in which Kress was able to create design alternatives was the fixed glove area of the variable sweep wing.

Waaland also remembered a visit to GD for a major design review that included Bill Schwendler and Robert Widmer, the chief engineer for GD. During the meeting, Widmer said he felt that the horizontal stabilizer should be moved up from the fuselage onto the vertical fin (maybe for lower drag). Waaland pointed out that the relocation would be a "fatal" change to the Navy version because it would guarantee high angle of attack (AOA) pitch up. The subject was then dropped. When Waaland later asked why the GD folks were silent at the meeting, they explained that their method of operation was not to challenge the chief, but to analyze any recommendation and write a memo to him on the conclusions. On the ride back to the airport, he asked Grumman management if "he had stepped on any toes" with his rebuttal of Widmer's suggestion. Their answer was an emphatic "Hell no—that's what we pay you to do!"

On the lighter side, Vinny Milano related two stories about the food in Texas and some of the "Lawn-Guyland" Grumman boys not being familiar with "exotic" dishes. He was invited to dinner one evening by his GD counterpart, Willard Caddell, in charge of weights and balance. Caddell explained that his wife made a chili for dinner and he wondered if Milano could handle the spicy way it was made in Texas. Being of Italian descent, he explained that he shouldn't have any trouble because Italian food was also spicy. The evening went smoothly, but the chili took its toll the following workday, much to the amusement of the GD folks.

Dane Lamberson was very taken by the Texas hospitality and lovely waitresses, and ended up ordering a dish at the Western Hills Hotel that he was not familiar with called "steak tartar." When served raw chopped meat, he became aghast and said "I can't eat this—it's raw!" The Grumman guys had a good laugh and wouldn't let him forget it; the Texas folks were very gracious and made him a Salisbury steak instead.

VFX, F-14

Ten variable sweep aircraft were designed worldwide before the F-14A. The F-14A was Grumman's third-generation variable sweep design, which evolved from the XF10F-1 and the F-111B. At the time of award in 1968, Grumman had 1500 engineers working on the design and over 9000 h of wind tunnel testing, including 3000 h associated with the inlet and nozzle design as well as other associated propulsion testing.

During the late 1960s, Mike Pelehach, chief designer, and his team (Fig. 6.4) worked closely with the talented and dedicated engineers at Naval Air Systems Command (NAVAIR), in particular George Spangenberg (Fig. 6.5), who was head of the Technical Evaluation Division. Other key NAVAIR personnel involved in the VFX/F-14 design evolution were Bill

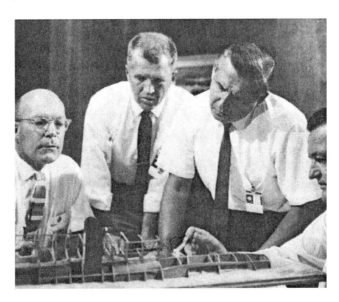

Fig. 6.4   Dick Hutton, Bob Mullaney, Mike Pelehach, and Joe Rees discuss aspects of the unique F-14 structural design concept.

Fig. 6.5   George Spangenberg (right center), the U.S. Navy's top designer, viewing the F-14A mockup in May 1969 along with Captain Ames (center); Fred Puglisi (left of Ames), Integrated Logistics Support; the author behind Puglisi; Ken Richardson; and Hughes (far left, partial view).

Kovin, Jack Linden, Keith Dental, and Fred Gloeckler. Notable Navy leadership included Admiral Thomas Moorer, Chief of Naval Operations (CN); Vice Admiral Robert Townsend, Commander Naval Air Systems Command (NASC); Vice Admiral Tom Connolly (Fig. 6.6), Deputy Chief

Fig. 6.6   Several generations of Grumman's top aircraft designers; (L to R) Mike Pelehach, Dick Hutton, Bill Schwendler, and Clint Towl (partial view), CEO; Lew Evans, president of Grumman; and Vice Admiral Connolly, Deputy Chief of Naval Operations, Air Warfare.

Naval Operations Air; Rear Admiral Jim Foxgrover, Fighter Branch, NASC; and Captains Scott Lamoreaux, John Weaver, and Mike Ames.

The following is an excerpt from a eulogy given by the author at Mike Pelehach's funeral on October 31, 2002, that recounts his design philosophy and several anecdotes relating to him, as one of Grumman's top designers, and his key teammates:

> I met Mike Pelehach some 40 years ago when I was a young engineer in Preliminary Design (PD) at Grumman. He had just returned to PD after some time spent as the program manager and chief designer of the Mohawk, the U.S. Army's premier surveillance aircraft of its day. We were all amazed with the stories of his flights in the experimental Mohawks with Army pilots that ultimately improved how the aircraft flew.
>
> He brought a new dynamic to PD with his drive, energy, and leadership. He didn't walk; he moved at a fast pace all the time! He had the uncanny ability to find the best in everyone and put a team together like a mosaic design while exhorting them with words like "let's make it happen." His drive and ability to see a design issue, and solve it quickly, were the foundations of all his future successes.
>
> During the early 60s when Pelehach took over PD, I happened to be in a design meeting with him and the PD staff. Usually Bill Tebo, head of PD propulsion, sat to his right. Tebo was a big man and liked to smoke a small pipe. Pelehach was conducting the meeting in his usual dynamic way and Tebo was attempting to relight his pipe and also tamping down the tobacco. Well unbeknownst to both of them some of the fiery ashes ended up in the cuffs of Mike Pelehach's pants leg and his pants started to smoke. Well "all hell broke loose" since he jumped up and Bill Tebo attempted to smother the smoldering pants cuffs. Needless to say he was very apologetic and an immense amount of energy was generated between the meeting, putting out the pants fire, and controlling hysterical laughter in PD.
>
> Mike Pelehach had the unique ability to size up people and let them run with an idea. The young forward swept wing design that eventually became the X-29 design team was given a timely boost in the late 70s when he approved the design of a radio-controlled model to test the concept.
>
> In the days of the (VFX) F-14 competition, Pelehach forged a unique link with key Navy admirals, the Navy's technical branch, and industry that helped guide and shape Navy requirements.
>
> He had three guiding principles as he evolved a new design and then developed and produced it:

- "Stay close to the field service and support people because they really know first-hand where the problems are and what the customer thinks."
- "Spend time with the people on the production line, know and understand their problems, and you will ultimately build the aircraft well."
- "Always tell the customer the problems first and your plan to fix them quickly."

You have heard of Napoleon's Imperial Guard and "Arnie's Army," well Pelehach had his "two percenters"(as he called them), and still does today. These were the people he would call on "to make it happen" no matter how difficult the job was or where they were located in Grumman. Here are some examples of his team's actions:

- Tom Kane spending untold days and nights in Washington on all Grumman programs including the VFX solving funding crisis issues.
- Howard Schilling finishing the wing drawings on the F-14 while suffering from the onset of appendicitis.
- Larry Canonico being thrown into the breach time and again when the inboard profile of a new aircraft design was not correct and the design had to be frozen to meet schedule. He was affectionately called "Cannonball" because he would pursue every job with speed and precision and not let anything slow him down.
- Pelehach calling me to drop everything and get a design team together to redesign the MIG-21s for Pakistan and China.
- Pelehach asking Admiral Tom Connolly, DCNO (Deputy Chief of Naval Operations) Air, to come to Grumman and address the entire design team during a critical phase of the F-14A design development when the drawing process was stopped in order to remove weight. Joe Rodriguez remembered having a "problem of the week" meeting with Renso Caporali, Bob Kress, Dick Cyphers, and other key technical managers. In many cases the problem was weight. At one point Grumman was going to adapt a new digital computer program that would shave each structural frame web thickness, but Dick Cyphers didn't think this process was ready based on his long experience. The team elected to bring each functional department in (mechanical systems, hydraulics, etc.) to modify the size and thickness of each bulkhead to save weight but not break at the design limits.
- Pelehach sitting up all night in the electron beam welding facility to watch the first titanium wing box on the F-14 being welded together.
- Mike Pelehach taking on the Air Force and going into Iran, over much resistance, to brief the Shah on the F-14.

With all of his drive and speed, he was also a caring man. He touched everyone from the production line mechanic to the CEO and he always asked how they and their families were feeling.

After the demise of the F-111B, the Navy, under the leadership of George Spangenberg, contracted with industry to examine the feasibility of using an advanced airframe combined with F-111B avionics and engines to satisfy the air superiority and fleet air defense missions. Joe Rees played a major role in Grumman's VFX success. He came to Grumman in 1965 after a distinguished career in the Navy including being the Navy's F-111B program manager. Rees, Pelehach, and Larry Mead spent considerable time in Washington working with their Navy counterparts. Rees (Fig. 6.7) credited the VFX win "as an obligation to the nation and to the future of the Company." Walsh summed it up as "we understood the Navy's requirements and got an early start; we achieved design simplicity, we amassed great substantiation."

These studies led to the VFX competition and many versions of Grumman Design G-303 including variable sweep designs 303-60, 303A, 303B, 303C, 303D, and 303E, and a fixed wing design 303F. Bill Phillips and Ed Happ were lead configuration designers on many of the Design 303 versions. Phillips was a colorful and passionate designer who flew P-51s in World War II. Dick Lu, head of Preliminary Design (PD) aerodynamics, worked closely with Phillips on the configuration layouts. All of the thousands of VFAX (predecessor to the VFX) and VFX configurations were evaluated by the PD aircraft weight group headed by Ed Tobin, Bob Keenan, and John Raha. In those days, each configuration was evaluated by the weights team to arrive at balanced configurations that met the selected design requirements. Ed Waeshe also led study efforts in 1969 on the VFX-2 (F-14B) and the F-14C as the F-14A began development.

Fig. 6.7 Joe Rees (left), deputy director F-14 program, and Dave Walsh, F-14 marketing manager.

Fig. 6.8   Mike Pelehach in front of the winning VFX configuration.

The winning VFX configuration (Fig. 6.8) featured two tails for greater directional stability and the removal of foldable strakes mounted on the lower portion of each engine nacelle, as recommended by the Navy. Renso Caporali recalled, "As submitted, Design 303E had a single vertical tail. Since the single fin was adequate for safe flight beyond Mach 2.0, Grumman proposed to add smaller vertical surfaces on the aft underside of the aircraft that would have to be folded for landings, takeoffs, and other ground operations. Calculations showed this arrangement was the lightest weight solution; however, the Navy would not bend and insisted on a more robust solution. We saluted, bit the weight bullet, and changed to a two tail solution."

Bob Kress played a key role in the design evolution of the F-14 as chief engineer, design innovator, and mediator. In many ways, he and Dr. Renso "Capi" Caporali, who at the time was technical assistant to Grant Hedrick, vice president of Engineering, made the necessary leadership decisions to balance design requirements with functional department demands (e.g., structures vs propulsion) without compromising key performance require-ments. Kress and Caporali moved into a local hotel called the Astro Motel with sufficient martinis to write the executive summary of the proposal. Capi was also responsible for the performance volume of the proposal.

An F-14 retirement ceremony was held on Long Island in June 2006 for more than 500 people, including many Grumman engineers involved with the F-14 development, the last F-14D squadron commander, other F-14D pilots, radar intercept officers (RIOs) and maintenance officers, and Vice Admiral David Venlet, Commander of the Naval Air Systems Command, himself a former F-14 RIO and pilot. I was asked to be master of ceremonies at the event and to introduce a dais made up of Grumman "pioneers" who made the F-14 a reality and success.

The author had the honor of reading reflections by the remarkable Bob Kress, who was ill at the time. Although he could not attend this event, he did attend the final F-14 retirement ceremony at Norfolk Naval Air Station in September 2006, and shortly thereafter passed on. Kress had a remarkable career at Grumman. He was able to attend MIT on a Grumman scholarship, and the way Kress put it, "Grumman made my life." He said he owed everything to Grumman. His career spanned 41 years in Flight Dynamics, and included being a key contributor to the Mohawk, the Lunar Module, the F-14, and vertical takeoff and landing designs. "These were the greatest years of aviation, and because of Grumman, I had a part," said Kress.

He joined Grumman in 1951 as a dynamicist in the Research Department engaged in aircraft and missile stability, control, and guidance. Kress was lead aero on the Mohawk, and became assistant chief of Aerodynamics in 1959, where he concentrated on the design of short takeoff and landing (STOL) and vertical takeoff and landing (VTOL) aircraft, as well as the TFX/F-111B. On the Lunar Module program, Kress played a key role as head of Systems Simulation, and Guidance and Control, culminating in becoming systems project engineer. He helped create the F-14A, as described in the following text, and served as engineering manager during development. He then went on to work on many VTOL projects, culminating in Grumman Design 698 and advanced versions of the F-14. Kress was also an expert radio-controlled model airplane builder, and actually designed and built a small jet engine for use in model aircraft.

Bob Kress kept a list of "white rabbits"—unique F-14 performance improvements—that in toto would make the aircraft a sure winner by virtue of superior aerodynamics and significant weight savings. His target was four, but by the end of 1968 the design team was sure they had seven:

- Variable sweep to achieve Mach 2.4, cruise efficiently, and land aboard the carrier at reasonable speeds.
- Automatic wing sweep to achieve big gains in air combat maneuverability (ACM).
- Wing pivot location to wipe out excessive high-speed pitch stability due to aerodynamic center shift with wing sweep that was detrimental to F-111 high-speed maneuverability. Dr. Gunther "Doc" Buchmann found this out by studying NACA archives.
- Widespread nacelles, endorsed by Mike Pelehach and Dick Hutton, were

selected to give the "bomber" type TF30 engines from the F-111 "straight line" air flow by removing the effects of the fuselage, and to permit the use of weapon rails or pallets. This configuration was also selected to distinguish the Grumman design from other competitors.

- Weapon rails that could be configured to carry Phoenix missiles and bombs to satisfy the three demanding missions (fighter escort with four Sparrow missiles, fleet air defense with six Phoenix missiles, and attack with a wide variety of bombs with sufficient fuel) called out in the F-14 type spec.
- Leading edge slats that doubled maneuvering buffet onset g's and greatly reduced turning drag.
- Glove vanes or swept canards for high-speed maneuvering.

These white rabbits also resulted in a significant weight savings compared to the F-111B. The VFX/F-14A airframe design benefitted from the lessons learned from the F-111B that required a beefed up structure, and as a result, the empty weight of the F-14A was almost 9800 lb lighter than that of the F-111B. Key design difference of the VFX/F-14A vs the F-111B were:

- The variable sweep wing in the aft position "laid" on top of the fuselage vs a wing that "cut" the fuselage.
- Weapon rails and fixed glove pylons vs the need for internal missile carriage and swiveling pylons.
- Tandem seating allowed for fuselage-length longerons for strength vs the side-by-side escape module utilized in the F-111.
- Titanium was used extensively in the wing covers, wing center section, and nacelles, amounting to almost 25% of the airplane manufacturers' planning report (AMPR) weight.
- Mach sweep programmer limited net wing bending moment.
- Electron beam (EB) welding saved considerable weight vs a bolted structure.
- Landing gear retracted into a glove area vs the fuselage.
- Widely spaced nacelles with straight flowthrough nacelles with 2-D inlets vs spiked inlets with engines side by side.
- Boron epoxy skins on horizontal tails vs an all-metal structure.

The F-14A made its first flight on December 21, 1970—23 months after contract award. Grumman won the contact in late 1968 and signed up to achieve the first flight in two years and initial operational capability (IOC) in 1973. Grumman met these dates. This was a remarkable achievement reminiscent of the first flight of the F9F-9 (F11F-1) Tiger that occurred 16 months after go-ahead from the Navy. Joe Cipp, head of the F-14A Product Development Center, recalled how the first flight happened.

Lew Evans, Admiral Connolly, and me were standing near the runway while Bob Smyth and Bill Miller were doing high speed taxi runs. It was getting dark and Lew (Evans) asked me if we could get a little flight in. I responded that we would have to see if all the inspections were in order and signed off by Navy inspection. Evans replied that we have the Navy's Chief Inspector with us (Admiral Connolly). I went over to talk to Bill Young, the plane captain, and said can we go? Well the F-14 took off, made a few turns around the field and came in with the landing lights on—nothing happened.

The second flight of the F-14A (Fig. 6.9), nine days later, was another story best recalled by Renso Caporali.

The second flight was perhaps the most photographed and best recorded crash of a tactical aircraft. The crew of Bill Miller and Bob Smyth ejected only 1.9 seconds before impact at the end of the northwest runway at the Calverton Flight test facility on Long Island. The cause was the fatigue failure of two 1/4-in. titanium hydraulic lines—one in each of the main hydraulic systems that powered the rudders, and other directional controls. After the accident and investigation we realized, full well, that the testing of these important systems was very hurried, rushed, and incomplete. The F-14 also had a third chance backup system that was designed to provide emergency control when the main hydraulic systems failed. It too failed.

Fig. 6.9   F-14A No. 1 on its second ill-fated flight is shown approaching the Long Island coast.

The problem was identified rapidly and F-14A No. 2 flew successfully five months later.

Renso Caporali discussed how the F-14 wing sweep management system evolved. The F-14 came into being due to the TFX program, which resulted in the variable-sweep-wing F-111A/B. The F-111B was found to be unacceptable for Navy use, largely because of its size, weight, and resultant unsatisfactory carrier suitability and air combat maneuvering (ACM) performance. In the case of the F-111, the wing sweep was controlled by the pilot with presumably enough structural strength, and consequent built-in weight, such that any wing sweep could be selected anywhere within the design flight envelope. However, it was intended that the pilot follow a schedule that near-optimized aerodynamic performance. The primary Air Force mission was low-altitude high-speed penetration of enemy airspace. The Air Force ran the program, hence the pilot control of the wing sweep was not unduly burdensome and the extra structural weight required in case of pilot lapses was not too much of a performance penalty.

When the Navy's requirements for the VFX were released in the RFP, the Fleet Air Defense Mission dictated the use of the variable sweep wing. One contractor, North American Aviation (NAA), did propose a fixed wing design, but Grumman's fixed wing design takeoff gross weight (TOGW) to satisfy all the requirements was about 5000 lb heavier than the variable sweep configuration. The other design mission, called Fighter Escort, put a premium on maneuvering performance that was extremely sensitive to weight. This meant that providing extra strength for improperly positioned wing sweep would severely penalize aircraft performance.

Grumman's approach to the potential weight problem during the proposal phase was that the weight and consequent performance estimates essentially assumed that the wing loads would be those of an airplane whose wing sweep was where it should be to match the flight condition, and just how that happened was not addressed at proposal submittal.

Subsequent to contract award, and after some serious design calculations, it became apparent that the difference in wing loads between a maximum g pullup with 20 deg of wing sweep while flying at Mach 0.7 and 35,000 ft (a necessary flight condition), and that same maneuver and configuration at essentially sea level at Mach 1.2 (an unwanted but unfortunately achievable combination) was such that, quite literally, thousands of pounds of useless aircraft weight growth would result.

In the case of the F-14, as in the Joint STARS program, a significant development had to take place after award to make the FSD and production programs a success. There were design assumptions and insufficient system design, development, and testing done of critical technologies (software systems in the case of Joint STARS) prior to award that would have severely impacted the chances of program success. I will discuss this crucial issue again in the Joint STARS E-8A, E-8C program development section of Chapter 8.

Grumman proposed a redundant system to limit the forward wing sweep as a function of Mach number so that the maximum wing loads at all flight conditions would not exceed those at the nominal Mach 0.7/35,000 ft point required for maximum range. The Navy was aware of these impacts and accepted the Mach Sweep Limiter approach with high redundancy built into the resulting system. Shortly after the acceptance by the Navy of the sweep limiter, it became apparent that the optimum wing sweeps for accelerating or maneuvering were very similar to the Mach Sweep Limiter schedule dictated by air load limitations. What followed was the incorporation of an "Auto" mode within the Mach Sweep Limiter system. By placing the switch in the Auto position, the system would position the wing to optimize or near-optimize performance as well as to keep wing loads within acceptable bounds.

Renso Caporali and Bob Kress worked closely with Bob Mohrman of Stress and his team to develop the Mach Sweep Limiter system concept. This concept was approved by Grant Hedrick, vice president of Engineering, who was highly respected by the Navy as one of our nation's foremost structural design experts. Bob Steele, head of F-14 systems, led the team effort along with Karl Jackson of Garrett AirResearch to develop the Central Air Data Computer (CADC) that controlled the wing sweep throughout the entire flight envelope.

As flight testing progressed, it became apparent that the inboard movement of wing air loads in high g flight was greater than had been anticipated, with the result that the aircraft strength was sufficient to withstand weight/g combinations well above the design limits. In fact, at least within the Mach Sweep Limiter envelope, it looked like the wings could quite literally not be pulled off. Some back-of-the-envelope calculations seemed to indicate that the most critical static strength serious damage might well be that the engine mounts would fail somewhere around 13 g! There were some instances during flight testing and operational service where the g meter was pegged at 10; however, when inspection occurred no damage was found and the aircraft was returned to service immediately.

Karl Jackson, Garrett vice president of Engineering, who was program manager of CADC at the time, recalled an event when a large contingent of Grumman engineers (Steele, Grobert, Dante, Holzapfel, Mennona, etc.) descended on Garrett in California for an important meeting after a major successful CADC flight test. Jackson hosted a dinner after work at a fine restaurant for all the involved engineers from Grumman and Garrett. After a few drinks, everyone ordered dinner and Jackson's came with soup. Jackson literally fainted into the soup and crashed to the floor. When he awoke he was being administered to by paramedics. Needless to say, the Grumman engineers always accused him of faking it to get out of paying the bill. He did try to recover from this event sometime later by scheduling another dinner with roughly the same cast of characters at the same restaurant. This time Jackson didn't even get a chance to order because he felt nauseous and immediately exited.

At a late night meeting at Grumman on Long Island, a Garrett engineer extolled the technical excellence of the Garrett CADC design with great confidence. Suddenly, Gerry Gottlieb, one of Grumman's senior engineering managers on the F-14 program, pointed to an area of the very complex electronic schematic diagram of the CADC and said, "But, if that component fails, we could lose an airplane!" Clearly defeated and deflated, the Garrett engineer looked at his diagram, agreed with the premise, and announced, "Well, that's why you buy more than one!" With that, the meeting just broke up with laughter. Garrett subsequently instituted a backup electronic circuit to correct the potential problem.

Jim Dante recalled how Bob Steele got him involved in project engineering and leading the development of a major system. Steele had an excellent rapport with the customer, understood people's motivations, and could read people well. During a meeting with the Navy on the CADC and air inlet control system (AICS), the Navy wanted to know how Grumman would incorporate the Tactical Air Reconnaissance Pod System (TARPS) on the F-14A. Without any hesitation Steele turned to Dante, who accompanied him to this meeting, and introduced him as "his number one computer systems guy" and the TARPS project engineer. Dante began the job with a few introductory viewgraphs (overhead transparencies), and did the initial design, software development, system demonstration, and carrier suitability trials successfully. This led to a three-year, $75 million program that delivered 35 production units.

Grumman President Lew Evans recognized that winning the VFX competition would be crucial to Grumman's future and that the competition from McDonnell Douglas would be fierce. Evans directed that Grumman's most experienced personnel would head up major proposal volumes. Joe Rodriguez, one of Grumman's most capable avionic engineering managers, who reported to Alex Alexandrovich, deputy director of Technical Operations, was selected to lead the avionics portion of the proposal that involved five volumes during the 1967-68 time period. The avionic architecture and suite of integrated black boxes of the VFX were key discriminators in the VFX proposal because it was imperative that proposed company-furnished avionic equipment be well integrated with the Navy-provided Hughes AWG-9 radar/Phoenix system. Hughes was an associate contractor who reported to the Navy along with Grumman on the F-14A program; this arrangement required strong Grumman leadership and excellent systems integration/engineering to make the F-14A weapon system a success as it was being developed.

The computer signal data converter (CSDC) was the heart of the F-14 avionic system because it was a junction box that enabled all the systems to talk to each other. Each avionic system or black box had a special interface, and each had its own set of coordinates (reference systems to measure parameters), so the CSDC was designed to provide coordinate conversions and common interfaces so information could be provided to all the avionic systems as required. For example, the CSDC formatted AWG-9 data and sent it to various displays. In like manner, the CSDC transmitted other avionic system data to the AWG-9 display.

Rodriguez remembered that the CSDC was created using a team approach that worked out the architecture and utilized inputs from many potential subcontactors as well as Hughes. Bob Kress played an active role in the CSDC concept, as did Bob Watson, Dan Collins, Newt Speiss, and Alex Alexandrovich. Rodriguez regards Kress as an "engineer's engineer," meaning he knew a little bit about some things and a whole lot about many things.

Bob Watson also worked on the navigation. Dan Collins, an electronic systems group leader, was a key proposal manager and concentrated on communications, autopilot, and flight controls. Joe Stump was involved in the avionic system design and systems engineering; Bob Branstetter, displays, and Vinny Devino, crew and equipment design (Fig. 6.10).

Fig. 6.10   Vinny Devino (left photo) and Bob Branstetter (right photo) with their Navy counterparts at the F-14A mockup inspection.

Fig. 6.11   Bob Nafis, program manager, and Rear Admiral (ret.) Emerson Fawkes.

Bob Nafis (Fig. 6.11) brought years of experience in developing major aircraft weapon systems to his position as program manager. He attributed the VFX win to "the superior design of Grumman entry." Rear Admiral (ret.) Emerson Fawkes had a distinguished career with the U.S. Navy that included being a chief project engineer, flight test at Navy Air Test Center (NATC), and performing a key role in the introduction of steam catapults on aircraft carriers. His experience in the fleet readiness of new naval aircraft was invaluable, and he attributed the VFX win to "a team effort."

Another key discriminator in the Grumman VFX win was the integrated logistics support (ILS) plan generated by a team that worked tirelessly to address all the carrier habitability and support issues involved with introducing such an advanced air superiority system into the U.S. Navy inventory. The ILS "elephant issues—those that could stomp the program" were:

- Government furnished equipment (GFE): Hughes AWG-9 radar/ Phoenix system and Pratt & Whitney (P&W) TF30 engines from the F-111B program with their own support systems. Hughes was an associate contractor on the F-14A program and reported directly to the U.S. Navy, and P&W was under contract to the Navy as well. Strong leadership by Grumman's F-14 program office and ILS technical management ensured all interfaces among the Navy, Grumman, Hughes, and P&W were developed to a high degree of accuracy to execute the program.
- The number and complexity of black boxes and subassemblies— avionic components/computers and cards with electronic chips, respectively—were substantially higher that those employed on previous aircraft weapon systems.
- Versatile Avionic Shop Tester (VAST): A wide variety of these black boxes and subassemblies, called weapon replaceable assembly (WRA;

black box) and shop replaceable assembly (SRA; subassembly or card with electronic chips) needed to be maintained on the Navy's VAST, located below deck in the aircraft carrier maintenance bays. VAST was a very complex electronic system to test and repair black boxes to the "chip" level; however, it was not fully capable during the F-14 early deployments.
• A vast new array of mechanical support equipment combined with existing equipment that had to be modified for the F-14.
• The F-14's variable sweep wing and twin engine configuration, combined with the world's most capable radar and missile system and extensive air-to-air and air-to-ground weapons, required extensive training programs (new and modified) comprising state-of-the-art operational trainers for the pilot and radar intercept officer, maintenance trainer units (MTUs), and publications.

The core ILS personnel on the VFX proposal were Dan Pliskin (Fig. 6.12), program manager; Bernie Yudin, deputy program manager, responsible for avionic and mechanical testing and support equipment, training, operational and maintenance training units, publications, spares, and field service personnel; Al Trabold, systems project engineering; Irwin Fishberg, system analyst; Cosimo Palazzo, mechanical test equipment; John Keenan, responsible for design of avionic system interfaces with the U.S. Navy's VAST system; and Ed Stroud, avionic support equipment. Dean Swain was appointed ILS program manager after the VFX proposal was submitted, and he interfaced with his Navy counterpart, Will Purdue, in the VFX/F-14A program office.

Dan Pliskin vividly recalled that the VAST system was not developed enough to properly repair the WRAs and SRAs of the avionic subsystems

Fig. 6.12   (L to R) Dan Pliskin, Bernie Yudin, Don Nelson, and John Keenan.

during the F-14's initial operational deployment. The first two squadrons of the F-14A (VF-1 and VF-2) were stationed at Naval Air Station (NA) Mirimar, California. Dan Pliskin had monthly meetings with Navy maintenance personnel, resolving supportability problems encountered with the aircraft. The F14-A was a maintenance nightmare, according to Pliskin, because the black boxes and subassemblies could not be properly maintained until VAST was fully operational. The VAST system was GFE, but Grumman was responsible for mission performance of the aircraft, so when an F-14 was down for maintenance, the onus was on Grumman. During this period the Navy called for a summit meeting at Grumman to address the intermediate-level problems using the VAST system. This meeting was with Navy flag officers; Navy program office, Program Manager Air (PMA); George Skurla, Grumman president; and the Navy's maintenance chiefs to identify the issues on each of the avionic subsystems on the aircraft. The Navy chiefs were exceptional 20-year veterans with a team of avionic maintenance technicians that worked 24/7 to keep the Navy's aircraft fully operational. Pliskin and Stroud gave a three-hour presentation, identifying in detail the problems encountered on each of the subsystems and their subassemblies using VAST. It should be noted that Grumman continuously provided this technical information to PRD (the supplier of VAST). The interim solution was better provisioning of spare parts. If a black box was down for maintenance (not operating properly), it was immediately replaced to ensure the F-14 was mission capable at the time of launch.

A key Grumman VFX proposal strategy developed by Alex Alexandrovich and Joe Rodriguez was the decision to test the AWG-9 radar and other avionic systems in a full-scale forward portion of the F-14A called a system integration test stand (SITS) at the Navy's Point Mugu, California. The SITS was located in an upper level of a laboratory near the Pacific Ocean. Testing was accomplished by opening large doors and rolling the SITS forward so the AWG-9 could track live targets over the Pacific. In addition, all the equipment bays represented the actual aircraft configuration with actual cable runs and cooling. Another major benefit was determining thermal and electromagnetic magnetic interference (EMI) effects on the avionic systems.

Rodriguez also formed a pilot/cockpit functionality team made up of Bill Miller, Charlie Brown (Fig. 6.13), and Navy pilots. Miller and Brown made significant contributions to the VFX preproposal and proposal efforts and during the F-14A mockup inspection after award relating to cockpit layout, display formants, and safety features. Another key to success was the memorandum of understanding that Grumman, the Navy, and Hughes forged. This type of agreement was, no doubt, established with all the

Fig. 6.13   John Arlin, mock-up manager, is shown conferring with Mike Pelehach and Charlie Brown in the F-14A mock-up hangar.

VFX competitors, but I believe from all the interviews and data reviewed that Grumman not only was in the forefront of developing a sound agreement, but also had established a thorough understanding of many of the key avionic system interfaces and other detailed issues. Rodriguez, Ken Richardson, the Hughes AWG-9/Phoenix system program manager, and John Weaver, the AWG-9/Phoenix system naval officer in the Navy's F-14A program office in Washington, met at least once per month. Rodriguez recalled flying to California from New York in the morning, landing in California about 1100 hrs, having a working lunch meeting, more meetings until a dinner break, followed by wrap-up sessions until it was time to catch the red-eye flight back to New York. Upon landing he would grab a quick shower, shave, and be back in the office to start a new day. This is the way development programs are—extremely intensive, exciting and demanding very long hours as the teams invent and wrestle to get the interfaces and details right for the thousands of engineers to execute the program.

John Arlin was responsible for the design and development of the mock-up and worked closely with the VFX design team and Joe Cipp, Product Development manager. The mock-up was very high fidelity because the wings swept, engine doors could be opened, the entire cockpit simulated all displays and controls, all access hatches—a key to maintenance accessibility of black boxes—were incorporated, and weapon rails with stores including Phoenix missiles and bombs could be raised and lowered.

Irv Waaland was lead aero on the F-14 and was responsible for integrating all the analysis and wind tunnel tests that led to the final VFX configuration. One of his aero team's notable achievements was a very efficient leading edge slat and innovative flap design utilizing the wing spoilers that resulted in excellent low-speed performance and very high roll response rates.

Jack Hassett and Ron Tindall played key roles in the propulsion integration of the Pratt & Whitney TF30 afterburning engine and the 2-D external compression inlet design evolution, respectively. Bill Greathouse, the head of Propulsion, a West Virginia gentleman according to his peers, was a referee of sorts trying to balance all the propulsion requirements during the preliminary design phase of the Grumman VFX design configurations. After the Grumman VFX proposal was submitted, but before award, Greathouse published an excellent paper on the integration of the TF30 turbofan engines, and the development of the 2-D external compression inlets and the convergent-divergent (CD) nozzles. There was panic within the Grumman program when the paper appeared because many felt that Grumman's unique propulsion, inlet, and nozzle design would be exposed to the competition. Dr. Dave Migdal was a major contributor to the design of the CD exhaust nozzle system that significantly reduced boat tail drag, described earlier as a technology shortfall in the F-111A design. Migdal also used his fundamental research on exhaust nozzle design and flow phenomena in his successful PhD dissertation.

Jim Dante recalled a hairy experience he had while at sea off the California coast troubleshooting headset noise that occurred when the F-14A was in afterburner operation. During the night, with the F-14A tied down on the deck and its tail pointing over the deck edge, Dante sat on top of the inlet taking measurements with the engines in full afterburner. Dante mentioned to the Navy technician that perhaps he should be wearing a flight jacket with a life preserver, and the technician said he would get him one in the morning. He did find a loose connection that alleviated the problem.

Larry Mead and Joe Cipp (Fig. 6.14), head of the Product Development Center that assembled the first F-14, played key roles in the manufacturing plan of the VFX/F-14 that integrated all the titanium manufacturing and composite facilities and unique manufacturing processes. Cipp started work at Grumman in 1941 at the age of 18. After returning from Navy service in 1943, he worked in the experimental manufacturing shop, and through the years became a leader in the Manufacturing department. Affectionately called Mr. Manufacturing, USA, Cipp was responsible for building the prototypes of the A2F-1, W2F-1, Mohawk, C-2A, and Gulfstreams.

Fig. 6.14 (L to R) Larry Mead, Bob Kress, and Joe Cipp discussing F-14 program plans.

John Michel, who was the head of the Weights department, headed up the VFX proposal effort and did an outstanding job of dealing with one of Grumman's largest proposals ever submitted to the DOD (Fig. 6.15).

Fig. 6.15 (L to R) Mike Pelehach, VFX program manager and chief designer; Dr. Tom Cheatham, vice president of Future Systems; Lew Evans, president of Grumman; and John Michel with the entire VFX proposal and the VFX mockup in the background.

ADVANCED STRUCTURES AND MATERIALS

Earlier in the chapter, I discussed the TFX/F-111B program and many of the airframe design issues that emerged during the program and for future consideration in new aircraft designs. Without question, Grumman benefited from design, test, and production of the XF10F-1 Jaguar and F-111B programs. It was fortunate that Larry Mead was directly involved with the Jaguar design, and that Mike Pelehach and Bob Kress were involved in the design evolution of the F-111B. On the down side was the fact that Grumman could not access data on the use of titanium on the A-12/SR-71 Blackbird, because the project was highly classified. (It also utilized a different titanium alloy due to its mission requirements.) Grumman, under the leadership of Grant Hedrick, established its own titanium development program that led to the purchase of the world's largest electron beam (EB) welding chambers from Boeing to carry out the development work preceding the VFX program. This titanium program coupled with experienced talent, Grumman's in-house VFX predecessor airframe studies, and a funded contract from NAVAIR to wrap a new airframe around the TF30 engines and the AWG-9 radar utilized in the F-111B led to the advanced F-14 airframe with over 24% of its weight in titanium, and boron epoxy composite skins for the horizontal tails.

Dick Cyphers made a major contribution in the evolution of the structural design of the VFX/F-14 airframe. In the late 1960s, and during the proposal in 1968, Cyphers and the structural design team worked closely with Grant Hedrick, Larry Mead, the multidepartmental Titanium Committee headed by Tom Main, and Advanced Development to conduct structural airframe design studies of variable sweep wing configurations. Cyphers was the project engineer, Nat Kotlarchyk his assistant for analysis, and Ron Heitzmann led materials and processes. Their studies indicated that the use of titanium in the design of the EB-welded wing carrythrough structure (wing box; Fig. 6.16), wing planks, wing pivots, and fuselage midsection would result in significant weight savings over the more conventional aluminum/bolted steel wing box approach used in the F-111.

Under Hedrick's leadership, the metallurgical and structural issues of EB welding of the F-14 titanium wing center section, the largest EB welded structure in existence, were successfully tackled. During the VFX proposal in 1968, a Grumman team designed, built, and tested a titanium box beam that was electron beam welded to provide meaningful data to the NAVAIR Structures Branch evaluators. Al Hallock, Ed Mulcahy, and Dietrich Helms led this effort during the VFX proposal. Hallock developed the sketches and drawings for wing box concepts and Mulcahy did the

Fig. 6.16   Early production titanium wing boxes with Tom Main, Bob Bohlander, and Dick Hutton.

stress analysis. Helms ran the EB weld facility in which the box beam was fabricated.

During the time between VFX proposal submittal and contract award in early 1969, Cyphers built up an airframe design team of key people: Bill Stewart, design of overall structure; Ed Mulcahy, stress; Frank Hardenburgh, fuselage; and Howard Schilling, wing. Al Hallock was in charge of the wing carrythrough structure, later renamed the wing center section (WCS). Carlos Paez (Fig. 6.17) reported to Al Hallock to develop the WCS structural arrangement. The VFX proposal had a general sketch for the WCS structure, and Paez's job was to improve and mostly define how the structure should be attached to the surrounding fuselage members, which were also not well defined. The Titanium Committee consisted of Tony Iopolo for producibility, Doug Hutchings for stress, Al Hallock and Paez for design, Ed Rolko for machining, Tom Tatarian for tooling, Dietrich Helms for EB welding, Steve Banks for materials and processes, and Al Wolfman for fatigue and fracture allowables. The committee met once a week with presentations by Paez on how the design was evolving. Then each committee member gave their opinion on the design status, followed by Mead asking for suggestions and improvements trying to define the way forward.

In the Grumman EB weld facility located on Long Island, titanium plates and structures were fused together in large vacuum chambers. Frank Drumm, Bob Witt, and Bob Messler developed weld inspection and

Fig. 6.17   Carlos Paez and John Grandy, producibility group.

evaluation techniques based on weld configurations developed by Paez; many electron beam welded specimens were made in this facility. Tony Marrocco was a key person in the effort to characterize the processing of titanium alloy Ti- 6AL-4V[*] in terms of its strength, machinability, toughness, ease of welding, and so on. Marrocco was ably supported by Steve DeMay, Joel Greenspan, and Tom Wolfe. Separately, a critical repair effort was started by Henry Beck from Liaison Engineering (these engineers provided critical and timely engineering data to Manufacturing and vice versa). He was concerned that no salvage capability, other than re-EB welding, was available. Secretly, Beck went to the Grumman library and searched all available weld journals. He soon discovered that plasma arc welding[†] in an argon gas environment produced a clean weld "puddle" (area of molten metal formed during welding) much better than the popular TIG[‡] welding. The plasma arc welding procedure for repairs was developed and it worked very well.

An extremely important design consideration of EB-welded titanium structures was damage tolerance—the ability of a structure to withstand

---

[*] Ti: titanium, AL: aluminum, V: vanadium.

[†] A jet of very hot plasma (heated gas), similar to TIG, but an advancement with greater energy concentration, stability, and deeper penetration.

[‡] Tungsten inert gas welds use arc welding with a tungsten electrode to produce the weld with an inert gas, usually argon or helium, to prevent contamination, and a filler material.

damage due to cracks. Small flaws, voids, and micro-cracks are inherently present in weldments and can rapidly develop into fatigue cracks and cause early structural failures. Therefore, a damage tolerance design approach based on fracture mechanics was introduced to ensure a safe, reliable structural design. Based on earlier experience in the aerospace industry with welded airframes, some weld failures did occur, and it was generally accepted by aircraft designers that welds were dangerous (e.g.,the F-111B D6AC steel[§] wing box was TIG welded, but the top cover was bolted together).

Grumman overcame the aerospace industry's lack of confidence in welding technology through pioneering work in several key areas of investigation: the nature of fatigue cracks, the prediction of structural fatigue life based on crack propagation, and the strength of cracked structure. Mechanical properties such as the fracture toughness and fatigue crack propagation rates in the base metal and in welds that held the structure together were developed. This effort led to structural design and damage tolerance of titanium structures criteria, EB welding procedures, and thorough inspection techniques, the result being that no aircraft service life structural failures in the welded titanium components ever occurred. Al Wolfman and Alex Gomza led the initial effort to determine the damage tolerance of titanium structures. Paul Bell and Harvey Eidinoff came on board later in full-scale development to continue this important work and developed a state-of-the-art damage tolerance computer program. At the time, damage tolerance criteria were not aerospace design tools. The Navy adopted these design tools for the F-14 program, followed by the Air Force for the F-111A program.

Paez remembers that the WCS received a great deal of technical management oversight through intensive reviews of the evolving design with Grant Hedrick. Hedrick would normally show up on Saturday mornings dressed in his white tennis outfit and sit with various members of the design team to review progress on design issues. Paez recalled that Hedrick, on one occasion, listened to various WCS design options being evaluated by Paez and then "sketched" out a path or potential solution but, in his quiet and caring manner, leaving the final solution to the design team.

Intensive F-14 design reviews were also held in Bill Schwendler's and Hedrick's conference rooms. Often the founding chief designer, Schwendler, would be present along with Dick Hutton and Grant Hedrick. Many of the F-14 program personnel, including me, attended some of these briefings. The

---

[§] D6AC is a high strength steel alloy used in applications that require fatigue strength and toughness like landing gear, axles, and shafts.

entire WCS design team, particularly those responsible for stress estimates, was called in at various times to review all aspects of WCS development and testing with Hedrick. Paez recalled:

> Most people felt this was the equivalent of a high school principal visit and went to each one with a great deal of apprehension. Hedrick for his part would do his homework ahead of time. He knew in advance where the soft spots were and waited to see if the presenters would acknowledge the issues. If one left the meeting "not bleeding too badly," it was considered a successful one. Hedrick had the ability to seek out the problems that others could not see, and always offered some guidelines on how to go about and solve them. He did refrain on giving specific directions; rather he described how the solution should be pursued. Of course, a return visit to show the final selected solution was inevitable to get his symbolic nod of approval. A slight smile from his face was considered a major win.

In 1967, Dr. Basil Leftheris of Research invented and developed the stress wave riveter (SWR), a unique electromagnetic tool that greatly facilitated installation of interference-fit fasteners and pins. Perhaps the most vital application of this unusual tool was to set large-diameter, interference-fit pins in the F-14 titanium wing center section at the ends of all electron-beam welds (12 or more in each box beam), to prevent cracking. Harvey Eidinoff, one of Grumman's senior material fatigue and damage tolerance engineers, recalled how Grant Hedrick directed the use of the stress wave riveter in the fabrication of the WCS. Analytical studies and test articles of WCS weld intersections indicated that there existed a probability of cracks; therefore, Hedrick directed that the probability be eliminated by drilling a hole at these intersections and inserting a high interference-fit titanium pin in the hole using the stress wave riveter—the result being that a failure never occurred as well as no fuel leaks.

At the time that the SWR became available for use in setting stainless steel rivets in the titanium wing skins, Grumman Manufacturing had already invested in "oversqueeze riveting machines" that had been qualified for F-14 wing fabrication. However, the SWR was a relatively mobile and versatile tool, and was used extensively to repair improperly set stainless steel and titanium rivets on the F-14 production line. Because the SWR was so novel, Leftheris had to campaign at great length with Manufacturing, and used the shop floor as his test laboratory to gain the confidence of the Grumman mechanics.

Hedrick also spearheaded the development of advanced composite structures. He formed the first composites group in Advanced Development (1964), headed by Artie August, to carry out development work that was led by Dick Hadcock and Sam Dastin. Their work led to Hedrick's decision to utilize a boron/epoxy horizontal stabilizer design in lieu of a conventional metallic design on the F-14 that saved approximately 225 lb. Carl Micillo worked on the development of an automatic tape-laying machine that eliminated the tedious process of hand layup of individual composite material sheets utilized in the early fabrication of horizontal tails. With the award of the VFX (F-14A) contract to Grumman in 1969, the world's first use of composites in primary flight-critical structure for a production aircraft became a reality.

THE F-14A (PLUS), F-14D STORY

The F-14 program conducted the Avionics Improvement Program (AIP) study, which was partially funded by the Navy in 1980-81. The program was under the direction of Bob Watson, program director of development; Hank Janiesch joined the F-14 program in September 1981 as the program manager for the ongoing AIP. Hughes Aircraft was investigating significant upgrades to the AWG-9 radar with a study entitled the Radar Improvement Program (RIP). Under Program Manager Jack Hassett, the flight testing of the GE F101 engine, which provided the F-14 with much more engine thrust and needed aero performance improvement throughout the flight envelope, was successfully concluded. All these studies and test efforts provided the foundation for the F-14D (Fig. 6.18).

Terry O'Grady was the AIP team leader, and Neil Gilmartin was one of the key engineers on the AIP study. During the full-scale development (FSD) program, Gilmartin became the system engineering manager. Should a system question or problem arise, he could invariably resolve the issue. He

Fig. 6.18   F-14D.

was tenacious and persistent in his pursuit of the F-14 system upgrade. With his sharp analytical mind, he showed the best way to address the magnitude of avionic and radar upgrades. Before long, he was recognized as the "architect" of the F-14D weapon system.

On the avionic hardware side, Jim Dante was the key engineer. He had a number of avionic equipment suppliers "lend" Grumman their prototype hardware for early lab testing in the Plant 14 Avionics Development Laboratory (ADL). He constantly kept NAVAIR informed of the evaluation and test results that proved the FSD hardware development schedule would be relatively low risk. Dante eventually became the subsystem engineering manager and the F-14D hardware guru. Mike Fusco was involved in the overall system-level development and was regarded as one of the best and brightest in developing the initial concepts in the AIP study. He also became the chief system conceiver of the weapon system.

Based on all the various studies being performed by industry and naval agencies, NAVAIR continued to refine the specific capability requirements for a major F-14A upgrade. By the end of 1982, the Department of the Navy Strategy Board agreed that an upgraded F-14A was more cost effective and less risky than designing a brand new Navy fighter/system. In August 1982, Rear Admiral (ret.) Paul T. Gillcrist, director, Aviation Plans and Programs, OP-50, recognized the need for engine, R&M, radar, and avionic upgrades and pushed for them, leading to the F-14A (Plus), the F-14B, and eventually the F-14D. Captain Norio Endo, F-14 PMA at the time, pushed hard for re-engining the F-14A and was successful. The Super Tomcat flew in July 1981 with the GE F101 derivative fighter engine (DFE; Fig. 6.19). Outstanding performance resulted, including a more than 60% increase in intercept radius compared to the F-14A with TF30 engines. The original intake and engine nacelles of the F-14A were designed to accommodate advanced engine airflow and installation requirements, as shown in Fig. 6.20.

During 1983, the pre-FSD studies, analyses, lab/flight test results, and improvement tradeoffs resulted in a solidified F-14 weapon system upgrade configuration—including new engines. The avionic upgrade was to be highly digitized (to take advantage of the emerging technology and to afford ease of future growth and expansion) utilizing two digital 1553B data buses and two Navy standard AYK-14 XN-6 system computers. The radar upgrade was to be based on the Hughes AWG-9 Block IVA configuration, and was eventually amended to include, wherever applicable, maximum hardware and software commonality with the Air Force F-15E Multi-Stage Improvement Program (MSIP).

By mid-1983, the Secretary of the Navy, John Lehman, directed that the F-14A be upgraded with new avionics, radar, and engines as well as much needed reliability and maintainability improvements. To minimize costs and

Fig. 6.19   The clean lines of the Super Tomcat are evident in this flight test photo.

share evolving technology, this Super F-14D was also to integrate other DOD programs, and thanks to Gilmartin and Dante, these requirements were already in our weapon system configuration. The program schedule was to accommodate the first F-14D production deliveries in early 1990.

In fall 1983, Grumman was contracted by NAVAIR to perform a six-month configuration definition assessment (CDA) study to define the F-14A

Fig. 6.20   This engine installation shows how the GE F101 fitted neatly into the nacelle that had been designed back in 1968.

airframe changes necessary to accommodate either the F100 or F110 engines under evaluation by the Air Force for the F-15/F-16 fighter aircraft. Jack Hassett was the program manager for all aspects of F-14 engine upgrades. Hassett laid the foundation for the F-14A (Plus) FSD engine effort. In addition to the CDA effort, he was a strong advocate of the preliminary installation fit check of the GE F110 engine mockups. Joe Burke was the leading experimental test pilot on the F-14A (Plus), F-14B program.

The new engine was comparable in weight to the TF30 engine in the F-14A; however, it was 50 in. shorter and produced 60% more thrust in afterburner. Maximum thrust in afterburner was increased from 41,800 lb with the P&W TF30 to 55,200 lb with the GE F110. In retrospect, the F-14A (Plus), or the F-14B as finally designated, finally achieved the excellent thrust-to-weight ratio that the F-14 was designed for. Equally important, the new engine provided rapid throttle movements necessary for dog fighting without the compressor stall that plagued the TF30 engine in the F-14A, and the F-14B achieved a 60% decrease in the time to reach altitude and a more than 60% increase in intercept radius.

NAVAIR was also tasked with generating an F-14D sole source request for quote (RFQ) to be available by December 1, 1983. Under the leadership of Bob Watson, Grumman was well into writing the response for the F-14D statement of work/proposal, and at the end of December delivered the finished "unsolicited" F-14D statement of work to the Navy without their RFQ. Bob Watson was very thorough, and worked hundreds of hours beyond the traditional hectic proposal period.

In January 1984, a Grumman core team was established by Bob Watson to reside in Washington, D.C., to work directly with NAVAIR to answer questions, discuss system alternatives, and generate the F-14D airframe/-system specifications. Bob Watson was the right man, at the right time, for the right job. With a sound engineering background, he was technically astute, was methodical by nature, and had a good appreciation for cost and schedule tradeoffs.

Janiesch remembered that at meetings, Watson never took longhand notes, but always printed them in real time. One day he asked the office secretary to type up his printed notes—and she refused! She reached into her desk drawer, pulled out a gold star, and after pasting it onto the top of his first sheet said in a sincere manner, "Your printing is as clear and legible as if I typed it—why waste my time and yours?"

Bob Watson led the effort to develop a descoped program due to a severe shortfall in funding. He assembled a great engineering team under the leadership of Neil Gilmartin, Jim Dante, and Pat Mennona (director of F-14 Engineering) in Washington to get the job done. The modified program included the Navy-selected GE F110-400 engine, and in June 1984, the

F-14A (Plus), F-14D contract was signed. In 1985, Bob Watson deservedly became the vice president of the F-14 program and Hank Janiesch became the director of the F-14A (Plus)/F-14D FSD program. Dave Kratz was the project test pilot and contributed to the proposal development as well as flight test relating to cockpit layout, displays, and safety.

The program got off to a good start, but two years into FSD the team uncovered a significant throughput problem with the recently delivered GFE AYK-14 standard executive software. Basically designed for shipboard use, Grumman's lab tests indicated the executive software at the time was not a mature standard and was more than 10 times slower than needed for airborne application. This problem was a major showstopper, because a Navy redesign would add about a year delay to the FSD and production aircraft schedules, along with attendant cost increases.

Dennis Carter, who at the time was the E-2C software project engineer, came on board and strongly advocated a new development that consisted of Grumman leading a CFE redesign of the executive software, which could therefore be uniquely tailored to our particular requirements and usage. After a tremendous amount of work and time by the program, numerous Navy evaluations, multiple schedules, and much testing, the system worked extremely well—a feat rarely accomplished for a lengthy (six-year) fixed price development program.

POST F-14D DEVELOPMENTS AND TOMCAT 21

A great deal of avionic system work was done by Hank Janiesch and his team on the F-14D program to extend the F-14 capability to a true air-to-ground mission derivative. Besides developing a new programmable tactical information display (PTID), and integrating the weapon delivery capability of the laser-guided bomb (LGB) series weapons, the big thrust was Quick Strike in the early 1990s. This would have given the Navy an air-to-ground capability compatible to that of the Air Force F-15E. Eventually the F-15E forward-looking infrared (FLIR) system, part of the Low Altitude Navigation and Targeting Infra-Red for Night (LANTIRN) system, was incorporated into the F-14D by fall 1996.

Another significant aerodynamic/propulsion achievement was the demonstration of supercruise with an F-14D during September 1989. Supercruise is the ability to sustain supersonic speeds (greater than Mach 1) without afterburner in level flight. The sophisticated aerodynamics of the F-14A airframe/propulsion system described earlier coupled with a low cross-sectional area for supersonic performance allowed the F-14A to achieve Mach 2.4 with an earlier generation, lower thrust turbofan engine (P&W TF30), as compared to the next generation engine P&W F100 turbofan engine employed in the F-15A engine. Tom Griffin, propulsion, led the effort under Jack Hassett, deputy program director. The F-14D achieved Mach 1.09 at intermediate rated thrust (IRT), non-afterburning that clearly showed that advanced versions (e.g., Tomcat 21) of the F-14 would have operational supercruise capability.

TOMCAT 21

In 1994 Grumman teamed with Northrop as prime subcontractor, along with Vought, for the forthcoming Advanced Tactical Aircraft (ATA) competition. The team lost the ATA competition in December 1987 after a grueling four-year battle with McDonnell Douglas/General Dynamics. Hundreds of Grumman engineers returned home to Bethpage, Long Island, and company management, advanced programs, and the F-14 and E-2 programs went through an intensive "lessons learned" process and developed strategies for the future. The ATA that became the A-12 was canceled by the DOD in 1992, and during the intervening four years from 1988 into the 1990s, Grumman aggressively proposed the Tomcat 21 (Fig. 6.21) as a highly cost-effective multimission fighter that would serve the U.S. Navy well into the twenty-first century.

Tomcat 21 preliminary design studies began in earnest in 1988 in Advanced Systems. Paul Bavitz and John McCabe led the effort, and Gus Sclafani was the configuration design engineer. Neil Gilmartin, who was the architect of the F-14D system, came on board to lead the system concept

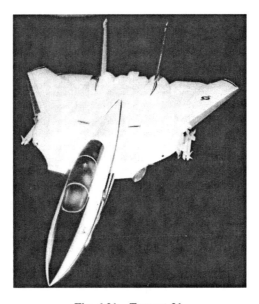

Fig. 6.21   Tomcat 21.

design. Doug Frei, Rudy Meyer, Mike Sturm, and Dave Richel were responsible for aerodynamic and performance estimates. A significant propulsion effort was devoted to an advanced version of the F110-GE-400 employed in the F-14D. The propulsion team included John Neiman, Cliff Callahan, Susan Dorfman, and Tom Griffin.

Basically, the F-14D and Tomcat 21's airframe and components were the same. Tomcat 21 was an evolutionary approach to minimize technical risk in development. Improvements over the F-14D included enhanced survivability, avionics, engine performance, and fuel capacity. The two significant airframe improvements were a larger wing glove from the engine intake to the leading edge of the wings and a more capable high-lift system. The glove vane was removed and replaced with an internal fuel tank that could hold about 2500 more pounds of fuel. The new high lift system involved adding an extendible flap, and incorporated a new leading edge. The predicted aerodynamic lift characteristics were verified by wind tunnel testing, which showed that the design takeoff gross weight would be 76,000 lb versus 72,900 lb for the F-14D.

The Tomcat 21 would have been a superior, long-range, all-weather, multimission fighter with enhanced air-to-air and air-to-ground capabilities due to high internal fuel capacity (over 18,500 lb) and low-drag weapon carriage via weapon rails. Future conflicts involving increased technological threats necessitated a long-range standoff strike role with large laser-guided bombs and advanced smart weapons. Avionics included the Joint Tactical Information Distribution System (JTIDS), significantly increased computer capacity, and blue-green light with night vision goggles.

Grumman worked closely with GE, the Navy, and the Air Force to develop a modification of the F110-GE-400 engine used in the F-14D. The resulting F110-GE-429D was a low-risk, high-reliability derivative engine that would deliver excellent performance growth. Tom Griffin was a major contributor to this effort with the propulsion team under Jack Hassett. The Super Tomcat 21 would have featured the 429D engine, which had about 80% parts commonality with the F-14D 400 engine, the B-2 F118-GE-100 engine, and the F-16 F110-GE-129 IPE (Improved Performance Engine). Significant increases in mission performance and specific excess power at transonic speeds were predicted. In addition, supersonic cruise at Mach 1.2 at 35,000 ft would be achieved due to a 35% increase in intermediate rated thrust.

CONCLUSION

The aircraft designers who created the F-14 gained valuable knowledge and experience from the design and flight testing of the XF10F-1 Jaguar and the F-111B variable sweep Navy fighters. Navy technical and flag officer leadership, including George Spangenberg and Admiral Tom Connolly, paved the way for the VFX/F-14 to become a reality. Four generations of designers participated in the evolution of the F-14: Bill Schwendler, Dick Hutton, Mike Pelehach, and Bob Kress. Hutton's generation also included Larry Mead and Grant Hedrick, who made significant contributions in the design, the use of advanced materials, and manufacturing technology. The F-14 was conceived as a totally integrated weapon system:

- An advanced airframe designed to accommodate growth in engine thrust and payload, as evidenced by the F-14D
- An advanced weapon system created by Grumman and Hughes Aircraft avionic and missile engineers with unprecedented radar range and unmatched missile range and payload variety
- A logistic support system conceived and demonstrated to maximize fleet readiness by ensuring excellent carrier suitability and mission effectiveness (the percentage of flight time that the weapon system is capable of achieving its mission)

The F-14D was retired in 2006 at the peak of its operational capabilities. Advanced versions proposed to the Navy held promise of long-range multimission capability well into the 21st century.

When the F-14A reached production maturity in the mid-1970s, Mike Pelehach became vice president of Future Systems, which was responsible for the pursuit and capture of all new business for Grumman. Pelehach brought key F-14 personnel with him to create requirements with new customers for advanced weapon systems as well as new product lines consistent with Grumman's inherent strengths. Bob Kress, Renso Caporali, Bill Rathke, Bob Steele, Herb Grossman, Larry Canonico, and the author were all assigned responsibilities within Future Systems. The F-14A, A-6E, E-2C, and EA-6B were in production, and derivatives were being created and developed by very capable program management organizations. New design teams were formed to pursue advanced aircraft and weapon system concepts, explore nontraditional business opportunities, and increase commercial/military subcontracting sales. The next chapter will attempt to capture some of the imaginative projects undertaken by Future Systems.

Chapter 7

FUTURE SYSTEMS

In 1976, Mike Pelehach became vice president of Future Systems, a division that brought together all the key departments in Grumman Aerospace in the pursuit and capture of new business. In the mid-1950s, Dick Hutton expanded Preliminary Design to pursue many new aircraft types. In the mid-1970s, Mike Pelehach had a vision to conceive new systems in Advanced Systems, Advanced Space, and Operations Analysis, which included work with the customer (government and other contractors) to create requirements and new business opportunities via Business Development. This vision also included:

- Pursuing critical advanced technologies in Research and Advanced Development that would lead to new products and advanced aircraft weapon systems
- Managing all company discretionary funds and proposals for new aircraft and space systems
- Bidding for new subcontracts with other companies
- Assisting and developing product improvements and new derivatives for ongoing programs (F-14, A-6, E-2, etc.) with Program Development, Operations Analysis, Proposal Operations, and Advanced Systems personnel
- Designing and building new hardware and demonstrator aircraft in a low-cost, self-contained, secure assembly and test area called the Product Development Center (PDC)

Figure 7.1 was taken in the Product Development Center in 1976 in front of F-14A test aircraft No. 5, which was being modified for the radar-guided weapon system (RGWS) demonstration program. Back row (L to R): Fritz Dunmire, Operations; Norm Gandia, Business Development, Navy liaison; Bob Kress, director, Advanced Concepts; Bill Tebo, director, Proposal Operations; Hal Moss, deputy director, Operations Analysis; Dan Lynch, director, Operations Analysis; John Cuniff, assistant to Mike Pelehach; Dave Walsh, director, Navy and Air Force programs, Business Development. Front

Fig. 7.1 F-14A test aircraft No. 5 being modified for the RGWS demonstration program.

row (L to R): Dr. Renso Caporali, director, Advanced Systems Technology, including Advanced Systems, Advanced Development, and Operations Analysis; Don Moyer, Advanced Space; Herb Grossman, director, Product Development Center; Tom Kane, director, Business Development; George Skurla, president, Grumman Aerospace; Mike Pelehach, vice president, Future Systems; Mike Ciminera, director, Advanced Systems; Dr. Charlie Mack, director, Research; Dick Hadcock, director, Advanced Development; and Dick Scheuing, deputy director, Research.

The Advanced Projects chart (Fig. 7.2) shows many of the demonstrator and full-scale model and systems tests that were performed and planned from 1980 through 2000. In Advanced Systems, a design team began pursuing a

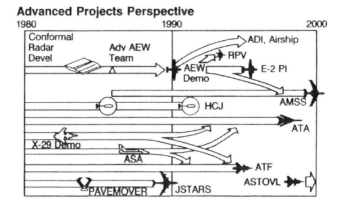

Fig. 7.2   The Advanced Projects chart.

forward swept wing technology plan in 1976 with the Defense Advanced Research Projects Agency (DARPA) that would lead to the X-29A demonstrator in the mid-1980s. The demonstrated technologies in the X-29 would be applied to the future Air Force Advanced Tactical Fighter (ATF) and the Navy Advanced Tactical Aircraft (ATA). During the mid-1970s, Advanced Systems funded an engineering systems design team that began work in the PDC on the design, simulation, and development testing of the radar-guided weapon system (RGWS) that would be tested in a modified F-14A. The RGWS led to the DARPA-sponsored Pave Mover program, which eventually became Joint STARS.

In addition, a vertical/short takeoff and landing (V/STOL) team was pursuing the U.S. Navy's subsonic V/STOL A and supersonic V/STOL B requirements. Another team was working closely with National Ship Research Development Center (NSRDC) on the A6 Circulation Control Wing (CCW) demonstrator program that flew in the early 1980s and dramatically reduced approach speed. An electronic warfare (EW) team was pursuing an advanced radar jamming system (ARJS) for the U.S. Army that would lead to the helicopter jammer (HCJ). An airborne early warning (AEW) team was pursuing conformal ultra-high-frequency (UHF) radar technology that would be demonstrated in a flying AEW demonstrator utilized in future programs: RPV, E2 PI (Product Improvement), Advanced Multi-Mission Surveillance System (AMSS), and an Air Defense Initiative (ADI) airship. Advanced Development and Engineering were pursuing key elements of the avionics system architecture (ASA) studies that would become part of the avionics architecture of the ATF and the ATA. The Future Systems business development provided excellent military service and governmental agency contacts and capture plans for all of Grumman's aircraft and Advanced Systems programs.

FORWARD SWEPT WING: X-29

During the mid-1970s, Grumman Advanced Systems engineers unsuccessfully bid on the U.S. Air Force (USAF) Highly Maneuverable Aircraft Technology (IIIMAT) program, which was won by Rockwell. However, transonic wind tunnel testing was continued by the Advanced Systems aero group headed by Mark Siegel, with Charlie McGloughlin as lead aero analyst. Disparities occurred between transonic wind tunnel tests at Mach 0.9 when compared with predicted analytical methods. After exhaustive analyses, it was found that by introducing the forward sweep angle into the equations, test results and predictions coalesced. Further analyses indicated that sweeping the wing forward while maintaining supercritical wing technology at transonic speeds (Mach 0.9) could significantly reduce transonic drag (greater than 20%) and increased sustained maneuverability-constant altitude turn where thrust equals drag.

This breakthrough in transonic performance was explained to Colonel Norris Krone of DARPA by Glen Spacht (Advanced Systems project engineer) in 1976. Colonel Krone was investigating the use of composites to avoid aero-elastic divergence in forward swept wing (FSW) aircraft. As a result of these discussions, the DARPA FSW program was born. Grumman's Advanced Systems department developed a technology and configuration development program in conjunction with DARPA that eventually led to Grumman winning the contract to build Design 712, X-29A demonstrator aircraft in 1981.

From 1976 to 1981, Grumman was involved in many internally funded independent research and development (IR&D) projects and contract-related advanced development (CRAD) contracts related to the FSW project. In 1977, the FSW design team determined that a demonstration of a powered model configuration would be a way to demonstrate basic flying qualities. Glen Spacht (Fig. 7.3) and his embryonic flight control system design team proposed to build a radio-controlled FSW model with moveable canards (Fig. 7.4). The author went to Mike Pelehach to plead their case, and he approved the $4000 project.

During the late 1970s and into 1980, Grumman was involved in many FSW configuration/engine studies, composite wing design studies, and wind tunnel tests that led to Design 712, which became the X-29A (Fig. 7.5). This was an integrated fighter demonstrator design that incorporated a forward swept wing with aero-elastically tailored composite construction, relaxed

Fig. 7.3   Glen Spacht holds the nose of the FSW model, with Mike Ciminera on the left. Russ Negri, FSW configuration designer; Jim Chin, flight controls; and Bob Kress and Nick Ziroli are behind the nose of the model looking at the inlet.

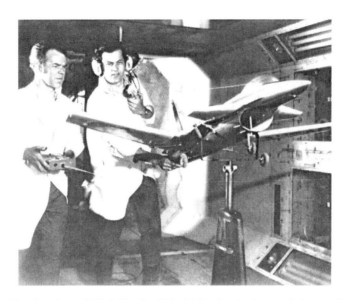

Fig. 7.4 Glen Spacht and Nick Ziroli of Model Design during a wind tunnel test of the FSW model.

static stability (35% negative margin—more than any aircraft), a triply redundant digital fly-by-wire control system, full authority, close-coupled variable incidence canards, thin supercritical wings with variable camber, moveable fuselage strakes, and a unique three-surface pitch control system.

There were two key discriminator tests that led to the Grumman win over Rockwell and General Dynamics. With DARPA funding, Grumman

Fig. 7.5 X-29A on an early test flight.

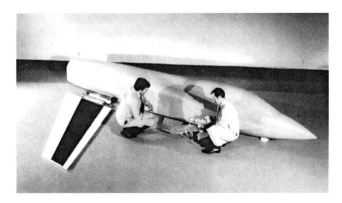

Fig. 7.6   Keith Wilkinson and Frank Rauch examine the aero-elastic FSW model prior to test.

designed and built a half-scale, reflection-plane model of an aero-elastically tailored composite wing model (Fig. 7.6) under the direction of Keith Wilkinson, and demonstrated that divergent speeds of FSW aircraft could be reliably predicted. In another crucial test, Doug Hutchings led the design and construction of the Design 712 full-scale, composite wing root test article that proved to DARPA that Grumman could successfully build such a structure involving the layup and varying orientation of hundreds of layers of composite material and still pass structural testing.

Figure 7.7 shows the design team, from left to right: Frank Rauch, Dynamics, aero-elastic model design; Dean Roukis, Dynamics; Augie Sarantonio, Mechanical Systems; Mike Ciminera, director, Advanced Systems; Keith Wilkinson, Dynamics/aero-elasticity/project engineer for wing divergence test; Mike Solan, Flight Control System Design; Arnold

Fig. 7.7   The winning Design 712, X-29A proposal team.

Whitaker, Flight Control System Design leader; Bob Roemer, director, X-29A program; Larry Canonico, senior designer; Ron Hendrickson, Aero; Russ Negri, configuration designer; Doug Hutchings, Stress, project engineer for full-scale composite wing root test; John Kohn, Loads; Glenn Spacht, FSW project engineer; Frank Halfen, composite wing layout. Not shown in the photo is Doug Frei, who became lead aerodynamicist on the FSW/X-29 when Spacht became project engineer. Spacht was involved with all aspects of the design as well as the DARPA proposal.

The X-29A/Design 712 was an outstanding technical success. The two X-29A aircraft were very reliable test aircraft, and were flown extensively over eight years from 1984 to 1992, totaling some 347 flights. Subsequent to these flights, Bill Mebes, X-29 program director, worked closely with the USAF Wright Aeronautical Laboratory, X-29 program personnel, and Advanced Systems to study the use of vortex control to provide more control when an aircraft is flying at high angles of attack. An additional 60 flights were conducted.

Connie Blyseth, one of Grumman's senior directors in Software Systems, Systems, and Advanced Engineering in the early to mid-1980s, recalled pivotal meetings of the X-29 Flight Control Advisory Board. This board was set up by Dr. Renso Caporali, who was directed by George Skurla to oversee the X-29 program for top management. The X-29 was Grumman's first venture into a digital software-driven flight control system. Blyseth was a member of the advisory board and voiced the concern of the systems and software community for the integrity of the software and the need to focus on such issues as generic software failures. The flight controls community was confident that on-board verification and testing of the vendor flight control software and hardware would be sufficient.

The systems world at Grumman had a long history of building ground-based systems and integration test stands (SITS) utilizing a substantial portion of the aircraft avionics as a primary mechanism for the integration, testing, and verification of the system. Proceeding without a SITS facility as an integral part of integration was not only a programmatic risk, but for the X-29, a major safety risk. The flight control system had components of both software and hardware redundancy. Given the inherent complexity of the X-29 flight control system, the systems community continued to voice concern for adequate testing. Late one night while out of town at the vendor's facility, Dr. Caporali, frustrated by the lack of convergence on the approach, essentially locked Blyseth and Whitaker into the hotel room and told them they could not rejoin the group until they had settled the issue. Around 0200 hrs, after Blyseth learned more than he wanted to know about flight control systems, and Whitaker the same for software, the two agreed on a plan to move forward with an integrated ground-based test stand to validate the integrity of the vendor's software and system. Not everyone was happy with this decision because it added to schedule and cost, but after over 400 successful flights, no one really wanted to look back and replay those tense sessions with the board. The X-29 program was a success, and provided a valuable stop gap for the preservation and honing of a broad spectrum of essential systems integration and vehicle design skills.

The two X-29s were flying aeronautical research laboratories that expanded the design options for designers of future generations of fighter and attack aircraft. They demonstrated high maneuvering and control at transonic speeds, reached a 67-deg angle of attack, and achieved Mach 1.8. The X-29 also represented the first new aircraft created in Future Systems by the Advanced Systems department and built in the Product Development Center (prototype shop) headed by Howard Schilling (Fig. 7.8).

Of equal importance was the fact that a new design team, with skills in advanced composites and digital flight control system technology, was formed and matured through the design, simulation, ground testing, and flight testing of the X-29A. This team, many of whom are not in Fig 7.7, along with other engineers, served Grumman well on future projects with other companies such as Northrop (e.g., the U.S. Navy ATA proposal from 1984–87).

Fig. 7.8   Advanced Systems department product development center (prototype shop).

V/STOL: DESIGN 698

In the late 1970s, the armed forces and industry were studying advanced vertical/short takeoff and landing (V/STOL) aircraft designs and utilization. The Defense Science Board Task Force on V/STOL Aircraft issued the following statements in the November 1979 final report: "The Navy must develop V/STOL aircraft in conjunction with appropriate surface ships and weapons systems... to be effective in the threat environment through 2000.... It is likely that a high altitude high speed (subsonic aircraft V/STOL aircraft configured for AEW, ASW and Missileer roles will produce the most immediate capabilities."

In response to the Navy requirements, Grumman began developing a V/STOL turbofan aircraft concept with vanes in the fan stream for zero speed control. The twin tilting nacelles contained all of the VTOL functions (thrust, thrust modulation, and control). The wing was sized to satisfy aerodynamic performance and control requirements and to house embedded radar for AEW functions. This concept was designated Design 698. Over four years of developmental tests culminated in a full-scale model test at NASA Ames in 1980 utilizing TF-34 engines (Fig. 7.9).

The Grumman V/STOL team was led by Bob Kress; Stan Kalemaris guided the configuration development and much of the wind tunnel planning. Kalemaris also played a major role in much of Grumman's V/STOL B supersonic design studies and testing. "Kress was the creative genius and

Fig. 7.9   Design 698 in a full-scale model test at NASA Ames.

head marketeer," according to Stan Kalemaris, "but Bill Rathke, as program manager, kept the train on the track and allowed the rest of us to concentrate on doing our jobs—he was critical to keeping the team together." Tony Bacchi and Wally Burhans did the configuration design studies of Design 698. Dr. Gunther "Doc" Buchmann was lead aero along with Vladimir Seredinsky, who "very elegantly established the vertical/horizontal flight transitional speed-altitude corridor and related propulsion scheduling," according to Mark Siegel, head of Flight Sciences. Dr. Dave Migdal of Advanced Systems led the intensive efforts on V/STOL jet-induced characteristics and effects for Design 698. Ray Rice tied all the testing together and played a lead role in the full-scale engine and wind tunnel model tests. Larry Canonico worked closely with Rice during an intensive eight-month period to design the full-scale tilting structure that supported the twin engine TF-34 turbo fan configuration. Bill Rathke commended Rice and Canonico to Grumman top management for the difficult and Herculean effort.

Doc Buchmann was an aerodynamicist at Blohm and Voss during World War II and came to Grumman after the war. He was a brilliant engineer who wrote all his equations in long hand. He always had a happy disposition and a good sense of humor, especially when he was playing the piano at parties. Dick Kita, one of Grumman's senior aeronautical engineers, reminded me that during a preliminary design meeting, I congratulated Doc for his excellent work on the Design 698 project. In return, Dr. Buchmann wished that I lived to be 100 and that the last voice I heard on my death bed was his. The meeting broke out in riotous laughter.

Grumman believed that airframe and engine technologies were in hand to build a subsonic turbofan V/STOL demonstrator in four years. The Defense Science Board Task Force on V/STOL Aircraft reached the same conclusion, stating that a demonstrator program could be initiated immediately. Figures 7.10 and 7.11 clearly show that if Navy funding was available, Grumman would have been in a strong position to win a development program that would lead to flying a demonstrator test vehicle followed by a full-scale development program when all the supporting technologies (e.g., embedded or conformal radar) were available. Dr. Dick Oman and his team from the Research department provided much help with the design of a unique tethered V/STOL A radio-controlled, transition model demonstration. Dr. Oman performed years of studies and experimental tests into complex jet stream and suck down effects associated with VTOL systems. Continued development was required in the areas of flight controls and avionics to build a practical operational aircraft. Grumman continued to develop the elements of conformal radar that held the potential for a highly capable surveillance system at a manageable size and weight.

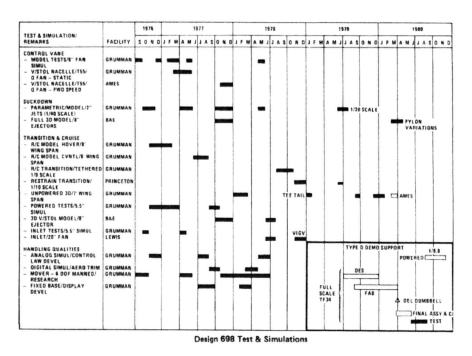

Fig. 7.10   The breadth of the Design 698 test and simulations program.

Walt Valckenaere and Doc Buchmann worked closely with the Navy and NASA during piloted flight simulations of Grumman's Design 698 twin turbofan, tilt engine V/STOL A configuration at the NASA Ames Research Center. The simulations were carried out in a vertical motion simulator with an interchangeable cab and a computer-generated image system with a four-window display. Of particular importance was simulating the hover mode and controlling the aircraft when a large amount of lateral and longitudinal control power, afforded by vanes located in the jet exhaust, was available to the pilot.

The Research department was heavily involved in investigating VTOL flying qualities to determine the requirements for an appropriate simulator. This device could be used by researchers and designers in realistically determining desirable handling qualities in hover, and in the evaluation of different VTOL configurations. There was much exploratory research work to be done on the simulator itself, to assure that the most realistic simulation was provided at reasonable cost. This research simulator effort, which was led by Harry Breul, was the result of close interaction with Advanced Systems design teams (V/STOL A and B) by providing first-hand experience with the kind of control responses actually being considered for the

Fig. 7.11   Design 698 tethered model test.

next-generation VTOL. In the mid-1970s, a 6-deg-of-freedom, large-amplitude, high-performance hover simulator became a reality, and provided a realistic operating environment for Advanced Systems and Advanced Development VTOL design activities (e.g., Design 698).

In the early 1970s, another research team headed by Oman began investigating VTOL jet flows in ground effect. They developed a simple, but highly instrumented, facility that enabled the acquisition of detailed data in the presence of multiple jets mixing turbulently in ground effect. Much was learned about flow entrainment around the aircraft and the variety of interactions with the ground, the resultant suck down and (often unsteady) fountain effects, and re-ingestion of exhaust products. To improve fundamental understanding of the unexpectedly large turbulent mixing rates observed in VTOL fountain flows, an extensive, detailed experimental program was successfully carried out in the mid-1980s. Data from full-scale and 1/7-scale Grumman VTOL Design 698 tests, generated in a joint program with NASA and the U.S. Navy, were utilized to ensure that scale effects were properly accounted for.

CONFORMAL RADAR: MMVX, E-2X

Grumman began working on conformal radar concepts in 1973. Fred Ganz was the leading project engineer responsible for the development of the conformal radar. Conformal radar is an antenna system that can be imbedded in the leading and trailing edges of an airplane's wings as well as in the sides of the fuselage. Fred Tiemann, in his *Memoir II*, touched on the pioneering work done by Ganz in his experiments with Yagi antenna arrays buried in the leading edges and trailing edges of wing airfoils. Grumman received a patent for the conformal radar antenna system in 1982. At that time, Ganz shared inventor honors with Dom Cermignani, a technical specialist in radio frequency (RF) design, and Richard Imgram, a principal engineer for computer-aided design. Side-looking lateral coverage was already demonstrated by cavity radiators mounted flush to the fuselage skin. Along with the patent, Grumman also received a $1.74 million Naval Air Systems Command (NAVAIR) contract for laboratory and ground testing.

The concept of replacing a rotodome with a 360-deg phased array system was the ultimate goal of a research and development (R&D) effort over many years. Bill Jorsch of Advanced Systems worked with Ganz on developing the conformal radar technology, and Pat Wiley worked with the Navy to obtain Navy R&D funds for rooftop testing of conformal radar elements and follow-on full-scale testing. After a series of successful rooftop tests performed in the Grumman Plant 14 Avionics Laboratory located on Long Island, Grumman won a $14 million Navy contract to test full-scale Yagi arrays in two E-2 outer wing panels in 1983. Bill Fehrs, one of Grumman's most experienced program managers, was responsible for this effort that entailed extensive modification to the wing panels in a "skunk works" product development operations environment where speed, accuracy, and cost control were essential. Larry Canonico was deputy for Engineering Management and Fred Ganz was deputy for Development. Canonico was awarded a patent for a modular antenna array invention. Aside from the near-term benefits of enhancing the anti-jam capability of current AEW aircraft, the phased array technology will be applicable for future AEW and tactical aircraft. Bob Steele was responsible for the avionics system concept for the V/STOL A, and Fred Ganz did the development work on the conformal radar configuration.

An E-2 outer panel, modified with conformal radar antennas, was tested atop a specially built ground test platform at the Grumman Calverton Flight Test facility on Long Island (Fig. 7.12). Harold Allen was the test project engineer.

Subsequent to these successful full-scale tests, Advanced Systems' design studies of MMVX (multimission, heavier than air, experimental) and

Fig. 7.12   An E-2 outer panel, modified with conformal radar antennas, sits atop a specially built ground test platform.

advanced E-2 configurations employing a conformal radar system were undertaken. Due to the elimination of the classical radar antenna rotodome installation employed on E-2 series aircraft, the aircraft designers had a field day exploring a wide variety of conformal radar configurations (Fig. 7.13). They wrestled with trying to minimize takeoff gross weight (TOGW) while maintaining good carrier suitability (takeoff and landing performance), radar coverage, deck spotting (the area the aircraft takes up on the carrier deck with wings folded), and low observables (LO).

These configurations led to two preferred designs. The first was a true multimission carrier-based design capable of cargo on deck (COD), AEW, and ASW missions; the other was a more radical-looking design that would perform AEW and ASW missions (Fig. 7.14).

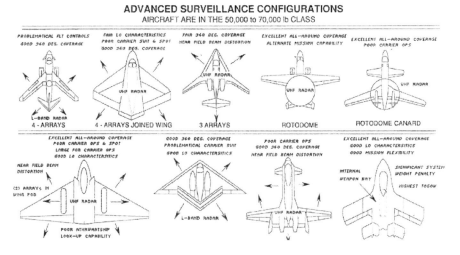

Fig. 7.13   A wide variety of conformal radar configurations.

Fig. 7.14   The two preferred designs in scale-model form.

The MMVX and subsequent E-2X design studies were carried out under the direction of Stan Kalemaris, director of Advanced Systems. Nick Dannenhoffer was program manager and Frank Dellamura was the configuration designer. Dellamura was ably supported by Vincent Crafa and John Protopapas of Propulsion; Victor Ciminera and Arnie Gersch, who carried out the sizing, performance, and weights analyses; and Dave Richel and Charlie Lundin, who developed aerodynamic inputs.

These innovative designs with 360-deg conformal radar coverage were presented to the U.S. Navy as part of an industry-wide response; after deliberation, the MMVX effort was shelved in favor of upgrading existing assets due to fiscal and budgetary constraints. The Navy subsequently turned to Grumman and requested that a derivative of the E-2C Hawkeye AEW aircraft system be developed using conformal radar in place of the existing radar and rotodome antenna currently being utilized. Harvey Fromer, E-2 program vice president, worked closely with Advanced Systems personnel as the team began to examine ways of successfully integrating a new 360-deg-capable UHF radar into the basic E-2C airframe while maintaining as much commonality of the existing airframe, landing gear, and subsystems as possible.

The E-2X was to be powered by two GE TF-34 engines, similar to those employed on the A-10 Thunderbolt II, and the conformal radar antenna arrays would be located in the wing leading edges, fuselage sides, and horizontal tail trailing edges. Figure 7.15 shows the extensive changes made to accommodate the conformal radar. In order to house the conformal antenna arrays in a level horizontal tail, the existing E-2C horizontal stabilizer that had dihedral was removed and replaced by the tail employed on the C-2 Greyhound COD transport, which had no dihedral. Dihedral is the

Fig. 7.15   The E2-X design for wind tunnel testing.

angle between horizontal and the upward angle of the horizontal that influences the amount of rolling moment the aircraft can achieve.

With the rotodome removed, a change occurred in longitudinal stability (pitch axis) that necessitated a wing glove, which housed additional fuel, to be added forward of the wing leading edge, as shown in Fig. 7.15. Ernie Ranalli, head of the Stress department, performed the preliminary structural analysis of the wing glove. Another big challenge of the design was to accommodate the TF-34 engines without changing the E-2C main landing gear. The solution was to "wrap" the TF-34 engine intake and exhaust ducts around the landing gear utilizing a split fan exhaust system that Frank Dellamura and Vin Crafa worked on intensely. It was rationalized that penalties due to additional internal drag would be overcome by a more powerful and efficient TF-34 engine variant, had the design reached a development stage.

The conformal radar offered the potential of a lighter weight and less "draggy" installation in a completely new airframe design compared to a conventional rotodome design. The installation of the conformal radar in the E-2X derivative revealed weight and volume penalties due to the distribution of the conformal arrays and transmitters in both sides of the fuselage, wing leading edges, and horizontal tail tailing edges. The number and weight of transmitter units, additional wing structural weight, required power and resultant cooling penalties, and the internal volume required to distribute power, signal, and cooling lines throughout the aircraft were many of the issues that had to be resolved based on available state-of-the-art technology. Harvey Fromer and the design team presented the results to the Navy, and the E-2X concept was also shelved. Historically, these efforts clearly demonstrated that Grumman was constantly trying to exploit advanced technologies by creating advanced aircraft systems concepts in the 1990 time period.

A-6A CIRCULATION CONTROL WING DEMONSTRATOR

In 1979, Grumman flew an A-6A circulation control wing (CCW) demonstrator that was the result of a two-year effort with the STOL Aerodynamics Group, Aircraft Division of the David W. Taylor Naval Ship Research and Development Center (NSRDC) in Bethesda, Maryland. The CCW is a mechanical high lift system based on the Coanda principle that employs tangential blowing over a rounded trailing edge of a wing, resulting in very high lift augmentation. The tangential blowing increases the velocity of the airflow over the leading and trailing edge of the wing using a series of blowing slots that eject high-pressure air that increases the jet momentum and mass flow. In the A-6 CCW demonstrator, air was bled from the 5th and 12th compressor stages of both J-52 engines that powered the A-6. The air was ducted along the wing trailing edge in a cylindrical duct attached to the underportion of the existing Fowler flap and fed into a plenum chamber that led to thin slots in the upper surface of the rounded trailing edge.

The work on CCW commenced at NSRDC in 1970. The NSRDC team that worked closely with Grumman was Bob Englar, lead engineer, and Jim Nichols, program manager. Englar had conducted extensive CCW investigations at NSRDC. The Advanced Systems engineering manager on the program was Horace Moore, and the Aero lead was Vladimir Seredinsky. Moore worked closely with Herb Grossman, who headed the Product Development Center to build the extensive wing, horizontal tail, and high-temperature ducting for the bleed air from the Pratt & Whitney J-52 engines in the A-6. Due to the very high pitching moments associated with "blowing on" on the A-6, the horizontal stabilizer had to be extensively modified. The area was increased 45% and incorporated "inverse camber and a slat" (Figs. 7.16 and 7.17). In addition, the wing

Fig. 7.16   The A-6 CCW with extensive modifications to the wing and horizontal tail.

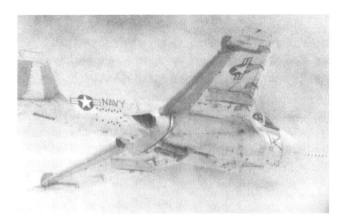

Fig. 7.17   The A-6 CCW showing the rounded trailing edge of the wing, wing fences, reverse camber of the horizontal tail leading edge, and external ducting from the engine to the wing structure.

glove strake at the fuselage junction had to be removed and replaced with a Kruger flap to avoid separation. Dr. Robert Melnik of Grumman's Research department performed exhaustive computational fluid dynamics (CFD) analyses to obtain the right geometry for the test conditions. In the late 1960s, Melnik and his team launched an investigation of subsonic and transonic airfoil theory, ultimately to enable design of airfoils and wings with improved performance throughout the speed range, including reliable prediction of low-speed stall and transonic buffet boundary. By the mid-1980s, the resultant computer code enabled design of complete wings with multi-element, high-lift devices for maneuvering at transonic speeds and for landing. This code became an industry standard, was utilized by Advanced Systems design teams., and greatly decreased expensive, time-consuming wind tunnel testing.

The resulting performance of the A-6 CCW was outstanding, with the A-6 flown as slow as 67 kt. Nominal approach speed on a standard day compared to a conventional A-6 on a standard day would be 76 kt vs 118 kt—a 35% reduction. The A-6 CCW actually reached a speed of 68 kt during approach; a company helicopter was the only vehicle that could fly slow enough to fly chase. In land-based operation, the landing roll and takeoff ground roll would be reduced by 65% and 60%, respectively. However, the resultant impact on weight empty on the A-6 configuration was in excess of 4000 lb. If CCW was to be employed successfully, the configuration would have to be part of the design evolution involving extensive tradeoffs and a much smaller trailing edge radius and the like.

Fig. 7.18 A model of the Goose G-711.

DESIGN 711: GOOSE REPLACEMENT

History repeated itself in the early 1980s when Grumman designed a modern replacement for the Goose, the G-711 (Fig. 7.18). The preliminary design of G-711 was carried out by Brad Griffin, configuration layout; Bob LeCat, aerodynamics (Fig. 7.19); Larry Canonico, inboard profile/final configuration/structural design layout; and Sam Dastin, composite fuselage/hull design. Preliminary development costs and flyway pricing were estimated by Gus Spanopoulos of Advanced Systems Pricing.

Design 711 showed the good lines of the fuselage, the excellent visibility and cargo access via the cockpit canopy, and the foldable wing floats' dockside access and cruise efficiency (Fig. 7.20).

Extensive low-speed wind tunnel tests were conducted that verified estimates of stall speed of 61 kt, cruise speeds of 175 kt, and a range of 800-900 statute miles. A powered wind tunnel model used to determine low-speed flight characteristics was tested in Grumman's low-speed wind tunnel facility on

Fig. 7.19 (L to R) Bob LeCat, Larry Canonico, and Mark Siegel, head, Preliminary Design Flight Sciences, discussing the aerodynamic configuration of Design 711.

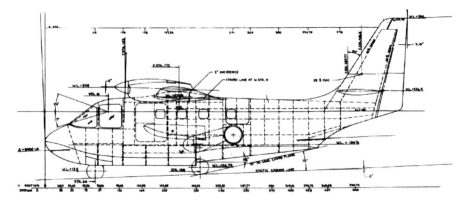

Fig. 7.20   The final side view configuration of Design 711.

Long Island. Mike Pelehach, ever the salesman, asked Hal Moss, director of Operations Analysis, if he would pose with the wind tunnel model to emphasize the size of the model under test (Fig. 7.21)—the implication to potential customers being Grumman was serious about the project. Moss was small in stature, but was one of Grumman's most gifted operations analyst engineers.

The flyaway price of a production Goose replacement was deemed noncompetitive until Grumman contacted Piper Aircraft and used Piper manufacturing methods. Larry Canonico of Preliminary Design actually laid out the structural design of an aluminum horizontal stabilizer using Grumman structural standards and estimated air loads and built the stabilizer in the PDC headed by Herb Grossman. He took the drawings to Piper, whose design personnel redesigned the tail using their standards—the result being a

Fig. 7.21   Hal Moss of Operations Analysis during Design 711 model tests.

Fig. 7.22 (L to R) Mike Pelehach, entertainer and aviation enthusiast Arthur Godfrey, and the author discuss Design 711.

dramatic reduction in labor dollars per square foot of tail area. The lesson learned was "know thy customer!"

Arthur Godfrey, of radio and TV fame and a great aviation enthusiast, was shown Design 711 (Fig. 7.22). He liked the aircraft and its roomy cabin very much. Herb Grossman, who headed the PDC, built a full-scale Styrofoam/-wood mockup in Plant 5 of the fuselage to show the excellent accessibility and "out-size" cargo capacity of the G-711. However, the board of directors decided against proceeding with the project due the high development cost, the fully equipped flyaway design price, and the estimated number of aircraft that could be sold.

AIRBORNE RADAR JAMMING SYSTEM (ARJS) DEMONSTRATOR

In 1980, Bob Salzmann, one of Grumman's foremost electronic warfare (EW) engineers, became part of Advanced Systems Technology as director of Advanced EW. He began working closely with U.S. Army programs in Business Development to expand Grumman's EW market with the Army. The U.S. Army has the largest aviation complement of helicopters and aircraft of any of the branches of the U.S. Armed Services, and the Grumman Mohawk was an important battlefield surveillance system for the Army.

At the time, the U.S. Army was still facing the Soviet threat in Europe and was deploying the Apache helicopter weapon system in support of combat infantry divisions. The Soviet surface-to-air threat was formidable, and consisted of highly mobile search and detection radars in combination with a wide variety of capable surface-to-air missiles.

Al Gurkewitz had become director of Advanced Avionics Systems in Advanced Systems. He and Wally Zepf worked closely with Bob Salzmann, Business Development, and Operations Analysis personnel on the requirements for an airborne radar jamming system (ARJS) and the effectiveness of such systems in support of U.S. Army operations in the European theater. These system approaches combined the use of tailored EW tactical jamming system technology developed on the EA-6B family of aircraft with U.S. Army helicopters, namely the UH-1 Iroquois (Huey; Figs. 7.23 and 7.24) and the UH-60 Blackhawk. The ARJS produced 1 million W of radiated power that represented a 10-fold increase over the EA-6B. The ARJS was designed to be a standoff jamming system, as opposed to being an escort jammer. It would stand off about 30-50 km (18-30 miles) and jam low-altitude surface-to-air missiles (SAMS) to allow the OV-1 Mohawk, and Scout and Apache helicopters to penetrate the battlefield.

Salzmann and Business Development began an intensive campaign with the U.S. Army Communications and Electronic Command (CECOM) under the direction of General Paige and the Electronic Warfare Laboratory (EWL) headed by Bob Giordano. They were able to gain the support of the EWL to fund the demonstration at Ft. Huachuca, Arizona. In addition, they worked with the Training and Doctrine Command (TRADOC) to develop preliminary requirements for an operational system. The result of this effort was an ARJS demonstrator consisting of "tailored" EA-6B EW components integrated into a

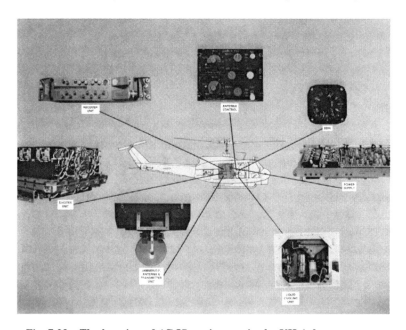

Fig. 7.23   The location of ARJS equipment in the UH-1 demonstrator.

Fig. 7.24   An in-flight side view of the UH-1 demonstrator shows the transmitter and antenna installation.

UH-1 helicopter. Joe Genovese played a key role in putting the system together and doing the system integration in the Grumman Plant 14 Electronics Center. Bob Fredette performed all the analytical work necessary to test the system at the radar site located at the Grumman test facility in Calverton, Long Island. Dr. Marty Golinski developed all the theoretical jamming techniques for the operational tests, and Ross Fleisig was the proposal and operations manager for ARJS. The UH-1 ARJS EW demonstrator program performed at Ft. Huachuca, Arizona, culminated in a series of very successful tests, totaling more than 42 h. The ARJS clearly demonstrated that EW support jamming could nullify Soviet-type technology in simulated combat situations during which attacking Apache helicopters and OV-1 Mohawk aircraft were able to effectively operate against simulated Soviet threats.

Several lessons were learned from this innovative effort. The close ties between Salzmann and the EA-6B team resulted in a cross-fertilization of technologies. More highly focused energy approaches and modulation techniques made their way into the final versions of the EA-6B, thanks to Bob Scholly and Bob Fredette. Another lesson was that the team did not fully understand the customer's process of introducing a new capability into operational units. In this case, the use of EW support jamming was not part of the ongoing Army TRADOC (Training and Operational Command) and, therefore, this capability was not allowed to be introduced into Ft. Lewis as a new capability to be tested in a larger Blackhawk helicopter. The Army formally terminated the ARJS in a memorandum of agreement with the Air Force in 1984.

The last lesson learned was by me, after being talked into spending $1200 for heavy boots to protect the Grumman team as it walked around the desert in Ft. Huachuca in the early morning hours to avoid snake and tarantula bites. This was a morale booster for the entire team, and many of the guys bought real Western-style boots.

COMPUTER-AIDED DESIGN IN ADVANCED SYSTEMS

Grumman was one of the first companies to experiment with Computer-Aided Design And Manufacturing (CADAM), which was developed by Lockheed. CADAM was a sophisticated computer-aided drafting tool with a limited ability to project geometry from one view to another. Points in one view, when selected with a light pen, would generate a line in another view much like the process a designer or draftsman does in manual drafting. The advantage of CADAM was that a designer could erase, move, scale, or insert geometry instantly and geometry could be transmitted to three-axis, numerically controlled machine tools.

In the early 1970s, Paul Weidenhafer was assigned by Grant Hedrick to investigate the use of CADAM. He was the key individual who introduced computer-aided design (CAD) to Grumman, which later became the Grumman Engineering and Manufacturing System (GEMS). Weidenhafer became a "disciple," and his enthusiasm and energy helped sell CADAM to Grumman's technical and manufacturing leadership. Two CADAM scopes were installed in Grumman's engineering building in Bethpage, Long Island. They were the size of large refrigerators and connected to company mainframe computers, according to Frank Dellamura, configuration design engineer.

Grumman's 10 senior configuration design specialists were from the "old school," meaning that aircraft designs were done on a drawing board in two dimensions with a great deal of artistic flair to get the shape and lines right for the chosen configuration. A bevy of engineers surrounded the designer to give starting points regarding fundamental dimensions, wing configuration, wing area and tail areas, internal fuel load, payload, and the like. They all worked on drafting boards in the time-honored process of vellum (drawing paper), pencils, triangles, scales, and pounce (powder eraser bag). Dellamura was the new kid on the block, assigned to the configuration designer corps by Ken Fitch and me to introduce CAD to the preliminary design process and fundamentally change the way the designers might perform their job in the long run. Fitch was one of Grumman's versatile engineers who transitioned from being project engineer on early missile programs that reached flight test to project engineer on aircraft programs.

Dellamura initially met with some intellectual resistance; however, the younger configuration designers, including Wally Burhans and Don Colquhun, were willing to listen and try it out. Early comments included:

"The screen is too small. It's got to be the size of a drafting table."
"You've got to see all the views at one time."
"Go-to-scopes are counterproductive."
"I get eye strain."

One of Grumman's most talented and artistic designers was Nate Kirshbaum, who graduated from Massachusetts Institute of Technology (MIT). He was a walking encyclopedia of aircraft history, specifications, and design characteristics of the entire world's aircraft. He is remembered as being a very kind and caring person as well as a brilliant designer. In those early days he said, "I'm holding up the design team. I can't turn out a configuration drawing as fast as they need it. Every time I finish a layout, someone has to transpose it into the computer. It's costing too much time."

As Dellamura, Burhans, Colquhun, and some of the other designers became more adept with the CAD system, the turnaround time to have a configuration ready for analysis got shorter and the configuration layout contained more information. Changes to a configuration came faster, and area and volume analysis became more accurate. Once they became comfortable using CAD, they started to abandon the old drafting board. As younger configuration designers came on board, CAD was used more widely and the requirements for a design position included proficiency in CAD as well as computer science.

The next step in CAD evolution was 3-D modeling that would allow a 3-D model to be quickly made by Grumman's model shop for either wind tunnel testing or radar signature analysis. Grumman had decided to wait for the release of a 3-D version of CADAM. Grumman's competitors were already developing proprietary 3-D systems, and Dassault, France's prime aerospace manufacturer at the time, was developing a 3-D system that eventually became Computer Aided Three-Dimensional Interactive Application (CATIA). With the emphasis on observables (radar and infrared signature), it was essential to develop a robust 3-D model to evaluate radar signatures at various radar frequencies. Evaluating a design for its radar signature involved building an expensive, exact scale model and testing it on a radar range.

Dellamura and Ken Fitch set about trying to develop a perspective on what the industry was accomplishing in 3-D computer-aided design. After many American Institute of Aeronautics and Astronautics (AIAA) conferences and interfacing with key industry experts like Dan Raymer from North American, they were convinced that Grumman should buy this capability in light of emerging programs that emphasized low observables for increased effectiveness against advanced airborne, ground, and sea-based threat systems. In light of Grumman's progress in the use of CAD systems and an expanded cadre of experienced personnel in this area, it was decided to develop this capability in house.

A research and development program was approved by me, and thus LEONARDO was born. Alfred Vachris named the project LEONARDO after Leonardo DaVinci, an artist/engineer. Vachris laid out the original high-level description of the program and how users would operate it. The Engineering department and the Grumman Engineering and Manufacturing Systems (GEMS) group supplied some very talented computer programmers, including Thomas Lazicky, Gerald Stoodley, and Joann Cipriano.

The project was started with a definite advantage. When Grumman acquired the CADAM license, it also received the complete computer code. The plan of attack was to modify CADAM to full 3-D wire frame and surface capability. After three years of work, users could develop a wire frame/surface model of an aircraft configuration that could be used to perform radar signature analysis. Grumman began an aggressive observables (stealth) program in the early 1980s, and the LEONARDO system was used by projects within a secure facility.

In retrospect, Grumman started the transition to 3-D computer-aided design too late. LEONARDO was a noble experiment that would have taken years to attain the level of maturity used by Grumman's competitors. Grumman gained considerable knowledge and expertise from LEONARDO, and the project terminated in the mid-1980s.

During 1983-87, Grumman teamed with Northrop as a major subcontractor for the U.S. Navy's ATA competition. Grumman's designers were required to use Northrop's Northrop Computer Aided Design (NCAD) 3-D system and workstations, with the result that the design team recommended that Grumman purchase or license it.

At the same time, Lazicky and Dellamura were sent to Dassault to review the first release of what would be known as CATIA—a superior CAD system with an operational manufacturing system. They recommended to the Engineering and Manufacturing departments that CATIA be adopted as Grumman's main CAD system over Northrop's NCAD system, and Grumman became one of the first U.S. aerospace companies to utilize CATIA for aircraft design.

CONCLUSION

From 1930 to 1970 many new aircraft starts and derivatives were solicited by the government and developed by Grumman per decade (an average of over 20 from 1930 to 1960 followed by 13 from 1961 to 1970). In contrast, during the 1971–1980 and 1981–1990 time periods only 10 and 4 aircraft were flown, respectively. Future Systems strategies were developed to address these shortfalls by creating requirements leading to new aircraft weapon systems concepts, increasing international sales of production programs, expanding subcontracting sales to both national and international customers, and creating new business opportunities by leveraging Grumman engineering and research expertise.

The major discriminators in making these efforts a reality were the versatility, creativity, and cohesiveness of Grumman design teams forged from major aircraft programs, Advanced Systems, the Engineering department, Flight Test, Research, Integrated Logistics Support, Business Development, and all functional departments including Contracts and Finance. In the 1950s, Dick Hutton made a strategic move by concentrating top engineering talent in Preliminary Design to create new aircraft. In the mid-1970s, Mike Pelehach and his team worked closely with major aircraft programs and departments, which resulted in top talent assigned to advanced aircraft weapon system development. Some examples of this cross-fertilization of talent were as follows: Bob Kress (Lunar Module and F-14A) headed the V/STOL- A, Dr. Renso Caporali (Engineering and F-14A flight test) became director of Advanced Air Force Programs, Bob Salzmann (EA-6B, EF-111) and a small team developed the ARJS concept and flew the demonstrator, and Al Gurkewitz (EA-6B) headed Advanced Avionics, was involved in ARJS, became program manager on Pave Mover, and was Joint STARS proposal manager.

This chapter has examined some programs that reached a level of maturity resulting in flight demonstrations (X-29A, ARJS, and CCW) or full-scale testing and mockup (V/STOL-A, conformal radar, Design 711). There were many significant design teams whose multiyear efforts did not reach a proposal win, full-scale testing/mockup, or flight hardware, including the ATF program, the ATA program, and the A/FX/JAST (Joint Advanced Strike Technology) program.

The next chapter examines the lineage of battlefield surveillance. The Joint STARS genealogy began with the RGWS demonstration in 1975. This aircraft weapon system concept demonstration was funded by Future Systems; designed by a team of Aircraft Program, Engineering, and Advanced Systems personnel in conjunction with Norden, the radar supplier; and the F-14A No. 5 test aircraft was modified and instrumented in Future Systems PDC.

Chapter 8

Lineage of Battlefield Surveillance: RGWS, Pave Mover, and Joint STARS

The Joint Surveillance and Target Attack Reconnaissance System (Joint STARS; Fig. 8.1) program was awarded to Grumman in September 1985, but its story began 11 years earlier in spring 1974.

In an attempt to capture all those responsible for "creating" Joint STARS, it is important to note that the "successes of this battlefield management system" were due to the leadership, program management expertise, and innovative and imaginative use of "critical technologies that were put into the hands of skilled engineers and scientists who understood the technology and how to take advantage of it." This is a quote from Jerry Norton's excellent published brochure, entitled, "From Concept to Combat—A Retrospective View of the Development of Joint Stars."

In the early spring of 1974, Israeli military representatives visited Grumman with lessons learned from the 1973 Yom Kippur war. Israeli losses were very high, and they were inquiring as to whether U.S. airborne systems had the capability to accurately detect and destroy first line defenses with precision at long standoff ranges. Grant Hedrick and Newt Speiss responded by asking Dan Collins, Gene Bonan, and Advanced Systems and Research for solutions. Hank Janiesch also had a meeting with key radio frequency (RF) engineers of several programs, including Gerry McNiff.

Radar Guided Weapon System (RGWS)

Within a week after the meeting, McNiff returned with three pieces of quadrule paper that laid out a "relative azimuth angle target detection and weapon delivery system utilizing real time synthetic aperture radar imagery for accurate target identification and location." He had a brilliant mind, was very innovative, and had a unique capability to explain abstract theory and convert it into meaningful and understandable engineering concepts.

Grant Hedrick and Newt Speiss possessed great foresight, and were very supportive of the concept. As a result, a small working group including McNiff; Sol Boles, RF Engineering; Walter Smerk, Systems Engineering; Frank Milordi, Flight Test; Jim Glover, Radar; and Joe LeStrange, Weapon

Fig. 8.1   E8-A maiden flight.

Systems began to help McNiff flesh out the concept. Dan Collins also came on board as director of Advanced Attack Engineering, and Hank Janiesch, who was head of RF Engineering, became the Advanced Attack Engineering manager. Through this period, McNiff was intensely developing algorithms and radar processing techniques, and giving technical presentations to senior Naval Air Systems Command (NAVAIR) personnel. In late 1974 the Radar Guided Weapon System program was born.

During early 1975, the team undertook an intensive investigation of the defense electronics industry's progress in synthetic aperture radar (SAR) and weapon delivery systems, which would lead to a joint venture to develop a "real time, standoff, precision attack system." Grumman selected Norden because it had designed and built the APQ-148 multimode radar with an elevation interferometer for terrain clearance elevation used on the A-6 Intruder. An interferometer is a very precise instrument designed to measure things with extreme accuracy. Norden pledged that it would contribute $10 million to a joint program. The resulting Grumman/Norden joint venture undertook a demonstration program that lasted 13 months; Grumman contributed $40 million to the venture.

RGWS was a multiphase program that Grumman initiated to develop the next-generation air-to-ground bombing system. It was to be installed in follow-on versions of the A-6 and have major enhancements over the F-14A in the air-to-ground mode. The initial phase of the RGWS was the concept demonstration phase. RGWS Phase I was to record in flight the radar amplitude and phase data from the radar receiver for postmission processing in the synthetic aperture radar processing station (SARPS). The following

RGWS phases would move the postflight processing to near real time and, eventually, real time. The processing of data took place in several stages or passes in the SARPS located in the automated telemetry station (ATS) at Grumman's Calverton, Long Island, facility The first pass was to reorder the recorded data from all the range increments as a function of time to all the time samples for each range increment. Pass two developed the motion compensation corrections for the selected time increment. Pass three applied the motion compensation corrections and performed the required signal processing. Pass four played back the processed data in real time for an operator to cursor the desired target. RGWS ended up being incorporated into the A-6F program but, unfortunately, the Navy cancelled this program.

In early 1976, the Phase 1 RGWS platform achieved a significant milestone with the delivery of a test F-14 aircraft. Herb Grossman headed the Product Development Center (PDC), in which a nine-month modification of the F-14 took place that led to the RGWS configuration. John Calandra was head of Vehicle Design and Jim Williams was in charge of Systems Design.

The F-14 RGWS demonstration aircraft system consisted of removing the AWG-9 air-to-air radar system, including all the wiring. A modified A-6 target recognition attack multisensor (TRAM) radar system was then installed along with the Norden azimuth interferometer, used to obtain the relative azimuth angle between the released glide weapon and the target, and a new radome (Fig. 8.2). The forward bulkhead and associated structure were also stiffened to minimize vibration and flexure for SAR motion compensation, and in-flight and ground processing instrumentation was installed.

Fig. 8.2   TRAM radar installed in the nose of the F-14 test aircraft. The rectangular device mounted below the antenna is the interferometer.

The intensive three-month test program achieved significant results based on the analysis of the flight test data by McNiff and his group. The data showed extreme azimuth accuracy in detecting and isolating ground targets over a wide swath of azimuth angles and ranges. Essentially, the RGWS demonstrated the ability of interferometric SAR to locate distant targets and to obtain range and angle measurements with sufficient accuracy for weapon guidance.

Frank Milordi and Gerry McNiff ran the tests and Jim Glover supported the program by selecting appropriate time slices as a function of range and radar gain control settings for processing in the SARPS. Glover also made sure that the radar and the A6 DIANE (Digital Integrated Attack Navigation Equipment) computer functioned properly. Frank Finnerty headed up SARPS, with Frank Milordi as his right-hand person. Unfortunately Finnerty passed away during the execution of the program, after which Frank Milordi took over.

Jim Glover recalled two stories about the RGWS program that speak to dedication and a "just in the nick of time" performance. Glover was working very late after a test flight on a bitter cold, "in the teens," January evening at Calverton, which is located at the eastern end of Long Island. He was exhausted when he drove home on a darkened country road and heard a "loud bang" from the engine that turned out to be a failed fan belt. Because it was so cold, his car was not overheating and he hoped that the battery would hold up. It didn't, and he stopped at the first place that was still open to try to call home. As luck would have it was a bar called the Crazy Clown that featured "go-go dancers." It was so cold in the bar that it was only occupied by the female bartender and a single dancer that would not dance because "it was so damn cold." Needless to say, Jim called his wife and managed to get home. The moral of the story? If you get stuck in the middle of nowhere and have to call your wife from a topless bar, do so only in the worst weather so she will believe you!

The second story involves Hank Janiesch. It was the final technical interchange meeting (TIM) for the RGWS Phase I program, and Hank was to present the flight test results. McNiff, Milordi, and the RGWS team were working through the night and into the morning trying to get the best test results in terms of relative location number. The results were not finished when the TIM started that morning, and Hank had to ad lib for what seemed like an eternity. This is not easy for engineers to do—they tend to be analytical and detailed in their thinking, and hence not good ad libbers. The SARPS team was feverishly working to get the best results. It was truly a nail biting moment, but the final numbers that came in were "spectacular."

As a result of the success of the RGWS program, the Grumman/Norden team was selected to compete with Hughes Aircraft to design and demonstrate a tactical airborne weapon delivery system (TAWDS), later called Pave Mover. The radar was installed in an F-111A. To support the Pave Mover program, Grumman also designed and built a mobile ground-based processing and control station, and performed systems and software integration to support a very successful flight test program with the Air Force from 1981 to 1983.

Hedrick and Speiss were very enthusiastic about the business potential of RGWS. Speiss wrote a very thoughtful and strategic memo to Bill Schwendler, one of Grumman's founders, in 1976 that addressed the long-term potential of RGWS, the need to improve the maintainability of the F-14A, and the multimission growth capability plan of the F-14A due to its inherent design capabilities. This is another example of quick and open access to top Grumman management with a new idea. Speiss wrote:

> There has been a move afoot both here at GAC (Grumman Aerospace Corporation) and at Hughes to "upgrade" the F-14. As one might expect from a system built around the mid-60's equipment, its reliability is not good and it is a "bear" to maintain. Experience with the A-6 and the E-2 shows you don't solve these problems by nibbling on the edges. By the time support costs are included and the airplanes in the field are modified, it costs the customer too much money and he gets only what he thought he paid for in the first place.... So what you have to do is mod [modify] the gear so it not only solves the R&M [reliability and maintainability] problem, but also gives him [the customer] a capability he can't refuse. RGWS does this for the F-14. Not only will it provide a much better, more reliable, and overall cheaper avionic air-to-air system ... but also provides air-to ground capability ... "the attack community has been looking for for the last 20 years!"... Bill it is my opinion (and perhaps only my opinion) that we will never sell more F-14s at home or abroad until we work something like RGWS into it. RGWS is recognized as being far superior to its competition in cost, reliability and performance ... an absolute natural for extending F-14 production.... In short, Bill, I have personally never seen a situation where a technical development gave us a more significant lead over our competition and was more timely and needed by our customers.... I think you can find some schools of thought that believe RGWS has hindered rather than helped us in marketing a multi-mission F-14 [F-14 program feeling at the time].... As things are shaping up, the business aspects seem tougher than the technical problems.

In retrospect, the U.S. Navy was very interested in a version of the A-6 with RGWS, but could not get the necessary funding to proceed. The F-14A also faced government funding problems, and upgrades did not begin until 1982, thanks to the navy Flag officer and F-14 program officer leadership.

The ultimate multimission F-14D effort began in 1983 and is discussed in Chapter 6.

PAVE MOVER

The Pave Mover program (Fig. 8.3) demonstrated that active engagement systems (aircraft, missiles) can be continuously provided with accurate targeting updates during their flight to target.

Grumman developed and successfully demonstrated its clutter suppression interferometry (CSI) concept for detecting and accurately locating very low speed targets in high land clutter environments. Gerry McNiff received the Engineering Outstanding Achievement Award in 1982 (Fig. 8.4) as the primary innovator for all the technologies demonstrated in Pave Mover. He received the award from Bill Bischoff, director of engineering, and Gerry Sandler, deputy engineering director, with Al Gurkewitz, Pave Mover program manager and deputy program director of Joint STARS. Gurkewitz worked closely with John Enzminger of the Defense Advanced Research Projects Agency (DARPA), who was instrumental in developing and managing a cutting-edge program for the U.S. government.

A joint Air Force/Army test took place at the White Sands, New Mexico, missile range. Gurkewitz discussed the Pave Mover's significant advantages:

> A unique feature of our system is its ability to detect and track targets that are moving slowly. To be able to pinpoint targets in those situations denies an enemy a once-effective means of avoiding detection. We learned quite a bit from our experience with A-6s in Vietnam. The enemy there learned to slow or stop their vehicles if they heard an A-6 making an attack run. When they did that, the plane often lost its target because the radar couldn't "see" the stationary target in the terrain.

The Pave Mover development work was done on Long Island and in Connecticut. Other key members of the Pave Mover team were Frank

Fig. 8.3   An F-111A modified for the Pave Mover radar and equipment installation.

Fig. 8.4   Gerry McNiff receiving the Engineering Outstanding Achievement Award in 1982.

Milordi, engineering manager; Jim Glover, radar development; Herman Binder, engineering management; Pat Reilly, software development; and Paul Richards, Frank Schifano, Harvey Sperling, and Leo Sledgeski, weapon guidance/weapons. Grumman utilized facilities at the Calverton, Long Island, production and flight test center, and in trailers at the Gyrodyne facility in St. James, Long Island. Norden's development work was carried out at its Norwalk, Connecticut, facility. This arrangement required that a signal tower be built at the Gyrodyne facility where the integration of the Pave Mover system occurred. The team was operating at such remote installations that it required long hours and much travel.

Al Gurkewitz not only was one of Grumman's finer engineers and program managers, but also had a good sense of humor. He called his teammates "Movers" to motivate them, and he would come up with a funny joke or situation that would keep the guys in stitches. The Long Island Railroad passed near the Gyrodyne facility, and there was a discarded toilet sitting near the tracks. One morning in the rain, Al went out and sat on the toilet with a raincoat and sunglasses on, and pretended to be reading the paper while the train roared by, which caused passengers to do a double take and his Movers to break out into raucous laughter.

The demonstrated Pave Mover concept formed the basis for Grumman's Joint STARS battlefield surveillance radar system, which was proposed to the Air Force in 1984. Actually, Grumman submitted two proposals—one being small radar on the OV-1 Mohawk and the TR-1 with extensive data links to ground processing stations, and another consisting of a large radar housed in a 24-ft, streamlined radome beneath a Boeing 707-300 series transport with all the data processing on board.

In September 1985, the Grumman/Norden team, with Boeing to handle the C-18 modification work, was awarded a $657 million fixed price contract for the development of two full-scale development aircraft systems with nine ground station terminals for integration into the Army's ground station module (GSM).

Key members of this winning effort were Al Verderosa and Al Gurkewitz as program director and deputy program director, respectively. Dan Terry was Joint STARS capture team leader, Frank Milordi was engineering lead, and Gerry McNiff, Jim Gover, and Dave Szakovitsitz played key roles in the system concept, architecture, and radar development. Pat Reilly took the lead on the software development with George Hummel. Key systems engineers were Sam Mackey, who guided the operations and controls effort, along with Bob Phear and Roger Moxham. Herb Landau had an important role in the proposal and subsequent development.

Joint *STARS* Development

A significant point about the Joint STARS program was that the U.S. government and Grumman entered into a fixed price contract for a huge and complex weapon system based on only a limited proof of concept demonstration for its radar (Pave Mover). The program absolutely needed a major development phase for the four subsystems (radar, operations and control, communication, and aircraft), and for its massive system software—none of which had been accomplished or was available at contract go-ahead. The full-scale development (FSD) was handled as a production-type program, as if the FSD was complete, design requirements and specifications were in place and well understood, and all that needed to be done was to build it.

Drawing from Jerry Norton's excellent publication entitled, "From Concept to Combat—A Retrospective View of the Development of Joint STARS," I have attempted to characterize the immensity of the Joint STARS development program.

> While evolving system and subsystem requirements and an extremely optimistic contract schedule were fundamental amid continuing problems, many of the difficulties being experienced were those associated with the development of what today is understood to be an unprecedented system.
>
> In 1989, a National Research Council (NFC) study defined an unprecedented system as one that has not been built before and for which no substantial implementation experience exists. It does not have a well-developed set of requirements and therefore does not have a

digital system architecture and software design that satisfies established requirements—an accurate characterization of Joint STARS in 1985 (although Joint STARS was not considered in the NRC study). The NRC study concluded that the conventional process for development of software systems, defined in government productionization standards (DOD-STD-1679 and MIL-STD-1521), was flawed for development of large unprecedented systems.

Grumman achieved success in FSD by utilizing the development processes successfully employed on the E-2A–E-2C airborne early warning (AEW) program. The development process featured incremental and orderly evolution preceded by prototyping and flight testing prior to production incorporation. In other words, the lessons learned by Grumman engineers and management during the E-2 development and variant evolution were applied to Joint STARS by these E-2 veterans, and prevented termination of that program.

The development team assembled by Al Verderosa and Marty Dandridge included many of the outstanding personnel from the Pave Mover program, including Gerry McNiff, Jim Glover, Frank Milordi, and Pat Reilly. Verderosa and Dandridge (Fig. 8.5) were, without question, one of Grumman's finer management teams. When Tom Guarino replaced Julie Cohen on the E-2C as program manager, he brought Al Verderosa with him as his "money guy" because Al was one of Grumman's top financial managers and negotiators. Verderosa came up through the ranks, and early in his career he was on the drafting boards of the E-1B program in the late 1950s. Marty Dandridge worked in contracts on the E-2 program and then became the Malaysian A-4 modification program manager (with Chuck Muller as his assistant). Verderosa recruited Dandridge as program director on Joint STARS FSD. His leadership made customers believe in Grumman Melbourne Systems Division (MSD) when the FSD program was massively over budget, far behind schedule, and headed for termination. MSD was established in Melbourne, Florida, for the development and flight testing of Joint STARS. He would run a meeting as long as necessary to understand and attack the most complex issues.

Fig. 8.5 Al Verderosa (left) and Marty Dandridge (right).

Verderosa and Dandridge had two very critical issues to deal with in getting the Joint STARS program underway at the Melbourne facility in Florida: the extended time between the finish of the Pave Mover program and the startup of the Joint STARS program, and the loss of some key Pave Mover engineers due to the move to Florida. In order to run key elements of the development program, Verderosa and Dandridge were able to bring key veterans from the E-2 program as well as some very key personnel from the industry.

Jerry Norton started on Joint STARS as systems project engineer just before the move to Melbourne in 1986. His biggest challenge at that time was to fill the void in the engineering staffing because many of the former Joint STARS team did not make the move to Florida. In July 1989, he was promoted to director of engineering and chief engineer, Grumman Melbourne Systems. Dr. Dale Burton took over that title/job when Norton retired in 1992.

Paul Coco moved from the E-2 to Joint STARS in 1986 at Al Verderosa and Marty Dandridge's "request." Coco worked initially in Avionics, then Systems, and then headed up the Engineering efforts leading to the successful system preliminary design review (PDR) in April 1986. He went on to become program manager. He later led the Desert Storm team in Saudi Arabia and ultimately was named vice president following the success of the Joint STARS aircraft in Desert Storm.

Dr. Dale Burton (Fig. 8.6) was the key system designer of Joint STARS in FSD. Burton had prior jobs with Hughes and Sikorsky. He had a PhD in Mathematics from Florida State University but had a penchant for hardware/software integration. He could discuss theory with the best of them, and

Fig. 8.6   (L to R) Pilot (unknown), Dr. Dale Burton, and Gerry McNiff with E-8 Joint STARS aircraft.

demonstrated great persistence in all his efforts. According to Jerry Madigan, this is "a trait that you can't be taught, can't buy, and either you have it or you don't." Early in the FSD program, Burton expressed his concern to Marty Dandridge and Paul Coco that the way Grumman and the Air Force were developing software by the "official DoD methods" could result in the aircraft being on the ground for some time. Dandridge was concerned that the program's budget was experiencing markups/downs from Congress, and a significant delay in the start of flight testing could mortally wound the program. He authorized Burton to grab a small number of people separate from the primary development team to develop early engineering flight test (EEFT) software. The idea was to get the aircraft up and flying as quickly as possible, and ensure that all the basic "wrapper" software around McNiff's radar software would be able to work in flight and demonstrate the radar modes. Burton formed a small group of special hired talent from outside Grumman along with some of the Grumman team to get the job done successfully.

Tony Guma arrived from the E-2 program, where he was an L-304/display expert, eventually becoming systems leader. On Joint STARS he was the systems project engineer and performed a key role in establishing a positive image of Grumman Melbourne Systems Engineering with Electronic Systems Division (ESD) at Hanscomb AFB and with Mitre, the U.S. government technical watchdog agency.

Tim Farrell was in the Integrated Logistics Systems (ILS) group before coming to Joint STARS. He fit right in managing Norden, the supplier of the radar sensor. Once the radar was delivered, Farrell played a key role in the EEFT effort. He took the lead in seeing that configuration control requirements of the flight test software releases were properly adhered to (a major Air Force concern).

Gerry McNiff (Fig. 8.7) was the "father" of Joint STARS, and Jim Glover was Jerry's right-hand man in the design of the radar and SAR processing algorithms.

Roy Schering was a contract engineer from the PAR company and a close associate of McNiff's for many years prior to Joint STARS. He was an expert software designer and a crucial EEFT team member.

Chuck Muller was an experienced E-2 program manager and served a similar role in helping to manage customer expectations in a late and overbudget program.

Jerry Madigan worked in the Communications, Self-Defense, and Computer Upgrades Engineering sections prior to becoming Engineering program manager. He worked closely with the Mitre chief engineer as well as the Air Force program manager. Madigan recalled some more of Dale Burton's small band of talented engineers that helped develop the EEFT

Fig. 8.7   On deployment in Desert Storm, 1991: (back, L to R) Gerry McNiff and John Faulkner (front, L to R) Pat Collins and Fernando Deribeaux, who were part of the Grumman team.

software: Cory Liang, a built-in test (BIT) software expert from Hughes who could understand hardware software interfaces; Mike Addison, a radar hardware engineer who was not afraid to get his hands dirty by opening avionics boxes, swapping line replaceable units (LRUs; avionics boxes), and making development LRUs work while the supplier's engineers were still thinking about the problem; Roddey Smith, an expert in displays who created the operating system displays with his team; and Min Tran, who programmed the radar signal processors.

Alan Van Weele was plucked from the Grumman Israeli hydrofoil boat program by Al Verderosa to become Grumman's lead on the vehicle side dealing with Boeing and the modifications to the 707 aircraft. Van Weele was instrumental in utilizing concurrent engineering involved in the refurbishment and modification of the Boeing 707-300 series aircraft into the Joint STARS configuration. Concurrent engineering replaced the traditional development process in which tasks are done in parallel that allowed all aspects of the system design to be considered up front in the design process. He would oversee the vehicle modifications that were being done at the Lake Charles, Louisiana, facility and continued as the vehicle design engineer for changes made during FSD.

Mike Kozak also came from the E-2 program, where he was vehicle engineer. On Joint STARS he was the vehicle engineer responsible for all the aircraft FSD drawings.

Tom Wood, Dave Szakovits, Jean-Marie Sanders, and Scott Spray were all former Hughes radar software designers who joined the Joint STARS team after Dale Burton came on board.

By late 1990, significant performance capabilities of the Joint STARS system were confirmed by flight test, early look, and operational field demonstrations in Europe. Although FSD was not complete, the Office of the Secretary of Defense (OSD), Air Force, and Army recognized the unique proven capabilities of the system and recommended that the two development Joint STARS aircraft be deployed to the Persian Gulf for Operation Desert Storm. In mid-January 1991, the aircraft arrived in Saudi Arabia (Fig. 8.8); two days later Joint STARS flew its first operational mission. In five years, the Joint STARS had gone from concept to combat, from a piece of paper to a combat-proven system. Upon landing at Melbourne from the combat deployment, Al Verderosa, Marty Dandridge, and Colonel Temple welcome the aircraft and crew home (Fig. 8.9). As a result of the success of the E-8A Joint STARS in Desert Storm, the USAF and Grumman crew received the Air Medal (Fig. 8.10).

Connie Blyseth, who was assistant to the corporate chief technology officer, remembered an event that occurred in November 1984 prior to the award of the Joint STARS program. Al Verderosa, Joint STARS program director, called him and said, "Connie, can you give a presentation to General Chubb [U.S. Air Force Joint STARS program manager] on Grumman and software?" Blyseth looked at his calendar and suggested the time to prepare would be about two weeks. Verderosa replied: "Where are you right now? I need you now." Verderosa was in Blyseth's office in a flash, and grabbed his arm as Blyseth scooped up his stack of viewgraphs (transparencies used for

Fig. 8.8   Joint STARS arrives in Saudi Arabia.

Fig. 8.9   Al Verderosa, Marty Dandridge, and Colonel Temple welcomed home the E-8A, with USAF and Grumman crew, from deployment in Desert Storm.

an overhead projector). The mood in the conference room was very somber—a number of blank faces, folks slouched back in their chairs, and General Chubb on the edge of his chair looking sternly down the conference table. Blyseth placed his pile of viewgraphs on the conference table and was greeted by, "Who are you?" from General Chubb, who was obviously impatient. General Chubb said he was concerned that Grumman could not produce the software system required and was hesitant to give us the award. "Look," he said, "I only asked three questions: What are you going to build?

Fig. 8.10   General McPeak presented the Air Medal to USAF and Grumman personnel for their service in Desert Storm.

From a management perspective, how do you know where you are? When will you be done?"

Blyseth remembered the drops of sweat running down his sides because General Chubb was an imposing individual and he was asking the right questions. Blyseth reached for his first chart and placed it on the viewgraph machine. On the screen were just four lines: *Software development at Grumman. How do you know what you're going to build? How do you know where we really are? When are we going to be done?* Without hesitation General Chubb turned, looked directly at Verderosa, and retorted, "Did you guys make that chart up on the way here?" "No Sir, as you can see it's a well-worn, much scratched up viewgraph," responded Blyseth. The presentation and discussion went well.

At the end there was a reflective pause, and General Chubb asked why the people on the program hadn't told him this. Blyseth replied:

> General, the people you see here today are the ones that designed the system for you. They are the best of Grumman. Unquestionably they have designed the finest airborne surveillance and tracking system ever to be offered to the U.S. government. That has been their job to this point, to assure you of the best design possible design. Now it is up to Grumman to deliver the product, and in doing that we will put the best processes and management technology that the company has to offer in place, to ensure its delivery to you.

Clearly the intense sense of anxiety seemed to have dissipated.

This core team understood how things needed to be done and was able to convince the Air Force to develop Joint STARS according to a Grumman proven Critical Program Decisions and Events process. This involved the following nine critical decisions and events that occurred during the Joint STARS development that were essential to the survival of the program, its success during Desert Storm, and the decision to proceed with production:

- Implement prototype plan, December 1986
- Delivery of aircraft No. 1, July 1987
- First flight, March 1988
- Militarized computer insertion, September 1988
- Radar demonstrations, December 1988 and April 1989
- Conduct early look of radar data, February 1990
- Conduct operational flight demonstration 1, October 1990
- Deploy to Desert Storm, December 1990
- Advanced technology insertion, March 1992

CONCLUSION

The evolution of Joint STARS began with the successful RGWS demonstration in the mid-1970s, followed by the Pave Mover program in the early 1980s. The award of the Joint STARS program in 1985 capped more than a decade of investment and the creativity, innovation, and perseverance of the engineering and proposal team. Joint STARS was a formidable undertaking because it was an unprecedented development of a battlefield surveillance system. Program and engineering management provided the leadership essential to attract top talent from Grumman and industry while guiding the program through its early development to successful deployment in Operation Desert Storm.

The next chapter examines how Grumman electronic warfare (EW) design teams developed a long line of EW aircraft systems. The EA-6A was developed in close cooperation with the U.S. Marine Corps, EW equipment suppliers, and a program/engineering team that skillfully modified an A-6A airframe, designed an EW crew station, and integrated EW and avionics systems. The EA-6B was the first dedicated, bottom-up EW system that began as a concept study briefed to top Grumman management as part of its open door policy to foster new ideas. It featured a highly modified and strengthened airframe, a crew of four, and a new EW avionics suite. Grumman was responsible for system software and total weapon system integration. Many variants of the EA-6B were developed, and it remains in service today. The USAF variable sweep wing EF-111A followed in 1974 as a tactical jamming system that featured outstanding aerodynamic and EW performance due to its ability to escort attacking aircraft as well as maintain a high loiter time standoff jamming orbit.

Chapter 9

LINEAGE OF ELECTRONIC WARFARE

EA-6A AND EA-6B

When the need arose for a standoff jammer, Grumman came up with the EA-6A, configured with the Navy Bureau–developed electronic counter-measure (ECM) system for signal analysis and jammer pod control. Lew Evans, vice president of Business Development at Grumman, was informed by Dr. Gene Fubini of Department of Defense Research and Engineering (DDR&E) of its "inadequacy," and suggested he look at the system being proposed for the North American RA-5C that was designed by Airborne Instruments Laboratory (AIL). Bob Miller was on educational leave at Massachusetts Institute of Technology (MIT), so Evans originally tagged Bob Nafis to detail the Navy mission using the EA-6A and see whether AIL management was interested in making a proposal to Grumman using its space, weight, and power provisions. About this time the RA-5C was cancelled due to overweight, and was unneeded as a nuclear delivery system; AIL became very interested. Tom Guarino and Bob Salzmann did advanced EA-6 (bowlegs) studies while Lew Scheuer, Don Cook, and Arnold Siedon did studies to improve the EA-6A. Miller returned from MIT and was made vice president, program manager for the EA-6B. It was a very successful program and continued in many variants, as well as new applications today, thanks to a team of creative engineers and managers from all disciplines.

EA-6A

The seeds for the EA-6A development (Fig. 9.1) were sown back in 1959 when the U.S. Marine Corps (USMC) developed follow-on requirements for the F3D-2Q Skynight (EF-10B), which was deployed to Vietnam in 1965 to support the first air-to-ground strike against surface-to-air missiles in history. Airborne electronic warfare (EW) was primarily conducted to support bombing missions in North Vietnam.

Grumman had won the A2F-1 attack aircraft development contract in 1959, and in 1960 Lew Scheuer, project engineer, performed a feasibility study for an A2F-1 ECM variant to replace the F3D-2Q. The USMC got what it wanted amid much push back from the Pentagon. Al Rogers, the A2F

Fig. 9.1   EA-6A.

program manager at the time, worked closely with several key USMC officers to make this program happen. The officers were Lieutenant General Phil Shutler; Lieutenant Colonel Ed Finlayson, A6A (A2F-1) program manager; Major Howie Wolf, project officer of EA-6A development; and Major Bob Farley, Bureau of Weapons (BuWeps) Avionics Branch—ECM systems. Further design studies were performed in 1961, and a congressional budget line was established for the EA-6A in Fiscal Year (FY) 1962, beginning in October 1961.

Late in the summer of 1962, the Joint Chiefs of Staff were to vote on the production go-ahead of the EA-6A. The U.S. Air Force (USAF) voted no, but the Navy/USMC gave their OK for production. However, Dr. Eugene Fubini, director of research in the Office of the Director, DDR&E, for all intents and purposes said if the military cannot decide, then he could not give the go-ahead on production.

Bob Salzmann came to Grumman in April 1962 from a small company that checked out the system and jammers for the B-52 fleet, and went to work on the EA-6A navigation system. He became ill with a burst appendix and was side-tracked for a while; as chance would have it, he began to do analytic studies of the effectiveness of jammers with Lew Scheuer and Arnold Siedon of Grumman. He basically took the jamming equations and began to analyze the effectiveness of the EA-6A jammers. Don Cook and Arnold Siedon undertook a study to improve the EA-6A using receiver technology from Loral.

The two Grumman people who acted as key technical leads as the EA-6A concept and design matured were Arthur Karle and Sal Migliore. When they came to Grumman, they brought with them a storehouse of knowledge based on the design, integration, and flight test of a USAF program to put a high-power, automatic support jamming system on a large aircraft. This aircraft system had integrated receivers and jammers and addressed the same frequency range of interest to the USMC and U.S. Navy.

The EA-6A was an ECM platform intended to blind and confuse adversary defenses as well as to suppress enemy air defenses. It carried a wide variety of ECM equipment that featured a very sensitive antenna system to detect enemy radar and communications frequencies, and a full spectrum of jammers that would disrupt enemy radars and communication systems.

The EA-6A design challenge was to incorporate a broadband receiving system (VHF to K band frequencies) that was originally intended as a reconnaissance system for ground and airborne application, and integrate it with existing ALQ-76 jamming pods the USMC was already using. These two systems were not designed to work together, so an effort was undertaken to provide some limited receive-while-jam capability, with Art Karle as the lead designer. Although Grumman was not a significant design agent in the EA-6A's jamming system, a lot of experience was gained. Fundamentally there was no "look through" capability in the receiver system when the jammers were turned on, and the jammers had to be steered in concert with each other. They could not be steered independently. The more advanced jamming techniques of pseudo-random noise generation could not be implemented with the existing magnetron technology, which is why the EA-6B jammers used the more advanced traveling wave tube technology.

Basically, the A-2F (A-6A) airframe design philosophy (i.e., heavy bomb loads carried on wing-mounted pylons, ample fuselage volume, high internal fuel capacity, and a large center of gravity range) allowed easy growth to the EA-6A and eventually the EA-6B. The EA-6A was outwardly distinguished from the A-6A by a large streamlined fairing mounted on top of the vertical stabilizer. This fairing housed signal surveillance and the receiver antenna system (ALQ-86). The fuselage was slightly increased in length to accommodate ECM gear, and the second seat was occupied by an electronic countermeasures officer, called an ECMO.

Specifically, the EA-6A carried the ALQ-41(X-band frequency band track breaker), the ALQ-51(S-frequency band deception jammer and track breaker), and the ALQ-55 (VHF data link jammer).This system was integrated with up to 15 steerable high-power radar jammers housed in five external streamlined podded units: the ALQ-31 jammer pod, the ALQ-54 expendable countermeasures passive decoys pod, and the ALQ-76 E/F frequency band noise deception pod. Each of the ALQ-76 pods had its own control panel; although it may have required all three of the transmitters in the pod to be steered to the same direction, each pod could be steered independently. These pods were mounted on wing pylons and the lower fuselage centerline. Two chaff dispensing pods (ALE-32 and ALE-41) could be interchanged with jammer pods on the wing pylons. The EA-6A could also carry and launch the AGM-45 Shrike antiradiation missile.

There is no question that the EA-6A weapon system, and the first-time use of such a system in a tactical ECM escort role, had a profound effect on reducing Navy and USMC strike and reconnaissance losses against the stiff Soviet-supplied air defense system in North Vietnam. Moreover, during Operation Linebacker, the EA-6As provided key ECM support for the B-52s, as well as completely protecting USAF reconnaissance drones when assigned as ECM escort.

EA-6B

The EA-6B Prowler (Fig. 9.2) was the first aircraft designed "wheels up" as an EW dedicated weapon system. Put another way, the EA-6B was the first aircraft designed as a fully integrated tactical jamming system (TJS). Designed in early 1966 to replace the EKA-3B Skywarrior for the U.S. Navy, the EA-6B differed from the earlier EA-6A in two major respects: the nose section was extended 54 in. longer to accommodate four crewmen, and it carried a more advanced TJS.

The U.S. Navy and USMC projections of the advancing threat through the 1970s resulted in the formal release of operational requirements documents in November 1965. Tom Guarino, who was in Operations Analysis at the time, was performing cost-effectiveness studies with Bob Salzmann. Salzmann had joined this team during the preliminary design effort, and played a key role during the Navy study. They illustrated how advanced tactical jamming systems in an advanced EA-6 (bowlegs) could dramatically

Fig. 9.2   EA-6B.

improve A-6 attack effectiveness while minimizing mission attrition. Guarino and Salzmann extensively briefed the Navy and got it interested in a similar program, which ultimately led to the EA-6B. An internal competition of sorts had developed in Grumman's EW world since the improved EA-6A study and the EA-6 (bowlegs) were both being briefed to the Navy and USMC. These "young tigers," as Lew Evans called them, had total access to his office. Tom Kane from Business Development knew all the key Navy and USMC personnel, and developed the marketing strategies and government briefings that were essential for the program success of both the EA-6A and the EA-6B.

Bob Salzmann became the architect of the new EA-6 (bowlegs) system; as a result, he looked at a wide variety microwave receivers and jammers from AIL, Melpar, and Raytheon as well as four major scenarios involving theaters of operation and threats. Initially the studies covered four frequency bands employed in operations in the Fulda gap (a key German area of strategic importance in the Cold War), in Central Europe, a Chinese scenario, and a Cuban scenario reflecting the Cuban missile crisis. At the time, Vern Kramer, USMC and Navy Plant Representative Office (NAVPRO) at Grumman was able to provide intelligence estimates to Grumman as part of the Navy-funded contract, and these data were very useful in defining the requirements for the basic EA-6B EW system. In addition to these four scenarios that were studied, the four frequency bands initially developed were selected because they were active in Vietnam. As soon as it became apparent that Grumman and its subcontractors could develop these high-power jammers, Grumman received a follow-on contract (EXCAP) for additional frequency bands that covered the remaining threats of interest from the four scenarios.

Grumman used this approach in an unsolicited concept development phase (CDP) proposal in June 1964. The EA-6B development was directed to Grumman as a sole source contract to save time and money, and covered the project definition phase ($5 million) as well as R&D work on long lead and high-risk items ($132 million). In October 1965, the Navy stretched the CDP contract schedule in order to allow the number of crewman to be increased from two to four, and to design a strengthened airframe design with increased fatigue life.

The four crewmen (a pilot plus three ECMOs) sat side-by-side in tandem cockpits. As in the case of the EA-6A, the EA-6B featured a streamlined antenna fairing on the top of the vertical fin that housed sensitive surveillance receivers and upper band frequency receivers. The airframe was substantially modified to extend fatigue life and to provide strength margins for long-term growth. It featured higher thrust J-52 engines that enabled it to match or exceed the performance of other strike aircraft. The EA-6B went through many development upgrades: Basic, EXCAP (expanded capability), ICAP

Fig. 9.3   ICAP 1 NPE Team.

(improved capability) I, ICAP-II, ADVCAP (advanced capability, which didn't go to production), and ICAP-III.

Figure 9.3 shows the ICAP-I NPE team. Standing (left to right) are Al Gurkewitz, Ed Cartosky, Bill Gorden, Tony Lawrence, Roy Driver, Ralph (Zeke) Zasdeskas, Larry Schadegg, Bill Dwinelle, unknown, Dan Henderson, Jim Vahelick, unknown, and Ed Binan. Kneeling (left to right) are Don Zielinski, Bob Scholly, Rich De Canio, Doug Hulsen, unknown, Fred White, unknown, unknown.

The ICAP-II development provided the EA-6B with the capability to fire HARM missiles that were more capable than the Shrike missiles. The ADVCAP was a very aggressive program to improve the EA-6B flying qualities and to upgrade the avionics and electronic warfare systems. Briefly, it consisted of a full-scale development (FSD) portion that developed a CFE Receiver Processor Group (RPG), a replacement for the ALQ-99 receivers, a GFE ALQ-149 communication jammer; a Vehicle Enhancement Program (VEP) to improve flying qualities and performance; and an Avionic Improvement Program (AIP) that included such systems as new multi-function displays for all crew positions and a heads-up display for the pilot. The ICAP-III version consisted of the ALQ-218 receiver, very precise selective-reactive radar jamming and deception, all-aspect rapid passive ranging, and a multifunction information distribution system (MIDS) that provided the Link 16 data link system. The MIDS was the terminal that enabled Link-16.

Artie Karle and Sal Migliore returned to Preliminary Design and worked closely with Tom Guarino and Bob Salzmann. There were many important contributions and contributors to the success of these developments. AIL was selected to provide the complete integrated jamming system that later became the ALQ-99. AIL subcontracted out much of the jamming subsystem to Raytheon and AEL. The Grumman technical team (Tom Guarino, Artie Karle, Sal Migliore, and Bob Salzmann) had great influence over the tactical jamming system (TJS) architecture during the study phase when the concepts were developed. Two of the key technical attributes of the ALQ-99 were jamming transmitters with 10 times the power of the ALQ-76 used on the EA-6A, and a receiving system that employed monopulse direction-of-arrival measurements. Both of these state-of-the-art systems were developed successfully.

Bob Salzmann and Bob Scholly recalled several events that occurred during the testing and deployment of the EA-6B. Several events involved Don King and Ed Cartosky, the EA-6B test pilots. King conducted test flights (Fig. 9.4) near the coastline of Cuba to collect data on the radars with Bob Scholly. During one of the final Navy preliminary evaluation (NPE) flights flown by Ed Cartosky, the Navy air traffic controller mistook the EA-6B as a reconnaissance flight and vectored the aircraft into Cuban airspace. Needless to say, the EA-6B exited the scene quickly, though it briefly became a State Department issue.

The EA-6B was a rugged airframe able to withstand very high sink rates during landing that emulated a "controlled crash." On such a landing test, Don King hurt his back and had to spend some time recovering from the incident. In the meantime, the test aircraft was taken aloft by an A-6 pilot who needed flight test time, but was not familiar with the EA-6B flight characteristics. The EA-6B was designed to have automatic spin recovery by simply letting go of the stick during a spin so the aircraft would self-correct and recover. This test aircraft also had a drogue chute that would be deployed during spin testing if anything went wrong during the test. The A-6 jock put the aircraft into a spin, fought the spin, and popped the drogue chute. The chute was released and the aircraft spun in the opposite direction, whereupon the pilot ejected. The aircraft then righted itself and crashed into the sea some 350 miles from shore. No pilot error occurred in the incident.

Fig. 9.4   EA-6B M1 test flight.

A pivotal event that occurred at the Bureau Inspection Survey (BIS) formal trials held at Eglin Air Force base in Florida simulated Soviet threats. Grumman had built into the system a new jamming technique called pseudo-random noise, which was developed at the Calverton flight test facility. Bob Salzmann and the EW team had quietly developed the theory and tested it against Nike sites on Long Island with outstanding success. During the very last mission of the BIS trials, the Navy allowed Grumman to test this new technology vs the more traditional noise jamming used by the Navy in its evaluations. The results were astounding or, to put it in a more common phrase by Navy ECMO, "Holy S–t!" These tests prompted major positive reviews at the highest levels of DOD.

The first EA-6B squadron, VAQ-132, went to war on the USS *America* in Operation Linebacker. The tactics development used in mission planning by the EA-6Bs was highly classified, and at the time only a few Grumman and Navy personnel had the necessary clearances. Several engineers, including Salzmann and Scholly, flew missions as back seat operators in the EA-6B during continental United States (CONUS) workups prior to deployment. When VAQ-132 aircraft stood off the Vietnam coast and collected electronic intelligence with the sensitive on-board receiver systems, some Grumman engineers were on board.

The last story had to do with the gold plating of the EA-6B canopy. During development of aircraft weapon systems like the EA-6B, testing of full-scale aircraft or aircraft components was carried out in an anechoic chamber used to house equipment for performing measurements of antenna radiation patterns, electromagnetic compatibility (EMC), and radar cross-section measurements. While testing of the EA-6B in Grumman's anechoic chamber (the largest in the world at that time), it was found that microscopic gold plating of the canopy provided significant radio frequency (RF) attenuation, and reduced jammer radiation below safe levels for the crew. Senator Proxmire was famous at the time for his Golden Fleece Award, which was given for wasteful government programs. The gold-plated EA-6B was unfairly singled out for this award.

In July 1965 Bob Miller was deputy program director reporting to Jim Zusi, vice president of the A6, EA-6A, and EA-6B programs. Miller would take over all EW programs in ensuing years. Tom Guarino became the electronic warfare systems program engineering manager with Bob Salzmann as technical assistant. Tom Brancati was systems project engineer and Gerry Gottlieb was subsystems project engineer. Artie Karl assumed responsibility of electronic warfare systems, and Sal Migliore had all onboard systems. Key people on the vehicle side were Richard "Bugs" Waldt, vehicle project engineer; Frank Hardenburgh, overall structural design; Bill Schooley, wing design; Cliff Hoelzer and Tom Griffin,

Fig. 9.5   Team photo taken during the NPE of the EA-6B in February 1970.

propulsion; Lou Byars, aerodynamics; and Ned Sweeney, crew and equipment.

Figure 9.5 is a team photo taken during the Navy preliminary evaluation (NPE) of the EA-6B in February 1970, which shows many key personnel responsible for the creation of the EA-6B, as well as members of the design and flight test team from Grumman, Navy, and Marine Corps. Standing from right to left in front of EA-6B No. 4 are Marty Lachow, Don King, Bob Salzmann, Pete Beresford, Tom Johnson, Fred Wilmont, Bill Peake, Bill Dwinelle, Tom Guarino, unknown, Al Gurkewitz, unknown, Jerry Mellman, Jim Vahelik, Bill Arnold, Cliff Lennon, Lenny Zambroski, Meek Kiker, Pete Kantor, Ken Moser, Ed Binan, Byron Lane, Nick Yokivich, Fred McCloskey, Tom Bamrick, Andy Brand, Ed McCormack, unknown, unknown, Ed Jackson, unknown, Ralph Rensfeld, Jerry Lang, unknown, unknown, unknown, unknown, John Kretzing, unknown, Arnold Seidon, unknown, unknown, unknown. Kneeling from right to left are Roy Henning, Charlie Dorchak, Bob Scholly, Mike Spenser, Tom McAlister, Al Russo, Morty Proper, Roger Bush, Jerry Hammer, Tony Lawrence, unknown, unknown, Frank D'Done, unknown, unknown, Tom Flores, unknown.

Another key decision that led to successive EA-6B developments involved the mission computer. The A-6A was having reliability problems with the rotating drum computer, so the EA-6B adopted the IBM 4Pi, which had a core memory/general processor (no moving parts) that could function as a 32-bit machine for the needed navigation precision, and a 16-bit machine for less-demanding tasks. The big decisions, based on cost, required AIL to use the Grumman computer for the signal processing algorithms, versus designing its own processor. As a result, the navigation, tactical jamming system, and some radar functions were all in the same processor. Initially, AIL was doing all the software related to the control of the tactical jamming system and Grumman was doing very little. The tactical jamming system was so high in power, with a lookthrough capability, that ground clutter was coming back into the system due to the large pulses of energy. During development, Grumman became very involved in all aspects of the mission software, at both AIL and Grumman. Grumman discovered many new and complex issues (e.g., earth effects) relating to the operation and jamming techniques that required very sophisticated software solutions. As the system and software architecture picture unfolded, the Grumman team put together a computer-controlled system with the whole aircraft integrated into the system. Bob Scholly managed the software development related to the receiver side of the EA-6B system and played a pivotal role in the development cycle. AIL had a very good design team that worked well with Grumman, and AIL produced very good state-of-the-art technology equipment.

Probably one of the most significant people who joined the team was Bob Fredette. He was a radar designer from Sperry who had worked on the Tartar and Talos shipboard surface-to-air missile (SAM) systems, probably the most modern SAMs of the day. While at Grumman he became a very effective radar jammer analyst, providing both an analytic and a practical foundation for new and effective jamming techniques. Bob Salzmann developed much of the ECM architecture as well as jamming techniques.

Al Gurkewitz also played an important role in the design team. He was a participant in the basic development as well as future variants, and he was instrumental in bringing Bob Fredette to Grumman. Gurkewitz was a physically large man with a great mind, and possessed a "big heart," as Salzmann remembered him. Recall the anecdots in Chapter 8 about Gurkewitz and his Movers (teammates) on the Pave Mover F-111 program, and in Chapter 7 regarding Gurkewitz's request for boots for the team testing the advanced radar jamming system (ARJS) in the desert. During the development of the EA-6B program, Bob Salzmann's house burned down in the middle of the Long Island winter. Salzmann had five children at home at the time, and Gurkewitz very kindly gave him warm winter coats for his children. It could be said that this kind act was part of the Grumman family tradition, but no one can deny Al Gurkewitz's care for his fellow employees.

A significant trend in the history of the EA-6B was that more and more of the functionality of the TJS was performed by mission software vs. hardware, and Grumman was responsible for the mission software. One of the key designers during this period was Gerry Mellman. He ran the System Design and Analysis group that conducted many of the studies that preceded the next development and led the development of the software requirements during these programs. Morty Proper became program manager and worked closely with Mellman until he retired. They were involved in many of the studies related to future developments.

The use of the AGM-88 High Speed Anti-Radiation Missile (HARM) grew out of a need to meet specific carrier deployments with various squadron combinations of A-6 and A-7 aircraft that were HARM capable. The A-6 HARM development program was proceeding slowly at the Naval Air Weapons Station, China Lake, California, so the Grumman EA-6B program, with Navy concurrence, came forward and said, "We can do it." From go-ahead on this development, the HARM met the carrier deployment schedule. Bob Scholly played a significant role in the HARM development. This was a model development program in that no requirements creep occurred in meeting the schedule on time. The HARM program was an excellent cooperative effort among Grumman, NAVAIR, and the HARM builder, Texas Instruments.

The EA-6B ICAP III development grew out of the aftermath of the fall of the Berlin Wall, the termination of EA-6A ADVCAP development, and the EF-111A Systems Improvement Program (SIP). Dan O'Neill took over the leadership of the EA-6B program. With his vast EA-6B program experience and logistics expertise, he brought stability to the program as well as an excellent rapport with the Navy. O'Neill led the charge on new EW developments as leader of the program. His philosophy was evidenced by his remarks in 1983, "Maintaining the status quo is not good enough in electronic warfare. Because the EW field is constantly changing at a rapid pace, we are continually revising the EA-6B system not only to meet today's threat but to anticipate tomorrow's threats."

Bob Scholly became chief technical advisor to the program. Grumman overcame program issues related to production EA-6B airframe structural fatigue problems and NAVAIR relationships due to the ADVCAP cancellation by proposing a winning technical solution, even though Grumman didn't expect to be the lowest bidder. Scholly was the capture team leader for the proposal. Under his technical leadership, the proposal process led to the selection of selective reactive jamming and all-aspect rapid passive location as Grumman's technical discriminators. This approach won the ICAP III contract, and was highly praised by DOD. It since has been integrated into the EA-18G Growler.

EF-111A

Bob Miller was director of EW programs, which included the EA-6B and EF-111 programs; as such, he was responsible for all new business pursuits and production EW programs. Bob Salzmann was Bob Miller's right-hand man from a strategic and technical perspective. Vern Kramer became program director of the EF-111 program when Miller left the program, and he provided excellent leadership in guiding the program through development, as well as developing new improvements to the system. Tom Street became the EF-111A program manager, and Bob Salzmann became deputy program manager.

The USAF wanted to replace the EB-66 and the EB-57 electronic warfare aircraft. John Cunnif took the lead in Advanced Systems to conduct conceptual EW design studies centered on threat requirements, system solutions, and suitable aircraft platforms. Studies were awarded to both Grumman and General Dynamics by the USAF, and Grumman was selected as prime contractor in late 1974. The EF-111A Raven (Fig. 9.6), a modification of the operational F-111A, was an excellent tactical jamming system (TJS) for the USAF. It could provide protection for strike aircraft by standing off from a target area in jamming orbit or by escorting the strike aircraft. With its supersonic penetration capability and long range due to its variable sweep wing technology, large internal payload capacity, night terrain following capability, and reasonable cost, the EF-111A was an effective TJS.

The primary EF-111A EW electronics were installed in the weapon's bay and in a 16-ft-long, streamlined, canoe-shaped radome located under the fuselage, much like that used on the F-111A Pave Mover program. The transmitters were located in the canoe-shaped radome, and the whole installation weighed about 6000 lb. Receivers were located in a streamlined pod mounted on top of the vertical fin, similar to the EA-6B installation. Extensive crew and equipment redesign occurred in the cockpit, with flight and navigation controls moved to the pilot's side, and all the EW

Fig. 9.6   EF-111A Raven prototype.

instrumentation and controls installed on the ECMO side of the cockpit. The EF-111A did not possess the Shrike or HARM missile capability of the EA-6B, but rather relied on speed, acceleration, and tactics for self-defense. In that regard, the P&W TF-30 engines were upgraded to the more powerful F-111D engines.

Because this was basically integrating the existing ALQ-99 into a new airframe, there was not very much new design in the TJS electronics. What was new was the exciter (which produces the jammer modulations) and the mission software (tailored to USAF requirements). The two key designers were Dave Tarbell, who provided the analytical basis for the exciter design, and Tony Pizzimenti, who was responsible for designing and developing the mission software. Tarbell's brilliance led to a new exciter and modulator design with optimized software. In his private life, Tarbell was a Unitarian minister; at Grumman, he was "business casual" in his dress way before its time.

The software controlling the modulation of the EA-6B and the EF-111 was traded back and forth between programs, and this process was instrumental in getting the most out of the system hardware. The EF-111A enjoyed a good service life from initial operating capability (IOC) in 1983 until 1998, at which point the EA-6B provided the electronic warfare role for the United States.

SYSTEMS INTEGRATION: *EA-6B* AND *EF-111A*

One of Grumman's inherent strengths was world class system integration capabilities and facilities that were developed and employed on all the key mission area programs, namely the F-14A (air superiority, multimission) and F-14D (air superiority/strike attack), the A-6 (all-weather attack), the E-2 (airborne early warning), the E-8 (battlefield surveillance), and the EA-6B (electronic warfare). Each of the aircraft weapon systems had a significant portion of its takeoff gross weight and cost devoted to the total avionic system. With the advent of the E-1B in the mid-1950s, this capability was carefully put in place as Grumman hired some of the best avionic engineers in the industry to help create the aforementioned programs and became totally responsible, as prime contractor, for the integration, management, and performance of these complex aircraft weapon systems. Basically, systems integration is putting together all the major avionic systems [CFE (contractor furnished equipment) and GFE (government furnished equipment)], subsystems, software, and supporting subsystems (e.g., cabling, data buses, installation racks, power, cooling, etc.) in a realistic operating environment of the aircraft weapon system that houses the systems, and thoroughly wringing out the total system prior to actual testing.

I have selected the EA-6B and EF-111A as representative examples of system integration capability and facilities that were developed. The basic EA-6B avionic system was almost 18% of takeoff gross weight (9700 lb out of 55,000 lb) and represented about 40% of the flyaway cost (i.e., the production cost of one aircraft in a production run that included the airframe, engines, aircraft subsystems, seats and furnishings, and the entire avionic system but no weapons). In like manner, the E-2C had 11,600 lb of avionic system weight in a 52,000 lb aircraft that amounted to 35% of the flyaway cost. Note the variations in the percentage of flyaway cost are driven by the type of avionic equipment, the number of aircraft purchased in a fiscal year, the fiscal year in question, and the rate of inflation.

The Systems Integration Test Station (SITS; Fig. 9.7) was a full-scale laboratory with real crew stations and equipment located to represent actual aircraft configuration. The SITS permitted avionic hardware integration and checkout with a large array of radar simulators. A computer setup was located near the SITS for checking out all the software in the entire computer subsystem.

The anechoic chamber (Fig. 9.8), the largest in the world at the time (1970s–1980s), could accommodate full-scale aircraft in a wheels-up configuration. Designed to allow full-power avionic system operation with all systems operating simultaneously, its use shortened development time by two to three years by allowing complete electromagnetic compatibility tests and full system operation 24 hours per day.

The electronic warfare test range (EWTR) (Fig. 9.9) was a group of radars and signal sources representative of varying frequencies in real operational

Fig. 9.7   EA-6B SITS.

Fig. 9.8 EF-111A suspended in the anechoic chamber.

scenarios, and was used in the systems integration of the entire system in the SITS as well as flight testing.

CONCLUSION

Grumman became one of the world's prominent aircraft electronic warfare system developers. Several key factors contributed to this accomplishment:

- Grumman's informal organizational structure allowed the EA-6B concept to quickly flow to top management allowing "young tigers" to run fast with adequate resources to develop the concept and brief the U.S. Navy.
- Innovation, creativity, and persistence resulted in Grumman becoming responsible for all major software and weapon system integration of the EA-6B.

Fig. 9.9 The EWTR used for the ground test of the SITS as well as flight testing.

- Leadership from a succession of program managers and engineering led to imaginative proposals resulting in new derivatives and product lines.
- World class system integration facilities, including the world's largest anechoic chamber and an electronic warfare test range, led to more rapid system integration, new system technologies to counter advanced threats, and considerable savings in test time and cost.

The first nine chapters of this book have identified over 555 people who helped create more than 70 aircraft, aircraft weapon systems, demonstrators, and a variety of advanced designs that spanned 65 years. The final chapter, Grumman in Perspective, discusses the past and present roles of the aircraft designer. Profiles of Grumman's designers are presented, followed by a discussion of the designs undertaken. The role of the "avionicers" (avionic engineers and many associated disciplines) and software engineers will be presented as Grumman transitioned to a premier integrator and manager of aircraft weapon systems. Lastly, the chapter will attempt to characterize the traits and achievements of the aircraft designers and their teammates in creativity, versatility, innovation, customer focus, and leadership, among other areas.

Chapter 10

GRUMMAN IN PERSPECTIVE

I have endeavored to remember and write down the names of Grumman's prominent aircraft designers and the key people who were involved with the creation of Grumman aircraft. Thanks to the inputs from so many Grumman and Northrop Grumman retirees and friends, and a lot of research, I have been able to highlight their contributions, provide insight into the design of the aircraft and its systems, and relate some anecdotes relating to the design teams. To date, over 555 people have been identified (more than 335 individual names) who were involved in the evolution of some 74 aircraft, aircraft derivatives, demonstrators, and selected future designs.

The nucleus of Grumman founders started work for Loening Aircraft in the early 1920s before they formed the Grumman Aircraft Engineering Corporation in 1929. The Grumman Corporation as a business entity lasted 65 years before being acquired by Northrop in 1994—an amazing achievement. Even more impressive is the fact that many of the design teams in airborne early warning (AEW), electronic warfare (EW), and battlefield surveillance/command and control/battle management are national assets, and are still producing new variants of aircraft weapon systems today as part of Northrop Grumman more than 80 years after Grumman was founded.

As we begin to characterize what makes good designers and summarize their traits and achievements, it is important to look at the historical progression in the role of an airplane designer to a more complex role of balancing a myriad of complex requirements to meet tomorrow's demanding environments. In identifying the prominent aircraft designers and their key teammates, I have used a classic definition of a designer from a brief article written by Joe Lippert in 1985, entitled, "Who Is an Airplane Designer," and a more broadened definition of the role of the designer and future challenges discussed by Irv Waaland in his 1991 Wright Brothers lecture, "Technology in the Lives of an Aircraft Designer." In addition, with the advent of more sophisticated aircraft weapon systems, the role of the avionic engineer and associated disciplines in radar, low observables signature, systems analysis, software, antenna system design, weapon integration, systems engineering, and the like were instrumental in the creation of major aircraft weapon systems (e.g., A-6A, E-2A, Joint STARS, EA-6B, F-14A) and their major variants (e.g., A-6E/F, E-2C, EA-6B ICAP, F-14B/D).

Joe Lippert said that it is difficult to define the line between preliminary designer, project engineer, manager, chief engineer, and so on. In most cases, all these principals were involved, and in some cases, one person established the configuration of the vehicle. He suggested that the term "designer" should be limited to the preliminary designer, who is the one who defines the original physical characteristics of the vehicle (i.e., transforms a concept into a drawing of the vehicle that he or she believes will satisfy the performance requirements).

The preliminary designer does not have to be an expert in all technologies that are involved in the design of a vehicle, but must be aware of the interaction of the various technologies and provide in advance a vehicle design that will permit later design detail changes such that the original definition of the vehicle is not compromised. The selected configuration is the result of the efforts of many designers, such as the structural designer, the aero and engine people, electronics designers, and so on. To this end, the team must estimate weights, size, aero requirements, structural requirements, power plant selection, accommodations for personnel and equipment, and the like. Hopefully, when the vehicle is finally turned over to detail designers, the estimates will be sufficiently good that no major changes will be required.

Irv Waaland stated that the basic tenets of good design have not changed since the Wright brothers, but our techniques have.

> When he entered the industry in 1953, the initial introduction of jet power and swept wings had occurred and most products reflected evolutionary growth in capability and complexity. Avionics were black boxes that were installed more than integrated into the airframe.... Designers were expected to understand the need for compromise and to be familiar with the requirements of other disciplines. The process was aided by the relatively small size of the design team, the frequency and similarities of subsequent designs, and the validity of many rules of thumb and empirical relationships. The individual engineer generally had a thorough understanding of his assumptions and results; reasonableness checks were frequent and natural. Good products needed good engineering, then as now, but the size, integration, and training of the design teams coupled with much, much less bureaucracy and security constraints, generally fostered a good understanding of the total task.

> Over time, we have witnessed significant increases in system requirements and aircraft complexity, as well as an explosion of technical sophistication in the arena of engineering tools and methods.

The complexity of both the product and the process has significantly increased the size of the design workforce leading to isolation of individual engineering disciplines... a major deterrent to "natural" concurrent engineering. The advances in technology have also led to increasing specialization. The need for broadly experienced integration engineers, people who are generalists in the mold of the Wright Brothers, has never been greater, but the reduced quantity of development programs coupled with the complexity of individual technology areas has inhibited multi-disciple training and growth. Aircraft design is a full-time task as illustrated by Kelly Johnson's penchant for focusing on one product at a time.... I believe the technology growth that allows us to design superior aircraft must be accompanied by full utilization of the ability of individuals to think beyond the output of a computer.

In the mid-1950s Grumman was not a hotbed of avionic engineering[*] talent, although Grumman had an excellent and adequate size staff of avionic engineers to satisfy program requirements at the time. There were brilliant aircraft designers at Grumman, but not so many "avionicers," according to Jerry Norton's recollections. Most of that category was still in the big electronic companies like General Electric, Hazeltine, Westinghouse, Hughes, and Sperry. Up until that time, the government dictated what electronic hardware would be utilized to satisfy a mission (or missions) requirement, and this hardware was furnished to the aircraft builder as government furnished equipment (GFE). Electronic hardware suppliers supported Grumman in the integration and testing of that equipment.

During the late 1950s, Grumman made the transition from an aircraft builder to an aircraft weapon system designer and integrator, commonly referred to as being the systems manager, who managed the total weapon system procurement and delivery to the government and guaranteed performance of the weapon system. With the advent of the E-1B Tracker, the W2F-1 Hawkeye, and the A2F-1 Intruder, Grumman was the prime contractor and the systems manager, and began hiring top talent from the electronics industry. These were the first big system integration jobs with Grumman as the systems manager. In the early days, Grumman landing gear designers were as good as the landing gear builders' engineers and dictated how the gear was to be designed. In like manner, Grumman avionics, subsystem, and software engineers became as knowledgeable as the well-known radar, antenna and "black box" houses. Grumman was one of the first companies that recognized and developed a strong systems engineering

---

* Avionics is often interchanged with electronics. Avionics refers to the science and technology of electronics and the development of electronic devices or systems as applied to aerospace applications.

department by virtue of the state-of-the-art avionics that were installed in the A-6, Mohawk, E-2, F-14, and so on. Initially, according to Joe Rodriguez, Grumman could not go anywhere to find system engineers that could tie all the systems, displays subsystems, and software together. Newt Speiss, Bob Watson, and Dan Collins were instrumental in laying the framework for systems engineering processes and the training necessary for Grumman's engineers. Grumman engineers dictated detailed system design requirements and specifications. This was followed by extensive simulation, systems engineering, component tests at the supplier as well as at Grumman, and complete systems integration and testing because Grumman was responsible for total systems performance. Most of the radar and black boxes were now supplied to the government as contractor furnished equipment (CFE) as a major portion (50–60%) of the overall contract to produce the aircraft weapon system. The bottom line was that on such programs as the A-6, E-2, F-14, Joint STARS, and EA-6B, Grumman developed what I refer to as a long line of in-house, world-class avionic and systems engineering talent.

DESIGNER PROFILES

The Grumman Aircraft Engineering Corporation experimental design, build, and test team in the 1930s was a gifted and experienced group that Roy Grumman hand-picked while many of them were working at Loening Aircraft and hired during the 1930s. Roy Grumman, Bill Schwendler, Jake Swirbul, and Julie Holpit were the nucleus of this team, which also included Dick Hutton, who was a mechanic in the Loening shop, and Ralston Stalb, a hydrodynamicist.

Roy Grumman (Fig. 10.1) designed and tested commercial and military aircraft at Loening, and he also designed and flight tested all Grumman aircraft through the end of World War II. His design philosophy was to protect the pilot, hence the ruggedness of the Wildcat and the Hellcat. Every new designer at Grumman was inculcated with the design principle that "the last part of the aircraft to fail will be the cockpit," in order to increase survivability in both a carrier crash landing and aerial combat. Grumman's design influence extended into the late 1950s with the Gulfstream I and the Ag Cat—a time span of over 40 years.

Fig. 10.1   Roy Grumman.

Bill Schwendler (Fig. 10.2) was chief engineer and a superb structural designer. His design philosophy was to "judiciously apply a factor of 2 (the Schwendler Factor) to a structure that met specifications to make it twice as strong as needed." From 1930 to 1950, his emergence as the chief designer of an engineering and manufacturing team that produced such formidable aircraft as the F4F Wildcat, F6F Hellcat, TBF Avenger, and F9F Panther paralleled the rise of Grumman to a preeminent position in this country's aircraft industry during World War II. The company earned the affectionate sobriquet Grumman Iron Works, but the salute from Navy and Marine pilots didn't come by accident. Mr. Schwendler, as we "young pups" addressed him, conducted bi-weekly design reviews well into the 1970s on the development

Fig. 10.2 Bill Schwendler.

of the F-14A—a span of over 40 years. The overarching design imperatives of Roy Grumman and Bill Schwendler to protect the pilot and design a robust structure were proven time and again in World War II and were carried out by all future design teams.

Although this book is devoted to the aircraft designers and key teammates that created the aircraft designs, it is essential to state that the fledgling Grumman Aircraft Engineering Corporation would not have been successful without the unique skills of Leon "Jake" Swirbul (Fig. 10.3), who was the part of the Grumman, Schwendler, Swirbul triumvirate that really made the company a reality. As I mentioned in Chapter 1, The Early Years, Jake

Fig. 10.3 Roy Grumman (left) and Jake Swirbul in front of a Widgeon.

worked closely with Roy Grumman as shop superintendent and "works manager" at Loening, and was the second largest stockholder of Grumman common shares when the company was formed in 1929. His outgoing personality combined with his unique skills in management, manufacturing, marketing, human relations, and communications enabled him to help Roy Grumman sell his new aircraft ideas in Washington; build a superb, well-motivated, and satisfied manufacturing workforce; and be a very effective chief operating officer for many years. He touched the lives of every person in the company as it was growing, and he became a leader and benefactor to all of the Long Island and state communities where Grumman was located. Swirbul's eulogy in 1960 said a great deal about the man and his life.

> As one seeks to understand the personality of the man who was a pioneer in airframe manufacture, outstanding industrial manager, dynamic community leader in health, education and welfare, an active sportsman, and personal friend of prominent citizens, he discovers a bold man with integrity and discipline whose steadfast faith in his fellow man never faltered.... This then is the lengthened shadow of one man, Leon A. Swirbul, which affected a multitude of individuals whose economic status has been improved.

Another key person who built the early mockups of the aircraft designs as well as the first prototypes was Julius "Julie" Holpit. Julie also worked with Roy Grumman and Jake Swirbul at Loening, and he was the first of a long line of very talented and experienced manufacturing operations personnel who worked closely with the preliminary and development design teams to build the wooden mockups and experimental test aircraft.

While discussing the prime reason for this undertaking, namely to remember and write down the names of those people who helped to create the design, I have been reminded by my very experienced and learned peers that without the entire organizational structure of the company these aircraft would not have been a reality. So very true! So at this time it is important to state that these unique creative capabilities by a handful of lead designers supported by key teammates could not have been sustained without the integrated effort of all functional disciplines. Business Development, Engineering, Quality, Integrated Logistic Support, Information Technology, Test and Simulation, Manufacturing Operations, Flight Test, and Supplier (Material) Management, to mention a few departments that were lead, and supported by Program Management, Financial Management, and Human Resources, made the development and production of these aircraft possible.

Under the leadership of Lew Evans, Gordon Ochenrider, and Tom Kane, Business Development played a key role during the evolution of a new design and subsequent derivatives of an aircraft. Business Development personnel knew the customer, a relationship forged over many years as the young officer or civilian came up through the ranks. Previous experience served them well as service pilots and officers, test pilots, engineers, program managers or having program experience, and field service representatives, to mention a few. They worked hand in hand with the design teams to make the right contacts in the services and government agencies and labs, helped secure important seed money contracts, participated on proposals, and were key members of each program management team like the F-14, S-2, A-6, and EA-6B.

In the early years Grumman was also blessed with a core design team that not only created new aircraft designs, but also did much of the experimental test flying. Roy Grumman and Bob Hall were very gifted in that sense, as well as fortunate in having Bud Gillies and Connie Converse, two very experienced test pilots, lead the way in a long line of outstanding and nationally recognized test pilots. If one takes a look at the names of Grumman's more prominent designers, beginning with Roy Grumman, we see a predominance of pure engineers, with three being experimental pilots and three who flew during their careers. Grumman, Hall, and Gordon Israel were experimental test pilots. Joe Lippert flew many of Grumman's commercial/crop dusting aircraft like the Goose and Ag Cat, Fred Tiemann flew in the E-2A on development test flights, and Grant Hedrick, in his eternal quest for knowledge, learned to fly in his 50s.

The names of Grumman's more prominent airplane designers that I have selected from preceding chapters are Roy Grumman, Bill Schwendler, Bob Hall, Grant Hedrick, Oscar "Pete" Erlandson, Gordon Israel, Dick Hutton, Larry Mead, Joe Gavin, Walter Scott, Mike Pelehach, Bob Kress, Bill Rathke, Leonard "Sully" Sullivan, Bernie Harriman, Dayton T. Brown, Arthur Koch, Joe Lippert, Ralston Stalb, and Glen Spacht. Roy Grumman and Bill Schwendler had 40-year careers that spanned the development of many aircraft. Each of Grumman's prominent designers had long and challenging histories involving many different aircraft as well as other avenues of success involving space, missiles, and marine systems.

Another key point is that many of the designers and their teammates who created the designs were model aircraft builders, including Dick Hutton, Bob Kress, Glen Spacht, and Joe Lippert, to name a few. As I mentioned before, this ability to visualize in scale form, examine fundamental flying qualities, and simulate actual key characteristics of a new design were invaluable. The flying model of the Jaguar that Joe Lippert built early in the program revealed poor inherent longitudinal flight characteristics that plagued the eventual aircraft. The V/STOL A transition flight control model that Bob Kress, the Grumman Research Department, and Nick Ziroli built demonstrated excellent transition from conventional flight to hover. When I got to know Bob Kress really well on the F-14 program and worked with him at his home, Bob showed me all of his radio-controlled aircraft, from World War I fighters to larger scale aerobatic designs. Later on Bob developed a small jet engine for model airplanes. During the conceptual design phase of the forward swept wing (FSW) program that led to the X-29 demonstrator, Glen Spacht and Nick Ziroli designed, built, wind tunnel tested, and flew a large-scale model of an FSW configuration.

Dick Hutton (Fig. 10.4) is regarded as one of Grumman's more outstanding designers because he had the remarkable ability to outline the preliminary design of an airplane, and the end result of all the estimates and detailed design was a good product that spoke for itself. He designed more successful airplanes than anyone else at Grumman, including the F4F Wildcat, F6F Hellcat, TBF Avenger, and F8F Bearcat, and also oversaw the preliminary design of many other successful Grumman aircraft—a testament to his talent for blending the best ideas into attractive high performance aircraft. Mr. Hutton retired in 1973 after 45 years of service.

Bob Hall (Fig. 10.5) was an aeronautical engineer, aircraft designer, and experimental test pilot. He already had 10 years of experience flight testing and designing aircraft prior to coming to Grumman in 1936, where he contributed heavily to the designs of the F4F, F6F, F7F, F8F, and TBF-1 Avenger, to mention a few. He flew the first flight of 10 Grumman aircraft. In 1950 he became chief engineer and was responsible for the design of the F9F Panther and Cougar jets. In 1954 he was appointed vice president of engineering. Later in his career, which spanned 44 years, he headed Grumman's marine efforts in hydrofoil craft.

Ralston Stalb (Fig. 10.6) was the first of many outstanding hydro-dynamicists and marine engineers that created and designed a long line of Grumman amphibians, hydrofoil boats, yachts, and recreational boats. Stalb was chief engineer at Loening Aircraft, where he designed the OA-1A before coming to Grumman. He was a brilliant, nationally recognized naval architect and hydrodynamicist. His work on the designs of the Widgeon, Goose, and Mallard amphibians resulted in beautifully proportioned hulls with good lines and excellent hydrodynamic and sea-keeping characteristics. Stalb insisted on strong and rugged designs in the Grumman tradition, and was a designer and a project engineer of the F6F Hellcat and the F8F Bearcat. He became the chief designer of the Albatross,

Fig. 10.4 Dick Hutton.

Fig. 10.5 Bob Hall.

Grumman's largest and most successful amphibian, which was adopted by the U.S. services as well as foreign countries. Unfortunately, his career was cut short due to debilitating arthritis.

Oscar "Pete" Erlandsen (Fig. 10.7) became the 47th Grumman employee after he graduated

Fig. 10.6 Ralston Stalb.

Fig. 10.7 Oscar "Pete" Erlandsen.

from Princeton in 1929. During World War II, Erlandsen was head of the stress department, and he made major contributions to the design of the F6F Hellcat as well as the F8F Bearcat. Larry Mead recalled in his memoir that Erlandsen was a "great intuitive structural analyst," and he demonstrated this with an innovative and intriguing idea to save a significant amount of wing weight on the F8F. After World War II in 1946, Erlandsen became chief designer and director of missile development that led to the Rigel missile. This was a leading-edge design that employed a ramjet engine with a rocket booster and a state-of-the-art navigation system called Loran C. This missile work also led to the Bendix/Grumman team winning the long-range Eagle missile contract that was to be carried by the Douglas F6D Missileer—both of which were cancelled by the Navy due to changing requirements. Erlandsen was also called upon later in his career to design Grumman's trailer truck with a special suspension, as well as high-speed trains.

Grant Hedrick (Fig. 10.8) was one of the United States' foremost leaders in the structural development of aerospace vehicles. As chief engineer and vice president of Engineering, he was intimately involved in the design of every Grumman aircraft, the Lunar Module, and the marine hydrofoil programs. Hedrick spearheaded the development of structure fatigue methods used by the industry and the Navy, developed advanced composite technologies used in major airframe structures, and developed electron beam welding of titanium structures. He also was instrumental in Grumman heavily investing in the Radar Guided Weapon System demonstrator program and follow-on radar technologies that led to the Joint STARS program. Hedrick retired in 1980 after 37 years with Grumman, and continued in a senior advisory capacity for the Grumman Corporation and as a Board member until 1985.

Fig. 10.8 Grant Hedrick.

Larry Mead (Fig. 10.9) came to Grumman in 1941 and was noted for his stress analysis work on all of Grumman's World War II aircraft as well as the XF9F Panther. He worked with Gordon Israel as assistant project engineer on the XF10F-1 Jaguar, deputy project engineer to Joe Gavin on the XF9F-9 Tiger, and project

Fig. 10.9 Larry Mead.

Fig. 10.10 Joe Gavin.

engineer on the F11F-1 Super Tiger. Mead became the project engineer on the A2F-1 Intruder preliminary design, proposal, and development, played a leading role in the design and development of the F-14, and led the development of the Gulfstream III. His career at Grumman spanned 52 years.

After World War II, Grumman was blessed with the hiring of many outstanding engineers from Massachusetts Institute of Technology (MIT), many of whom are mentioned in this research on the aircraft designers and their teammates. After graduating from MIT and serving in the U.S. Navy, Joe Gavin (Fig. 10.10) joined Grumman as a design engineer on the XF9F-2 Panther in 1946. In rapid succession he became project engineer on the F9F-6 Cougar in 1950 and the F9F-9 (F11F-1) Tiger in 1952, followed by chief experimental project engineer in 1956. Gavin was destined for leadership roles in space and with Grumman; he became chief missile and space engineer in 1957, director of the Lunar Module program in 1962, director of Space Programs in 1968, and president of Grumman Aerospace Corporation in 1972. He retired from Grumman in 1985 after 39 years with the company.

Bill Rathke (Fig. 10.11) was in many ways the epitome of an excellent engineer and designer who had exceptional skills in developing leading edge aircraft systems with a quiet yet tough determination. Coming to Grumman in the early 1940s and retiring some 40 years later, Rathke worked on a long series of aircraft: F6F Hellcat, TBF Avenger, F7F Tigercat, Mallard amphibian, F9F Panther series of jet fighters, and F11F-1 Tiger. He was project engineer for the preliminary design, proposal, and development of the S2F Tracker, the TF-1 (C-1) Trader (a cargo on deck delivery aircraft), WF-2 (E-1B) Tracker, W2F-1 (E-2A) Hawkeye, and C-2 Greyhound. Rathke played a major role in the development of the Lunar Module as engineering and program manager before becoming program manager on the F-14A Tomcat.

Fig. 10.11 Bill Rathke.

Joe Lippert (Fig. 10.12) built gasoline engine–powered model airplanes as a youngster, and this became a lifelong hobby. He always wanted to design aircraft, came to Grumman in 1942 after graduation, and retired in 1976. He participated in the design development of aircraft programs from the F4F Wildcat up to and including the F-14 Tomcat. Lippert spent 10 years in Preliminary Design as a senior aerodynamicist

and designer. During this period he was a major
contributor to the design configuration of the WF-2
Tracer Airborne Early Warning Aircraft, Dick Hutton's
assistant in the configuration development of the S2F
and F9F series of jet fighters, and the designer of the Ag
Cat along with Arthur Koch.

By the age of 10–12 years, Arthur Koch (Fig. 10.13)
was drawing layout plans of model airplanes from
photos and dimensions available of actual aircraft,

Fig. 10.12   Joe Lippert.

because no model kits were available. Koch and Lippert both graduated from
the prestigious New York University Guggenheim School of Aeronautics.
Koch started work at Grumman in 1935 and did the power plant installations
on the XF4F-1 and the J2F-1 Duck amphibian. Koch was the preliminary
designer and project engineer of the TBF Avenger torpedo bomber as well as
the AF Guardian series of antisubmarine warfare aircraft. He also laid out
the initial configuration of the G-21 Goose and codesigned the Ag Cat with
Joe Lippert. He was one of Grumman's very talented designers because he
had a remarkable ability to transform a collection of ideas into a design
drawing quickly. Koch retired from Grumman in 1972 after 37 years, but
continued on as a consultant designer with Grumman American and then
worked permanently for Schweizer Aircraft.

Gordon Israel (Fig. 10.14) worked for Grumman in the period from 1941 to
1953. Israel had a gift for designing very streamlined aircraft with excellent
lines. He was project engineer on the F7F Tigercat, which was a graceful and
high performance twin engine fighter. Other Israel design trademarks of
outstanding appearance and gracefulness were the G-73 Mallard and the F9F
Panther and Cougar series of jet fighters. His last assignment was project
engineer of the variable sweep wing XF10F-1 Jaguar—a unique design with
many new technologies including variable sweep wing technology and flight
controls combined with an underpowered engine. It should be noted that after
leaving Grumman, Israel was hired by William Lear and he redesigned the
Lockheed Lodestar to achieve remarkable performance, as well as
participating in the preliminary design of the LearJet.

Dayton T. Brown (Fig. 10.15)
and his codesigner R.D. MacCart
did some fine design work at
Brewster Aircraft when a contract
for a 300 mph carrier-based fighter
was put out for competition in
1935, and the resulting F2A Buffalo
was the first monoplane fighter to
enter service with the U.S. Navy. In

Fig. 10.13   Arthur Koch.

Fig. 10.14   Gordon Israel.

Fig. 10.15   Dayton T. Brown.

1943, design work began on Grumman's first attempt to enter the light plane field with the Kitten landplane series, G-63 and G-72, and the G-65 amphibian. The design team of Brown and Hank Kurt laid out the designs under Roy Grumman's personal supervision. They were good performing aircraft using the latest Grumman proven technologies in aerodynamics and manufacturing; however, the post–World War II market potential did not materialize, and the projects were terminated.

Bernard J. (Bernie) Harriman (Fig. 10.16) had been with the company almost 29 years when he died at the age of 48 in 1968. Harriman signed on with Grumman in 1939 after attending Hofstra University and Pratt Institute. He started in the shop and in 1941 moved to Structural Design Engineering, where he worked successively on the F6F Hellcat, F7F Tigercat, F8F Bearcat, A2F-1 Intruder, Mallard, and F9F Tiger. Then, in 1957, he began work on the design of Grumman's corporate aircraft, the Gulfstream I, for which he was project engineer until 1965 when he became project manager of the Gulfstream II. One of the large corporate owners of the Gulfstream I remarked that "whenever we fly our Gulfstreams, we are reminded of the great contribution made to this fine airplane by Bernie Harriman."

After graduating from college in 1959, I started to work in Preliminary Design (PD); Walter "Scotty" Scott (Fig. 10.17) was manager of Preliminary Design and Leonard "Sully" Sullivan was deputy manager. In those days, a new member of PD had to sit in a holding area until clearances were completed. I remember on my first day in PD, Scott came out to welcome me with a quiet smile and a firm handshake. Sullivan's recollections in a letter to Joe Lippert in 1985 stated that Roy Grumman and Jake Swirbul were determined to keep up with changing times, and they gave many junior engineers some extraordinary opportunities to follow their own capabilities. Preliminary Design was expanded from about 30 people in 1954 to about 300 people in 1964.

Scott was trained at Webb Institute as a naval architect; however, for the next 30 years he spent most of his time as an aeronautical engineer. He designed the post–World War II Mach 2 XSSM-7 Rigel missile. After Sputnik was launched in 1957, Grumman formed the Advanced Space Department in PD headed by Al Munier, and Scott wrote some of the early space proposals. After

Fig. 10.16   Bernie Harriman.

Fig. 10.17   Walter Scott.

winning the Orbital Astronomical Observatory (OAO) proposal, Scott became the program manager. He went on to become director of Ocean Systems, and retired in 1970 to begin a new career as a designer and builder of yachts.

Leonard "Sully" Sullivan (Fig. 10.18), manager of Preliminary Design, came to Grumman in 1950 after serving in World War II and graduating from MIT. Sullivan went to work on the Mach 2 Rigel missile

Fig. 10.18 Leonard "Sully" Sullivan.

program under Pete Erlandson. He became the project engineer on a tactical version of the missile as the program was canceled by the Navy, and many members of the Rigel team became the core of an expanded Preliminary Design department under Dick Hutton. As a member, and eventually manager, of Preliminary Design, Sullivan was responsible for all Grumman technical proposals for new business including the Eagle missile system, A2F-1 (A-6A), W2F-1(E-2A), OV-1, EA-6A, Tri-service VTOL aircraft, Nimbus and Apollo spacecraft, the Navy F-111B/Phoenix, the Lunar Excursion Module (LEM), and the early work on the VFX that led to the F-14. He was responsible for all future systems studies and for the output of Grumman's Operations Analysis department in all phases of advanced vehicle studies, antisubmarine warfare (ASW), air defense, attack, reconnaissance, space uses, transportation, and so on. Sullivan was, without question, an inspiring, eloquent leader who was highly respected by the government and industry. Both he and Russ Murray, deputy director of Operations Analysis, accepted important positions in the Department of Defense (DOD) in the early 1960s and went on to have long distinguished careers with the U.S. government in various capacities.

Mike Pelehach (Fig. 10.19) came to Grumman from Vought Aircraft in 1950, where he did structural and power plant installations on the F6U Pirate Navy Fighter as well as working on other Vought aircraft including the XF5U. If Arthur Koch is remembered as one of Grumman's more proficient and fastest designers, then Mike Pelehach's preliminary design capabilities were on an even higher level of design imagination, creativity, and speed. Pelehach laid out Design 98J, which became the F11F-1F with the J-79 afterburning engine, and Design 118, a supersonic all-weather fighter concept that "was pedaled in Washington as Grumman's version of the F4 Phantom that was unsuccessful but demonstrated to Washington and the Navy that Grumman had a new design team that could come up with a very hot new technology design," according to Leonard Sullivan. Pelehach went on to design the W2F-1 proposal

Fig. 10.19 Mike Pelehach.

configuration and the C2 Greyhound, as well as the winning OV-1 Mohawk design. In Sullivan's opinion, Mike Pelehach was clearly Grumman's top designer.

He was chief designer of the VFX/F-14 Tomcat and spearheaded the whole relationship among the Navy, Grumman, and major subcontractors with an excellent team that included Joe Rees as his deputy. Pelehach went on to become president of Grumman International, where his design genius was sought after by many countries, resulting in significant foreign sales of Grumman aircraft systems as well as avionic and propulsion upgrades to other operational aircraft.

Dick Hutton and Mike Pelehach were truly remarkable designers, as I have tried to portray. Hutton began his career as a mechanic at Loening and completed his engineering studies at night at Pratt Institute. Pelehach started designing structures and power plant installations at Vought after completing a two-year aeronautical engineering program at the LaGuardia School of Aeronautics. Both men rose to some of the highest leadership positions in Grumman—a testament to their innate genius of design and leadership.

Bob Kress (Fig. 10.20) defines versatility at Grumman, making the transition from being an aerodynamicist, to performing a major role in the development of the Lunar Module, to becoming a chief aircraft designer, an engineering manager, vice president of Grumman's Advanced Programs, and an entrepreneur after he retired from Grumman. Bob was affectionately called Kaiser von Kress by his close associates, because he was someone who could provide firm leadership and direction, and he was never afraid to stand up for what he thought was right, especially when it came to the fighting capabilities of the F-14 Tomcat that he helped create. Kress could delve into the deepest technical problem, from both a vehicle and an avionic standpoint, and he was highly respected by government and military officers and experts. He was the lead aerodynamicist on the OV-1 Mohawk, and provided aerodynamic oversight and developed innovative lift augmentation devices for the TFX/F-111B. Kress became the Lunar Module Systems project engineer, was part of the core design team that developed the F-14 Tomcat and became engineering manager during development, and led the design evolution on the Navy's V/STOL A, which utilized jet vane control.

Fig. 10.20   Bob Kress.

Glenn Spacht (Fig. 10.21) joined Grumman in 1968 as an aeronautical engineer and showed great promise in advanced design, along with many other fine young engineers and designers working in conjunction with seasoned PD veterans. Dr. Renso Caporali, who became director of Advanced Technology, and myself, who became director of Advanced Systems in 1976, recognized the great potential of these teams and "let them run" in much the same way as Roy Grumman and Jake Swirbul did in the early 1950s. Spacht played a leading role in the evolution of the forward swept wing (FSW) from 1976 to 1980, which led to Grumman winning the X-29 contract in December 1981. He worked closely with Colonel (Dr.) Norris Krone of Defense Advanced Research Project Agency (DARPA), led an excellent team that won several critical design and wind tunnel test contracts related to the Grumman/ DARPA technology road map, led the design effort during the preproposal period, and worked closely with Bob Roemer during the proposal period as the program transitioned from Advanced Systems to the Product Development Center. After award, Spacht became deputy program manager of the X-29 program, while Bob McGuckin was program manager. Spacht became vice president of Engineering in 1990 and retired from Grumman in 1994 when it was acquired by Northrop.

Fig. 10.21   Glenn Spacht.

DESIGN PERSPECTIVES

The X-29 was the last new fighter aircraft that Grumman designed, built, and flight tested in its 65-year history, and it was the only new aircraft flown in the decade from 1980 to 1990. There were, of course, very significant developments and production of aircraft weapon systems programs including Joint STARS and major variants of the A-6, E-2, F-14, EA-6B, and EF-111 that followed the X-29. From 1930 to 1940 there were 18 new aircraft and variants; from 1941 to 1950 there were 24 new aircraft and variants; from 1951 to 1960 there were 21 new aircraft and variants; from 1961 to 1970 there were 13 new aircraft and variants; from 1971 to 1980 there were 10 new aircraft and variants, excluding the three Grumman American light planes; and from 1981 to 1990 there were 4 new aircraft and variants, with 5 more variants and Joint STARS from 1991 to 1994 (see Fig. 10.22).

The X-29 not only demonstrated the outstanding transonic maneuvering and high angle of attack performance associated with the forward swept wing due to the integration of several leading edge technologies, but it also was an extremely reliable demonstrator, as attested to by 347 flights conducted by Grumman, Air Force, and NASA pilots from 1984 to 1992. Grumman wisely invested in this demonstrator program (a nominal 50% investment of the original $100 million contract) not only to ensure it successfully met all program milestones on schedule, but also to allow the birth of a new experienced design team. Over the course of the program, a cohesive mature team emerged with proven skills in advanced aerodynamics, composites, and

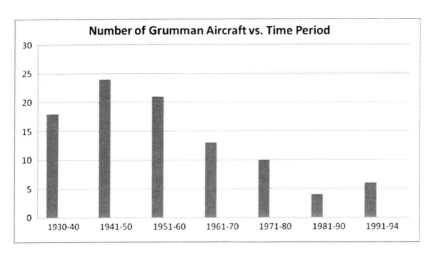

Fig. 10.22   The number of Grumman aircraft built from the 1930s to the early 1990s.

flight control technologies combined with the management capabilities, technicians, and streamlined processes of the Product Development Center (Grumman's version of the Skunk Works or Phantom Works) to build a new aircraft demonstrator and flight test experience with a new aircraft.

Renso "Capi" Caporali remembered being called into George Skurla's office, who was president of Grumman Aerospace, about the time that the X-29 was being prepared to be shipped to Edwards Air Force Base (AFB) in California. Skurla asked Caporali how the program was going and commented that he was concerned about not having a lot of experienced people around anymore who could get a new aircraft up in the air for the first time. Capi got the message and asked Skurla, "Do you want me to go?" Skurla said yes, and Caporali spent about four months with the team at Edwards AFB.

From a historical perspective, Grumman did attempt to get involved in V/STOL technology in the 1960s. Several unsolicited tilt wing and ducted fan in wing V/STOL designs of the Mohawk were submitted to the government, as well as formal competitive bids to the Navy and Army for the Tri-Service Transport and the Advanced Aerial Fire Support System (AAFSS), respectively. In both bids Grumman teamed with Kaman unsuccessfully. Grumman was also offered the opportunity to become involved with the "Americanization" of the English Harrier VTOL fighter and decided not to pursue the opportunity. McDonnell Douglas became the prime on the AV-8A and AV-8B Harrier for the U.S. Marine Corps (USMC). As discussed in Chapter 7, Future Systems, Grumman mounted an exhaustive and industry-leading effort in response to the Navy's V/STOL A program from the mid-1970s through 1981, during which time Grumman's Design

698 reached full-scale wind tunnel and propulsion testing at NASA facilities. Bob Kress led this effort, and Grumman had developed a very experienced preliminary design and development team that would have formed the nucleus of a full-scale development team, assuming the Navy had gone ahead with this program and Grumman had won the program.

Lockheed won the VSX (Navy designation for heavier than air, search, experimental) competition in August 1969, which took place during the time of the VFX/F-14A competition. It is important to mention that Grumman was a leader in carrier-based antisubmarine warfare (ASW) with the S-2 series aircraft, the work of George Klaus and his team in submarine detection technology and equipment, and ASW Operations Analysis expertise. In 1965, the CVS (antisubmarine) aircraft carriers were under fire in the Office of the Secretary of Defense (OSD); hundreds of Russian submarines were tracking our attack carriers, and the Navy wanted a new jet ASW aircraft with a superior detection and tracking system that OSD wanted justified. Grumman fielded a strong Operations Analysis and Engineering team to work with the Navy. This multiyear effort resulted in excellent data bases for CVS operations with S-2 aircraft from Grumman, and land-based and ship-based ASW assets from other aerospace contractors and the Navy. Grumman led the briefing to top OSD, Navy flag officers, and the Navy Technical Branch, with the result that the cost–benefits analyses of the VSX program were justified and the program was given the go-ahead.

In the stealth technology area, Grumman made some early decisions that in retrospect cost the company a prime contractor role in forthcoming competitions more than a decade later. In 1973, Grumman did not become involved in DARPA's stealth program; however, in the mid-1970s Grumman formed an Advanced Air Force Group in Advanced Systems (Preliminary Design) that involved pre-ATF (Advanced Tactical Fighter) studies [e.g., the Configuration Development of Advanced Fighters (CDAF) as well as compartmented stealth studies]. Grumman's Advanced Air Force team participated heavily in many of the pre-ATF-related company-sponsored conceptual design and wind tunnel studies, as well as winning its fair share of contract-related advanced development (CRAD) studies funded by the Air Force. In 1983, Grumman proposed a forward swept wing ATF configuration, but was not selected for the demonstrator phase of the ATF program.

In 1981, understanding that it was behind in stealth technology, Grumman made a major investment of research funds by hiring Dr. Alan Simon and Dr. Ken Perko of Global Analytics to perform a thorough review of its stealth technology programs and research. Dr. Renso Caporali, director of Advanced Systems Technology at the time, was instrumental in bringing them on board. Drs. Simon and Perko, both former senior DARPA officials, were nationally recognized for their expertise in this critical technology area. The review found that Grumman was several generations behind in stealth technology, and the two recommended a more aggressive technology roadmap that Grumman implemented. This enhanced Grumman's ability to have a more fruitful dialogue and contracts with the U.S. government and services. Gregg Kutz and Herman Erbacher, Advanced Systems, provided the leadership for Grumman's stealth technology team. Positive examples of these efforts were the design and construction of a state-of-the-art radar cross-section testing facility in Rancho Bernardo, California, that Kutz, Dick Anderson, and the stealth team developed with Alcoa, and the construction of modern secure facilities and hangars in Grumman's Plant 5 facility in Bethpage, Long Island.

However, when the Navy's Advanced Tactical Fighter competition began in 1984, Northrop was the prime contractor with Grumman as the major subcontractor. Grumman mounted a major four-year design effort, peaking at 500 personnel, and contributed heavily with its expertise in aircraft-related technologies honed on the X-29 program; avionic and system integration personnel from its aircraft weapon system programs (F-14, E-2, EA-6B, Joint STARS); and the use of a state-of-the-art Product Development Center on Long Island that built a significant portion of the ATA preproposal and proposal test and mockup hardware. The Northrop/Grumman team lost the competition to the General Dynamics/McDonnell Douglas team in late 1987. At award, the ATA became the A-12, which was subsequently canceled in 1991. Northrop purchased Grumman in 1994, and the Northrop Grumman Corporation, utilizing many of Grumman's former ATA design personnel, teamed with McDonnell Douglas and British Aerospace to successfully pursue A/FX and Joint Advanced Strike Technology (JAST) studies programs that led to the Joint Strike Fighter (JSF) program in 1996. Boeing and Lockheed Martin were eventually selected in late 1996 to proceed to the next concept demonstration phase, and Northrop Grumman teamed with Lockheed Martin, who became the winner of the JSF program in 2001.

Even though the number of government starts in new aircraft had diminished from 1970 to 1990, Grumman's Future Systems Organization (Business Development, Advanced Systems, Advanced Development, Operations Analysis, Research, and Product Development Center) developed long-term technology programs with the U.S. government agencies and services, funded them, won their fair share of contract research and development (CRAD), and developed several significant design teams that worked together, in some cases for many years, in the pursuit of Advanced Air Force programs, the Navy's V/STOL A program, the ATA, and the AF(X)/JAST, while demonstrating the Airborne Radar Jamming System for the U.S. Army, developing and testing the conformal UHF radar for the U.S. Navy, and winning the X-29 forward swept wing demonstrator program.

There were many imaginative and creative Preliminary Design engineers who performed numerous conceptual design studies throughout Grumman's history. Some are not mentioned in this book because many of these projects did not reach full-scale flying status, full-scale wind tunnel testing, and/or the full-scale mockup stage. I had the honor to know and work with many of these men who contributed to Grumman design numbers that reached into the 700s. In Chapter 7, Future Systems, I discussed Design 698, V/STOL A; Design 711, a new amphibian to replace the Goose that was designed in 1937; and Design 712, which became the X-29, because these projects reached the level of maturity described. I also included design studies of the MMVX and E-2X, based on the use of conformal radar technology developed at Grumman that opened wide avenues of design possibilities. In Chapter 6, I touched on Tomcat 21, which did not reach flight hardware but held great promise to maintain the long-range fighting punch of the U.S. Navy. Again Grumman blended its best talent from Advanced Systems and the F-14D program to form an excellent design team that energized the U.S. Navy over a four-year period to request proposals based on the superb ongoing performance of the F-14D and a strong supplier base.

The last perspective in this area is derived from research and discussions with many Grumman veterans including Irv Waaland, who went on to become the chief of design and the chief designer of the B-2 at Northrop Grumman. Grumman had a unique culture—individuals were free to express and demonstrate their capabilities. There was no evidence of *Dilbert* managers. Grumman management, beginning with the founders and continuing until 1994, encouraged direct access. Some examples were Joe Lippert going to see Roy Grumman with the Ag Cat concept and Tom Guarino and Bob Salzmann meeting with Lew Evans about the EA-(bowlegs) study that led to the EA-6B. Criticism was constructive, never demeaning. As a result, the company enjoyed the often sought, seldom realized, benefits of brainstorming ideas and concepts. Waaland recalled dealing directly with Bill Schwendler in the design reviews of the Gulfstream II.

Throughout Grumman's 65-year history, the U.S. Navy remained one of its most important customers. NAVAIR, BuAer, and today's Naval Air Systems Command had a similar culture. The NAVAIR engineers were very knowledgeable about what worked and didn't work in their unique environment, and treated the contractor as a team member. Together, the Navy/Grumman team usually delivered excellent products with substantial growth potential to meet the Navy's worldwide commitments, and operate safely and efficiently in the aircraft carrier environment.

THE AVIONICERS AND SOFTWARE

Another very important historical perspective regarding Grumman is the change from being a traditional Navy supplier of rugged aircraft to one of the world's leading aircraft weapon system developers involved in the integration and management of complex programs. As discussed in Chapters 4–6, 8, and 9—devoted to the development of the A-6 all-weather air-to-ground attack weapon system, the lineage of airborne early warning, the F-14 air superiority and mutimission weapon system, battlefield surveillance, and electronic warfare, respectively—Grumman aggressively began to hire the best and brightest from the avionics and electronics industry in the mid-1950s to supplement an excellent core staff of avionic engineers. The term "avionicers" has been coined to describe the avionic system engineering profession, which includes many areas of specialty; the term is written with much admiration and respect.

In addition, Grumman developed unique state-of-the-art (SOA) facilities for each mission area featuring system integration test stations (SITS) with complete cockpit and fuselage crew stations and computer complexes, dedicated test ranges (e.g., EWTR; electronic warfare test range), and the world's largest anechoic test chamber. As a testament to this transformation, the main product lines for Grumman in the 1990s were the A-6 Block 1A, the E2C Group II, the F-14D, the EA-6B AV CAP, the EF-111 SIP, and Joint STARS. Unique national asset teams emerged at Grumman in the mission areas of air superiority/strike–multimission, all-weather air-to-ground attack, airborne early warning, battlefield surveillance, and electronic warfare.

In the aforementioned chapters, I identified many key avionic, software, and system engineers who were an integral part of the design teams that created the aircraft or variant. In the ensuing paragraphs, I have selected some key people for summary purposes, while fully recognizing those who made contributions in earlier chapters.

On the A2F-1 proposal, Bob Nafis was the lead engineer in the systems group, ably supported by Gene Bonan, Newt Speiss, and Dan Collins. Speiss actually did some flight experiments with a private plane to improve the pilot's and bombardier navigator (BN) displays for weapon delivery. Dan Collins became "Mr. A-6" because he played such a key role in the development of subsequent A-6 variants.

In the lineage of the E-2 family, Bob Nafis put together the systems approach on the W2F-1 proposal, and Fred Tiemann came on board right after award and was instrumental in Grumman becoming the systems leader on the E-2A development. Fred Tiemann, along with Dick Anderson, Ken Koehler, Dennis Carter, and Gerry Norton, played a key role in the E-2B variant development. Gerry Norton and Jim MacManus were responsible for the initial radar upgrade to the E-2 (the APS-111). When Fred Tiemann returned to Advanced Systems in 1976, he spearheaded the Corsiga overland concept, and during flight testing he and Gerry Norton demonstrated the concept. The E-2C development that gave the Navy excellent overwater and overland AEW capabilities was led by Tom Guarino, Dick Anderson, Gerry Norton, Dennis Carter, and Tony Guma.

The VFX proposal avionic architecture that led to the F-14A avionics configuration was led by Joe Rodriguez, with significant contributions by Alex Alexandrovich, Bob Kress, Dan Collins, Bob Watson, Vinny DeVino, Bob Branstetter, Joe Stump, Bob Steele, and test pilots Bill Miller and Charlie Brown. The F-14D development that resulted in one of the Navy's most versatile and effective strike fighters was led by Bob Watson, who worked tirelessly with Neil Gilmartin, Jim Dante, Pat Mennona, Dennis Carter, and Dave Kratz, development test pilot, to make the program a reality.

The lineage of the Joint STARS began with the radar guided weapon systems (RGWS) demonstrator that was the invention of Gerry McNiff. He came up with a relative azimuth angle target detection and weapon delivery system utilizing real-time synthetic aperture radar imagery for accurate target identification and location. Hank Janiesch, Newt Speiss, and Grant Hedrick recognized the vast potential of this development, and were instrumental in assembling an excellent engineering team to flesh out the concept and have Grumman invest heavily in the proof of concept; this led to the Pave Mover and eventually the Joint STARS program. The Pave Mover successful demonstration was due to the technical prowess of Gerry McNiff, Frank Milordi, Jim Glover, Sam Mackey, and Bob Phear, with Al Gurkewitz as project manager. The Joint STARS proposal was led by Al Verderosa, Al Gurkewitz, and Gerry McNiff. The rather incredible Joint STARS development was led by Al Verderosa and Marty Dandridge, who combined their vast program and technical management talents to bring the program through a very difficult development phase. The outstanding demonstration of the Joint STARS system in the first Gulf War was due in part to the technical leadership and innovation of Gerry McNiff, Dr. Dale Burton, Paul Coco, and Gerry Norton.

Grumman's ascendency to become a premier electronic warfare systems provider began with the EA-6A, whose requirements were championed by the U.S. Marine Corps and the Grumman development team, led by Al Rogers with key engineers Art Karle and Sal Migliore. Pivotal operations analysis and system studies that led to a fully dedicated next-generation EW system were performed by Tom Guarino and Bob Salzmann. Salzmann went on to became the chief architect of the resulting EA-(bowlegs) configuration that eventually became the EA-6B. The technical team of Guarino, Salzmann, Karle, and Migliore were instrumental in the design of the tactical jamming system. Guarino became the EW systems project engineer. Bob Miller would eventually take over and lead all EW programs, including the EF-111, with Salzmann as technical assistant. Bob Fredette and Gerry Mellman contributed heavily in the development of jamming techniques and systems design, respectively, employed in the development of new EA-6B variants under the technical leadership of Al Gurkewitz. Bob Scholly had a major role in the EA-6B because he led the overall proposal and development of several new EA-6B variants. When Miller retired, Dan O'Neill led the overall EA-6B program and the pursuit of new variants. In like manner, Vern Kramer and Tom Street led the EF-111 program with Bob Salzmann providing technical oversight as deputy program manager and Dave Tarbell responsible for the unique TJS equipment design.

Software and computer technologies became major drivers of aircraft weapon system design following the growth of avionics. Tactical systems of the 1970s (E-2C, EA-6B) with hundreds of thousands of lines of code gave way by the late 1980s and early 1990s to trainer/simulations (A6E-WST, Weapon System Trainer) and surveillance systems (Joint STARS) driven by millions of lines of code (Fig. 10.23). Software offered unlimited vistas of

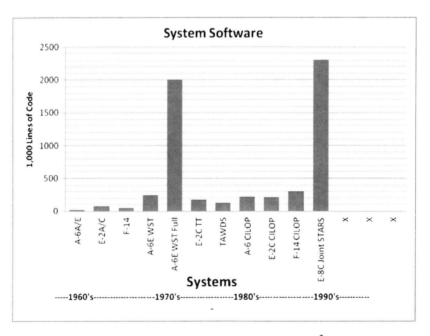

Fig. 10.23 Software lines of code vs. time.*

---

* WST: weapon system trainer; TT: tactical trainer; TAWDS: tactical air weapon delivery system (Pave Mover); CILOP: conversion in lieu of procurement.

functionality (e.g., what a software application can do for the naval aviator) from flight controls to surveillance and situational awareness. These new software challenges required changes in management and technical organizational structure to answer the three fundamental software performance questions, namely: How do you know what you are going to build? How do you know where you are? When are you going to be done? Major aircraft programs and derivatives (sometimes called upgrades) occurred on 5- to 10-year centers. Technology advances, and determining when specific technologies would be available for aircraft weapon system upgrades (referred to as TAD, technology availability date) and/or if there was a technology gap became major thrusts for engineering centers of excellence.

In 1970, Grumman Aerospace Corporation (GAC) transferred 90% of the tactical software personnel to Grumman Data Systems. When the burgeoning software problems of the A-6E-WST occurred in the late 1970s, it was recognized that the tactical software skill base needed to be an integral part of engineering in GAC.

In 1978, the Software department was established within GAC, headed by Gerry Sandler and Deputy Connie Blyseth. With the delivery of the A-6E-WST and the establishment of the Software Support Facility at Orlando, Florida, Blyseth returned to head up the Software department. At the same time, Engineering was restructured to meet the challenges of managing both vehicle and systems technologies. A new dynamic organization was formed in Engineering—Vehicle Engineering under Norm Lewin and Systems Engineering under Dick Anderson. Technology management within GAC would undergo another reconfiguration with the establishment of Corporate Technology. Software and systems disciplines remained distinct and at the appropriate organization levels, and research and development funds were invested in software for the first time.

DESIGNER TRAITS

So how does one characterize the Grumman aircraft designers, aircraft weapon system designers, and their teammates who created all the fine aircraft and variants that I described in the preceding chapters? Several key words come to mind, namely versatility, creativity, curiosity, innovation, customer focus, quick response, leadership, and longevity. These words, though, do not fully capture the advantages of the informal, less structured relationships that allowed a fluidity of ideas to be nourished in a less formally structured company. Grumman's organizational structure allowed ideas to be explored and encouraged communication on all levels and across all levels of the organization. Examples of this are Joe Lippert and Arthur Koch meeting with Chairman Leroy Grumman with an idea for a new agricultural crop dusting aircraft that became to Ag Cat, and Tom Guarino and Bob Salzmann having direct access to President Lew Evans's office with the EA-(bowlegs) electronic warfare concept that became the EA-6B. There is a downside, of course, that a more formal and accountable program structure is needed to run complex aircraft weapon system programs; Grumman, like other companies, responded with well-managed programs like the F-14D and Joint STARS, to mention a few.

I have selected only a sample of names to represent the key characteristics, recognizing that many people could fit into many categories.

- Versatility: Bob Kress (aircraft, space, aircraft), Joe Gavin (aircraft, space), Walter Scott (missiles, space, aircraft, marine), Bill Rathke (aircraft, space, aircraft), Leonard "Sully" Sullivan (missiles, aircraft), Pete Erlandson (missiles, aircraft), Bob Hall (aircraft, hydrofoils), Tom Street (hydrofoils, aircraft)
- Leadership: Roy Grumman, Bill Schwendler, Grant Hedrick, Dick Hutton, Al Verderosa, Marty Dandrige, Tom Guarino, Bob Miller, Joe Gavin, Larry Mead, Leonard Sullivan
- Creativity, curiosity, innovation: Roy Grumman, Bill Schwendler, Dick Hutton, Mike Pelehach, Bob Kress, Bob Salzmann, Grant Hedrick, Newt Speiss, Joe Gavin, Gerry McNiff, Gordon Israel, Glen Spacht, Joe Lippert, Dick Anderson
- Quick response: Mike Pelehach, Art Koch, Julie Holpit, Herb Grossman, Howie Schilling
- Customer focus: Roy Grumman, Julie Holpit, Mike Pelehach, Marty Dandridge, Tom Guarino
- Longevity: Roy Grumman, Bill Schwendler, Grant Hedrick, Dick Hutton, Larry Mead, Julie Holpit, Bill Rathke, Bob Hall

I hope you enjoyed reading about the hundreds of Grumman people who created over 70 aircraft in a 65-year timespan. One of the great pleasures of this undertaking has been re-establishing contact and renewing old friendships with almost 80 people throughout the United States. It has been an emotional journey because many of the Grumman pioneers are no longer with us, and some of them passed on or became incapacitated during my communication with them. Memories of them and their accomplishments will sustain us now. For those who remain, we are all a little grayer now, many are fully retired giving back as they can, and a few are still on the front lines. Grumman will always be a part of us, and at times we will remember and reminisce about those exciting years when we accomplished so much as part of the Grumman family.

Appendix

AIRCRAFT DESIGNERS AND KEY TEAMMATES

CHAPTER 1: THE EARLY YEARS

Loening OA-1A	Grover Loening, Leroy Grumman
XJF-1 to J2F Duck	Roy Grumman, Bill Schwendler, Jack Neady
XFF-1, XF2F-1, XF3F-1	Bill Schwendler, Roy Grumman
G-21 Goose	Roy Grumman, Bill Schwendler, Ralston Stalb, Arthur Koch, Tom Rae
Design G-22, Gulfhawk	Roy Grumman, Bill Schwendler, George Titterton
XF4F-2	Dick Hutton, Bill Schwendler, Roy Grumman

CHAPTER 2: THE WAR YEARS

G-44 Widgeon	Roy Grumman, Ralston Stalb, Tom Rae
XF5F-1, XP-50	Dick Hutton, Bill Schwendler
XTBF-1 Avenger	Bill Schwendler, Arthur Koch (PE), Bob Hall, Oscar Olsen, Bud Gilles
XF6F-1 Wildcat	Roy Grumman, Bill Schwendler, Dick Hutton
XF7F-1 Tigercat	Dick Hutton, Gordon Israel, Bob Hall
XF8F-1	Roy Grumman, Bill Schwendler, Dick Hutton, Bob Hall, Pete Erlandsen
AF-2S, AF-2W Guardian	Bill Schwendler, Dick Hutton, Bob Hall (XTB2F-1), Arthur Koch (XTB3F-1), Earl Ramsden (PE), Harold Kressly, Jack Erickson, George Klaus, Ed Pholig, Basil Papa

CHAPTER 3: THE POSTWAR YEARS: FIRST JETS

XF9F-1 Panther	Bill Schwendler, Dick Hutton, John Karanik, Gordon Israel
XF9F-6 Cougar	Joe Gavin, Dick Hutton
G-73 Mallard	Gordon Israel, Hank Kurt, Ralston Stalb, Tom Rae
XJR2F-1 Albatross	Bill Wange, Ralston Stalb, Tom Rae
G-63, G-72 Kittens	Roy Grumman, Dayton T. Brown, Hank Kurt
G-65 Tadpole	Roy Grumman, Dayton T. Brown, Hank Kurt, Dave Thurston
XF10F-1 Jaguar	Gordon Israel, Larry Mead, Joe Hubert, Gene Wade, Al Munier

CHAPTER 4: THE DYNAMIC 1950S AND 1960S, AND THE GULFSTREAM LEGACY

XF11F-1 Tiger	Bob Hall, Dick Hutton, Joe Gavin, Larry Mead, Bob Miller, Bob Mullaney, Walter Scott, Joe Hubert, Tom Kelly
F11F-1F Super Tiger	Mike Pelehach, Bob Miller, Bob Mullaney, Arnold Whitaker, Dr. Richard Kopp, Tom Keller, Dr. Henry Kelly, Bob Kress, Norm Lewin, Ed Kelly, Gene Baird
A2F-1 Intruder, A-6A	Larry Mead, Leonard Sullivan, Horace Moore, Bill Murphy, Bugs Waldt, Bob Nafis, Gene Bonan, Bob Carbee, Newt Speiss, Bill Beese, Bob Watson, Larry Vandercreek, Herman Wenz, Lou Arsenau, Dan Collins, Ren Witte, Joe Rodriguez, Chuck Darling, Jerry Ryan, Bob Harvey, Hal Moss, Doug Hill, Don Cook, Bill Fehrs, Walter Smrek, Rich Capria, Dick Feyk, Joe Cagnazzi, Joe Ruggiero
S2F Tracker	Bill Rathke, Joe Lippert, George Klaus, Jack Saxe, Jack Mooney, Skip Courtney
Precursor S-2 Turbo-prop Designs	Bob Bram, Dane Lamberson, Bill Tebo
S-2 Turbo Tracker	Gerry Maurer, Dick Crowell, Steve Wineberg, Herman Wenz, Jack Kellet, Joe Witko
C-1A	Bill Rathke and PD team (Joe Lippert, Lloyd Skinner, Roy Wood)
OV-1 Mohawk	Mike Pelehach, Bob Kress, Don Terrana, Ed Harris, Jonas Bilenas, Herb Grossman, Larry Canonico
Preliminary Design	Walter Scott, Leonard Sullivan, Joe Lippert, Joe Hubert, Dick Hutton, Mike Pelehach, Al Munier, John Michel, Art Koch, Dick Thurston, Dick Cyphers, Howard Weinmann, Vinnie Milano, Pete Viemeister, Lloyd Skinner, Bob Englert, Fritz Dunmire, Sam Rogers, Arnold Gersch, John Harvey, John Protopapas (see Figs. 4.15 and 4.16)
Operations Analysis	Dan Lynch, Hall Moss, Russ Murray, Hank Beers, Doug Hill, Bruno Maiolo, Bob Evans, Jim Tedesco, Gerry Ryan, Bob Harvey, Mike Ciminera, Pete Schwartz, Hugh Lowery, George Duffy, Fred Roffe, Ed Schoenfeld, Al Glomb, Bernie Buc, Tom Doherty, Tony De Ruggiero, Joe Cubells, Hank Suydam, Sam Rogers, Ed Conroy, Harry George
Ag Cat	Joe Lippert, Arthur Koch
C-2	Bill Rathke, Mike Pelehach, Frank Perley, Lloyd Skinner, Al Kuhn, Paul Weidenhafer, Larry Canonico
Gulfstream I	Mike Pelehach, Don Terrana, Charlie Coppi, Fritz Dunmire, Roy Grumman, Vinny Milano, Dick Hutton, Bob Englert, Henry Schiebel, Bernie Harriman, Al Rogers, Grant Hedrick
TC-4C	Bill Fehrs, Larry Canonico, Larry Kipnis, Jim Koschara
Gulfstream II	Bernie Harriman, Charlie Coppi, Irv Waaland, Dick Hutton, Rudy Meyer, Grant Hedrick, Walt Valkeneare
Gulfstream II STA	Mark Siegel, Dick Kita, Walt Kohloff, Bill Barhart, Jack Klafin, Bill Gentzlinger
Gulfstream III	Larry Mead, Bill Gentzlinger, Steve Dondero, Dick Kita, Paul Bavitz, Ed Curtis, Pete Hellston, Charlie Coppi, Sam Dastin

CHAPTER 5: LINEAGE OF AIRBORNE EARLY WARNING SYSTEMS

WF-2, E-1A, E-1B	Bill Rathke, Joe Lippert, Sam Rogers, Lloyd Skinner, Joe Gavin, Bob Nafis, Bill Burns, John Lenz, Mark Mellinger, John Cunniff, Tom Wolfson, Bob Watson
W2F-1, E-2A, E-2B, E-2C	Bill Rathke, Mike Pelehach, Frank Perley, Leonard Sullivan, Lloyd Skinner, Jim Brennan, Grant Hedrick, Bob Nafis, Fred Tiemann, Bill Zarkowsky, Basil Papa, Alex Alexandrovich, Julie Cohen, Bob O'Donohue, Joe Rodriguez, Barney Tichy, Jim Corbett, Jerry Norton, Ken Koehler, Bernie Farber, Dennis Carter, Paul Coco, Chuck Muller, Dick Anderson, Jim Murphy, Mike Kozak, Marty O'Connor, Dick Lebitz, Larry Michelon, Deac Jones, Tom Attridge, Jim McManus

CHAPTER 6: THE F-111B AND THE LINEAGE OF THE F-14

TFX, F-111B	Leonard Sullivan, Gene Bonan, Vinny Milano, Dane Lamberson, Dick Feyk, Ted Zach, Paul Anbro, Mike Pelehach, George Petronio, Bob Roemer, Bob Kress, Joe Rodriguez, Irv Waaland, Paul Weidenhafer, Don Terrana, Grant Hedrick, Dick Hutton, Frank Visconti, Dick Kita, Phil Brice, Ed Waesche
VFX, F-14A	Mike Pelehach, Joe Rees, Larry Mead, Bill Phillips, Ed Happ, Ed Waesche, Bob Kress, Renso Caporali, Irv Waaland, Paul Marterella, Dr. Gunther Buchmann, Dick Cyphers, Grant Hedrick, Tom Main, Joe Cipp, Carlos Paez, Al Hallock, Ed Mulcahy, Dietrich Helms, Dick Hadcock, Sam Dastin, Tom Kane, Jack Hasset, Ron Tindall, Bill Greathouse, Dr. Dave Migdal, John Michel, Tom Cheatham, Joe Rodriguez, Bob Watson, Dan Collins, Joe Stump, Bob Branstetter, Vinny De Vino, Dick Lu, Bob Mohrman, Bill Miller, Charlie Brown, John Arlin, Basil Leftheris, Bob Nafis, Rear Admiral (ret.) Emerson Fawkes, Dan Pliskin, Bernie Yudin, Al Trabold, Cosmo Palazzo, John Keenan, Ed Stroud
F-14A (plus), F-14B, F-14D	Bob Watson, Hank Janiesch, Neil GilMartin, Jim Dante, Jack Hasset, Pat Mennona, Dennis Carter, Terry O'Grady, Mike Fusco, Joe Burke, Dave Kratz
Advanced Structures and Materials	Grant Hedrick, Dick Cyphers, Larry Mead, Tom Main, Nat Kotlarchyk, Ron Heitzmann, Al Hallock, Ed Mulchahy, Dietrich Helms, Bill Stewart, Frank Hardenburgh, Howard Schilling, Carlos Paez, Tony Iopolo, Doug Hutchings, Ed Rolko, Tom Tartarian, Steve Banks, Al Wolfman, Frank Drumm, Bob Witt, Bob Messler, Tony Marrocco, Steve Demay, Cliff Shaver, Joel Greenspan, Tom Wolfe, Henry Beck, Al Wolfman, Alex Gomza, Paul Bell, Harvey Eidinoff, Basil Leftheris, Artie August, Dick Hadcock, Sam Dastin, Carl Micillo
Tomcat 21	Bob Kress, Paul Bavitz, John McCabe, Gus Sclafani, Neil Gilmartin, Doug Frei, Rudy Meyer, Mike Sturm, Dave Richel, John Neiman, Cliff Callahan, Sue Dorfman, Tom Griffin

CHAPTER 7: FUTURE SYSTEMS

Future Systems Organization	George Skurla, president; Mike Pelehach, vice president; Fritz Dunmire; Norm Gandia; Bob Kress; Bill Tebo; Hal Moss; Dan Lynch; John Cunniff; Dave Walsh; Renso Caporali; Herb Grossman; Tom Kane; Mike Ciminera; Dr. Charlie Mack; Dick Hadcock; Dr. Dick Scheuing
X-29A	Glen Spacht, Russ Negri, Mark Siegal, Charlie McGloughin, Keith Wilkinson, Doug Hutchings, Frank Rauch, Dean Roukis, Mike Ciminera, Mike Solan, Arnold Whitaker, Bob Roemer, Larry Canonico, Mel Garelick, Frank Halfen, Jerry Kohn, Howard Schilling, Doug Frei, Augie Sarantonio, Jim Chin, Bill Mebes, Dick Bartholome, Dennis Romano
Design 698 V/STOL A	Bob Kress, Stan Kalemaris, Tony Bacchi, Wally Burhans, Dr. Gunther Buchmann, Vladimir Seredinsky, Ray Rice, Bob Steele, Dr. Dick Oman, Walt Valkeneare, Bill Rathke, Dick Bartholeme, Harry Breul
Conformal Radar	Bob Steele, Fred Ganz, Dom Cerlignani, Dick Imgram, Pat Wiley, Bill Jorsch, Bill Fehrs, Larry Canonico, Harold Allen
MMVX and E-2X	Stan Kalemaris, Nick Dannenhofer, Frank Dellamura, Vincent Crafa, John Protopappas, Ernie Ranalli, Victor Ciminera, Arnie Gersch, Dave Richel, Charlie Lundin
Circulation Control Wing	Horace Moore, Vladimir Seredinsky, Dr. Bob Melnik, Herb Grossman
Design 711 Amphibian	Mike Pelehach, Brad Griffin, Bob LeCat, Larry Canonico, Sam Dastin, Gus Spanopoulos, Herb Grossman
Airborne Radar Jamming System	Bob Salzmann, Joel DiMaggio, Paul McDermott, Al Gurkewitz, Wally Zepf, Joe Genovese, Bob Fredette, Ross Fleisig
Computer Aided Design in Advanced Systems	Paul Weidenhafer, Frank Dellamura, Al Vachris, Mike Ciminera, Ken Fitch, Wally Burhans, Don Colquhun, Nate Kirshbaum, Tom Lazichy, Gerald Stoodley, Joann Cipriano

CHAPTER 8: LINEAGE OF BATTLEFIELD SURVEILLANCE: RGWS, PAVE MOVER, AND JOINT STARS

Radar Guided Weapon System	Gerry McNiff, Newt Speiss, Grant Hedrick, Dan Collins, Gene Bonan, Hank Janiesch, Sol Boles, Walter Smerk, Frank Milordi, Jim Glover, Joe LeStrange, Herb Grossman, John Calandra, Jim Williams, Frank Finnerty
Pave Mover	Gerry McNiff, Al Gurkewitz, Frank Milordi, Jim Glover, Herman Binder, Pat Reilly, Paul Richards, Harvey Sperling, Leo Sledgeski
Joint STARS proposal	Al Verderosa, Dan Terry, Frank Milordi, Gerry McNiff, Jim Glover, Dave Szakovitz, Pat Reilly, George Hummel, Sam Mackey, Bob Phear, Roger Moxham, Herb Landau
Joint STARS	Al Verderosa, Marty Dandridge, Jerry Norton, Paul Coco, Dr. Dale Burton, Tony Guma, Tim Farrell, Gerry McNiff, Jim Glover, Roy Schering, Cory Liang, Mike Addison, Roddy Smith, Min Tran, Chuck Muller, Jerry Madigan, Alan Van Weele, Mike Kozak, Tom Wood, Dave Szakovitz, Jean-Marie Sanders

CHAPTER 9: LINEAGE OF ELECTRONIC WARFARE

EA-6A	Lew Scheuer, Al Rogers, Bob Nafis, Bob Salzmann, Don Cook, Arnold Siedon, Artie Karl, Sal Migliore
EA-6B	Tom Guarino, Bob Salzmann, Tom Kane, Artie Karl, Sal Migliore, Bob Miller, Tom Brancati, Gerry Gottlieb, Bugs Waldt, Frank Hardenburgh, Bill Schooley, Cliff Hoelzer, Tom Griffin, Lou Byars, Ned Sweeney, Bob Fredette, Al Gurkewitz, Gerry Mellman, Bob Scholly, Morty Proper
EF-111	Bob Miller, Bob Salzmann, Vern Kramer, Tom Street, Dave Tarbell, Tony Pizzimenti, Danny O'Neill, John Cunnif

CHAPTER 10: GRUMMAN IN PERSPECTIVE

Introduction	Joe Lippert, Irv Walland
Designer Profiles	Roy Grumman, Jake Swirbul, Julie Holpit, Dick Hutton, Bob Hall, Ralston Stalb, Oscar Erlandsen, Grant Hedrick, Larry Mead, Joe Gavin, Bill Rathke, Joe Lippert, Arthur Koch, Gordon Israel, Dayton T. Brown, Bernie Harriman, Walter Scott, Leonard Sullivan, Mike Pelehach, Bob Kress, Glen Spacht
Design Perspectives	Renso Caporali, Greg Kutz, Herman Erbacher, Dick Anderson
The Avionicers and Software	Bob Nafis, Gene Bonan, Newt Speiss, Dan Collins, Fred Tiemann, Dick Anderson, Ken Kohler, Dennis Carter, Gerry Norton, Jim McManus, Tom Guarino, Dick Anderson, Tony Guma, Alex Alexandrovich, Bob Kress, Dan Collins, Bob Watson, Vinny DeVino, Bob Branstetter, Joe Stump, Bob Steele, Bill Miller, Charlie Brown, Gerry McNiff, Hank Janiesch, Frank Milordi, Jim Glover, Sam Mackey, Bob Phear, Al Gurkewitz, Dr. Dale Burton, Paul Coco, Arte Karle, Sal Migliore, Bob Salzmann, Bob Fredette, Gerry Mellman, Bob Scholly, Dave Tarbell, Gerry Sandler, Connie Blyseth
Designer Traits	Versatility: Bob Kress, Joe Gavin, Walter Scott, Bill Rathke, Leonard Sullivan, Oscar Erlandsen, Bob Hall, Tom Street
	Leadership: Roy Grumman, Bill Schwendler, Grant Hedrick, Dick Hutton, Al Verderosa, Marty Dandridge, Tom Guarino, Joe Gavin, Larry Mead, Leonard Sullivan, Bob Miller
	Creativity: Roy Grumman, Bill Schwendler, Dick Hutton, Mike Pelehach, Bob Kress, Bob Salzmann, Grant Hedrick, Newt Speiss, Jerry McNiff, Gordon Israel, Glen Spacht, Joe Lippert, Dick Anderson
	Quick Response: Mike Pelehach, Arthur Koch, Julie Holpit, Herb Grossman, Howie Schilling
	Customer Focus: Roy Grumman, Joe Gavin, Mike Pelehach, Tom Guarino, Larry Mead, Julie Holpit, Marty Dandridge
	Longevity: Roy Grumman, Bill Schwendler, Grant Hedrick, Dick Hutton, Larry Mead, Julie Holpit, Bill Rathke, Bob Hall

About the Author

As a young boy of 12, I began to try to design airplanes with very limited knowledge other than what I gained by going to the public library in Port Washington, New York, and looking at aviation books, old issues of *Aviation Week*, and scanning *Jane's All the World's Aircraft* in the reference section. *Jane's* became my bible, and my drawing board replaced the baseball diamond as I began to make sketches by approximating aircraft geometrical relationships from *Jane's*.

During my early teens, my mother and father worked for an English couple, Charles and Elizabeth Hobley, as head housekeeper and gardener, respectively. My job was to babysit for their young son, David, and as a result they became aware of my keen interest in aviation. They became my sponsors over several years by providing me English aviation magazines as well as letters of recommendation as I competed for scholarships to attend college. I received copies of *Aeroplane* and *Flight* magazines, which contained wonderful descriptions of many of the world's aircraft as well as cutaway drawings. I grew up on British aviation. Fast-forward to the mid-1990s, when I was vice president of the Grumman JPATS (Joint Primary Aircraft Training System) program and meeting with Martin Baker senior management, I was able to name many of the British aircraft in the history hall at Martin Baker, much to the astonishment of their chief engineer.

When I was a junior in high school, I saved enough money to purchase my first edition of *Jane's All the World's Aircraft* (1952–53). My designs were maturing, and I began to submit them to aircraft companies like Douglas and Grumman, where I became an engineering apprentice at the age of 17. My designs included a subsonic transport with an aero-isoclinic wing shape similar to that used on the Handley Page Victor bomber, a twin turboprop feeder liner transport, a supersonic fighter, and a small jet-powered amphibian. I received comments back from Carlos Wood, chief engineer of Douglas, and Warren Allen and Fritz Dunmire, chief engineer and aircraft designer, respectively, of Grumman, who encouraged me to continue to

233

understand more of the basics of aerodynamic theory and create more designs.

In my senior year of high school in 1955, my guidance counselor told me to apply to only one school, Rensselaer Polytechnic Institute (RPI), to study aeronautical engineering. When I became a senior at RPI in 1959, I completed a year-long conceptual design, structural layout, and aero-performance of a jet-powered amphibian with the help of engine data and hydrodynamic basics supplied by Grumman.

In 1959 I became the youngest engineer ever hired into Preliminary Design (PD). I was given this chance because I was an engineering apprentice for Grumman for four years and had demonstrated my deep desire to design aircraft by submitting conceptual designs to PD personnel for review. In those days, most of the personnel in PD had long, established careers working on other programs and brought honed knowledge of what it takes to get a design off the drawing boards and into hardware. I was surrounded by some of the most imaginative, brilliant, creative, and experienced people in the aerospace industry from the United States and abroad. Many were veterans of pre–World War II aviation developments in Europe, as well as World War II veterans. I came to know Joe Hubert, chief aerodynamicist of the ME 163 in World War II; Dr. Gunther Buchman of Blohm and Voss; and Stanislaus (Stosh) Rogalski, who designed, built, and flight tested aircraft in Poland in the 1920s and 1930s.

At that time, Preliminary Design was run by Walter Scott; he was succeeded by Leonard "Sully" Sullivan. Sully left Grumman in the 1960s to take a position at the Department of Defense, and he was succeeded by Mike Pelehach. I was assigned to work for Hal Moss, who was head of the Advanced Vehicle Design Group in the Operations Analysis department, which was a key organization in PD. And so began an exciting nine-year journey of investigating all types of vehicles: subsonic and supersonic fighters and attack aircraft, surveillance and antisubmarine warfare (ASW) aircraft, product improvements of military and commercial aircraft, conventional and advanced helicopters, missiles, supersonic transports, hydrofoil boats, ground effect machines, dirigibles, and more. Hal was a brilliant aeronautical engineer who was educated at MIT and RPI. While at RPI getting his masters in aeronautical engineering, Hal also taught young aeronautical engineering students. This experience, combined with his ability to generalize vast amounts of technical data, his writing skills, and his patience, made him a great teacher. Hal was highly respected by the hardware-oriented project managers, as well as the designers who would lay out (draw) the selected design points in 2-D that were generated by Hal and his team.

In order to synthesize generalized families of vehicles to satisfy varying mission requirements, I had to interface with every major engineering function that was employed in designing a new aircraft (e.g., aero, propulsion, power plant installation, structures, materials, mechanical systems, hydraulics, landing gear, weight estimating, crew and equipment, avionics, payloads, etc.). These data were than generalized and entered into Grumman's Generalized Aircraft Design Program via thousands of key punch cards.

We tackled extensive studies on helicopters and competing vertical and/or short takeoff and landing (VSTOL) configurations (compound, rigid rotor, tilt wing, fan in wing, etc.), hydrofoil boats (semisubmerged and fully submerged hydrofoils, gas turbine/supercavitating propellers, and water jet propulsion), ground effect machines, missiles, and advanced dirigibles in much the same way as we did aircraft design studies. I got to know and work closely with Chuck Ellis, chief engineer of Kaman Helicopter, and we developed a generalized helicopter design program that enabled the Grumman/Kaman design team to compete for the Army's rigid rotor Advanced Aerial Fire Suppression System (AAFS) program. In like manner, I worked closely with Tom Street, chief hydrodynamicist for Grumman at the time, to develop an extensive generalized hydrofoil design program that included all the hydrodynamic drag and performance parameters of hydrofoil boats. This effort enabled Grumman to perform an extensive design contract for large oceangoing destroyer-type hydrofoil ships for the Navy Electronics Lab. The hydrofoil design team was able to take our design points and layout and weigh selected hydrofoil designs that met Navy requirements.

During the mid-1960s, Mike Pelehach became chief of PD and we began a furious effort on the heavier than air, Fighter Attack Experimental (VFAX) followed by the VFX (precursor F-14 designation) parametric design studies that culminated in several candidate Design 303(Grumman design number) candidates (variable sweep and fixed wing) that were selected for more detailed design. Through Mike, I got to know George Spangenberg, chief of the Technical Development Branch of NAVAIR and the Navy's chief designer, and Fred Gloeckler, head of Mission Effectiveness for NAVAIR, by briefing them extensively on many design tradeoffs of design missions, design payloads, wing configuration, engine type and bypass ratio, and so on.

In late 1968, Mike Pelehach, then F-14 chief designer, was promoted to become vice president and program manager of the F-14A Tomcat program. He asked me to come and work directly for him and told me "he would show me how real airplanes are built." And so began another chapter in my 50-plus years with Grumman and Northrop Grumman. I returned to head up PD, now called Advanced Systems, in 1976. Notable achievements during the next five years were design teams working on the forward swept wing (FSW) design studies leading to the X-29 Forward Swept Wing Demonstrator; Advanced Tactical Fighter (ATF) design configuration studies, wind tunnel tests, and technology development for the U.S. Air Force; developing subsonic and supersonic VSTOL carrier-based designs for the U.S. Navy; developing conformal ultra-high-frequency (UHF) radar technology through full-scale test; proposing the F-14A for the Next Generation Fighter program for Canada; and developing the next generation advanced aircraft design process.

On the FSW we won a series of design, wind tunnel, and aero-elastic wind tunnel tests with the Defense Advanced Research Projects Agency (DARPA), and performed full-scale structural tests on the complex, composite wing root of our forward swept wing design, which enabled Grumman to win the X-29 Forward Swept Wing contract to build two demonstrator aircraft. In addition, with the advances in computer technology, we began to develop the next generation advanced aircraft design process that eventually led us to a fully integrated process from parametric vehicle design to a selected design point and the fabrication of a wind tunnel model.

Bob Kress was Grumman's answer to Burt Rutan in those days. His design genius was once again displayed in a series of full-scale subsonic VSTOL engine/flight control tests, full-scale NASA subsonic wind tunnel tests, and a series of tethered VSTOL scale model tests with our Research department that confirmed transition flight control laws. Three excellent design teams emerged and matured in this time period—the FSW/X-29 design team, the VSTOL design team, and the ATF design team.

The role of the chief engineer/designer was expanding. We still needed the aircraft configuration design engineer who could make a 2-D, three-view drawing representing the selected design points. He was surrounded by a very experienced design team of the chief engineer, aero, propulsion, weights, and crew and equipment people to make the design stable and balanced. The big difference was that from a conceptual design point of view we were generating thousands of design points that could be rapidly sized, used in Operations Analysis effectiveness studies, and priced through life cycle cost. Cost-effectiveness studies using advanced avionics systems, payloads (ordnance), and varying levels of stealth and Defense Electronic Counter-measures (DECM) technology were key design drivers. Selected conceptual design points from the myriad of tradeoffs were then put through their paces in sophisticated campaign analyses that involved varying threat levels, multiple aircraft carriers, varying carrier force complements driven by spotting factor, and the like to arrive at the most cost-effective solutions.

I spent almost 51 years with Grumman and Northrop Grumman, and more than half of my career was devoted to the front end of the business, which included Advanced Systems/Preliminary Design, Operations Analysis,

Advanced Technology, Advanced Programs, overseeing new opportunities in all business areas, leading major proposals to the government, building demonstrators, and managing research and development dollars. Grumman management appointed me vice president of Advanced Programs in 1985.

I was able to take many of the skills honed in these years, including strategic planning, communication, leadership, managing diverse design teams, technology planning, national and international customer focus, financial management, and business opportunity analysis, and successfully employ them managing large programs across diverse business areas with total quality emphasis.

My management assignments were vice president of the Systems Group (Electronics, Space, and Joint STARS divisions), senior vice president of the Electronic Systems division, and vice president of JPATS (Joint Primary Aircraft Training System). After Grumman was acquired by Northrop in 1994, I became vice president, program manager of the F-18A/B/C/D Hornet program in 1995, followed by vice president, program manager of the Joint STARS (Joint Surveillance and Target Attack Reconnaissance System) program in Lake Charles, Louisiana, in 1997. From 2000 through 2009, I was a sector consultant for Northrop Grumman and provided continuous technical and program management oversight of many programs, including unmanned autonomous systems such as the Fire Scout, UCAS (Unmanned Combat Air System), and X-47B.

I continue to consult in aerospace, lecture, write, and serve on several boards, including the Legacy Engineering Advisory Council; chair of the Leadership Board of the School of Engineering at Rensselaer Polytechnic Institute; advisor to the Western Museum of Flight in Torrance, California; and the COA (Christian Outreach in Action), a nondenominational center in Long Beach, California, that cares for those in need.

BIBLIOGRAPHY

Anderton, D. A., & Watanbe, R., *Hellcat*, Crown, New York, 1981.

Bernstein, J., "Grumman Eyes Amphibian Goose," *Newsday* (Grumman Photo).

Biographical data of Grumman personnel, Northrop Grumman History Center Archives.

Ciminera, M., *A Perspective on Military Fixed Wing Aircraft*, Industrial College of the Armed Forces, 1988.

Ciminera, M., *The Development of a Twin-Turbofan V/STOL Aircraft*, AHS, 1980.

Door, R. F., *Grumman A-6 Intruder*, 1987.

Francillon, R. J., *Grumman Aircraft Since 1929*, Naval Institute Press, Annapolis, MD, 1989.

Gillcrist, P. T. (Rear ADM., USNRet.), *TOMCAT—The Grumman F-14 Story*, 1994.

Grumman chronology picture of aircraft to 1994, Northrop Grumman History Center Archives.

Grumman personnel, photographs, Northrop Grumman History Center Archives.

Grumman Plane News, articles, Northrop Grumman History Center Archives.

Grumman prototype aircraft, photographs, Northrop Grumman History Center Archives.

Hutton, D., letter, Northrop Grumman History Center Archives, 1985.

Koch, A., letters, Northrop Grumman History Center Archives.

Lippert, J., letters and documents, Northrop Grumman History Center Archives.

Mead, Jr., L. M., *My Fifty Two Years at Grumman*, 1998.

Meyer, C. C., *F11F-1F Super Tiger*, 1998.

Meyer, C. C., *Grumman Swing Wing XF10F-1 Jaguar*, 1993.

Meyer, C. H., *Corky Meyer's Flight Journal: A Test Pilot's Tales of Dodging Disasters—Just in Time.* Specialty Pr Pub & Wholesalers, 2006.

Miller, J., *The X-Planes*, Aerofax, 1988.

Nichols, J. H., Englar, R. J., Harris, M. J., & Huson, C. G., *Experimental Development of an Advanced Circulation Control Wing System for Navy STOL Aircraft*, David Taylor Naval Ship Research and Development Center.

North, D. "Grumman Studying Amphibian Market," *Aviation Week*, 1978.

Norton, S. G., *From Concept to Combat*, 1994.

Paez, C., *The Development of the F-14A Wing Center Section*, 2008.

Pelehach, M., Research by Ciminera, M., *Future Military Aircraft Needs*, 1984.

Salzmann, A. R., *Airborne Electronic Warfare in the Modern Age*, 1978.

Seybel, R., *Grumman Manufactured Aircraft as of 1994*, 1994.

Seydel, R. *Grumman Manufactured Aircraft as of May 1994, Parts I, II, III*, 1994.

Spacht, G., *The Forward Swept Wing: A Unique Design Challenge*, AIAA, 1980.

Sullivan, L., letter, Northrop Grumman History Center Archives, 1985.

Thomason, T., *Grumman Navy F-111B Swing Wing (Navy Fighters No. 41)*, Steve Ginter, Simi Valley, CA, 1998.

Thruelson, R., *The Grumman Story*, Praeger, 1976.

Tiemann II, F., memoir, Northrop Grumman History Center Archives, 2005.

Waaland, I. T., *Technology in the Lives of an Aircraft Designer*, Wright Brothers Lecture, 1991.

INDEX

Note: Page references in *italics* denote figures.

SUPPORTING MATERIALS

To download supplemental material files, please go to AIAA's electronic library, Aerospace Research Central (ARC), and navigate to the desired book's landing page for a link to access the materials: arc.aiaa.org.

A complete listing of titles in the Library of Flight series is available from ARC. Visit ARC frequently to stay abreast of product changes, corrections, special offers, and new publications.

AIAA is committed to devoting resources to the education of both practicing and future aerospace professionals. In 1996, the AIAA Foundation was founded. Its programs enhance scientific literacy and advance the arts and sciences of aerospace. For more information, please visit www.aiaafoundation.org.